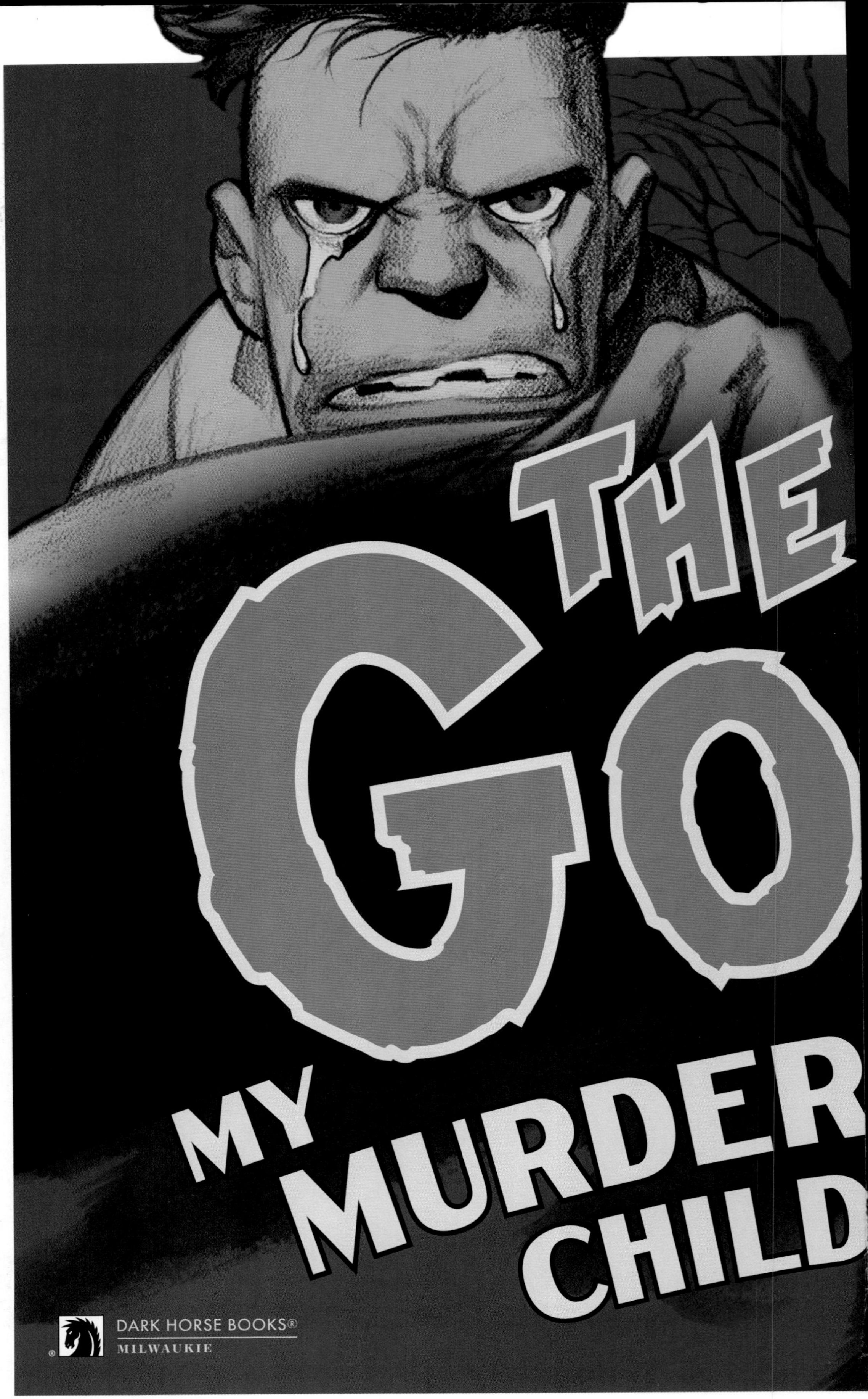
THE GO
MY MURDER CHILD

DARK HORSE BOOKS®
MILWAUKIE

WRITTEN AND ILLUSTRATED BY
ERIC POWELL

ART FOR
"THE ABOMINABLE BOGGY" BY
KYLE HOTZ

COLOR ASSISTS BY
**ROBIN POWELL, SHAYNNE CORBETT &
BARRY GREGORY**

ON™ IN

OUS
HOOD

(And Other Grievous Yarns)

First Edition:
editors SCOTT ALLIE & MATT DRYER

Second Edition:
editor SCOTT ALLIE

assistant editor BRENDAN WRIGHT

designer AMY ARENDTS

president & publisher MIKE RICHARDSON

Neil Hankerson *executive vice president* • Tom Weddle *chief financial officer* • Randy Stradley *vice president of publishing* • Michael Martens *vice president of business development* • Anita Nelson *vice president of business affairs* • Micha Hershman *vice president of marketing* • David Scroggy *vice president of product development* • Dale LaFountain *vice president of information technology* • Darlene Vogel *director of purchasing* • Ken Lizzi *general counsel* • Davey Estrada *editorial director* • Scott Allie *senior managing editor* • Chris Warner *senior books editor* • Diana Schutz *executive editor* • Cary Grazzini *director of design and production* • Lia Ribacchi *art director* • Cara Niece *director of scheduling*

THE GOON™: MY MURDEROUS CHILDHOOD (AND OTHER GRIEVOUS YARNS)

This volume collects issues #1–#4 of the Dark Horse Comics ongoing series *The Goon*, as well as the short story "The Goon Meets the Brothers Mud" originally published in DHC's *Drawing on Your Nightmares* one-shot.

Published by
Dark Horse Books
A division of
Dark Horse Comics, Inc.
10956 SE Main Street
Milwaukie, OR 97222

darkhorse.com

To find a comics shop in your area,
call the Comic Shop Locator Service toll-free at (888) 266-4226.

First edition: May 2004
Second edition: October 2010
ISBN 978-1-59582-616-9

10 9 8 7 6 5 4 3 2 1

Printed at Midas Printing International, Ltd., Huizhou, China

INTRODUCTION

What can I say about Eric Powell that the Tennessee State Police Department hasn't already said. Let's face it, Eric Powell is one bad mother~~fucker~~! And I mean that in a good way.

Never have I seen an artist arrive on the comic scene so completely polished and mature in his writing and art.

When I first saw *The Goon*, I ~~shit~~ my pants. I kid you not. My laundry lady will back me up.

It wasn't his lush line work or his writing that caught my eye. Those came later. It's his beautiful oil-painted covers that made me fall in love with the book. Jesus Christ on a pogo stick! Can this boy paint!

Then I opened up the book and read it. I became an instant fan on that day. The man combines horror, comedy, and action with such deftness and bravado, it's downright scary.

What else is scary is that he's from Tennessee.

That's right. Tennessee. The state where they just found the joys of making a right turn at a red light, and the polio vaccine. This just goes to show you that geniuses come in all sizes and shapes—and places.

Now, I can go on raving about his talent and how he's the next big thing in comics, but I won't. I'm going to let you judge this boy's brilliance yourself. So go ahead, take a step further and read this magnificent book.

And prepare to drop a load.

Enjoy.

Frank Cho
Liberty Meadows
January 20, 2004

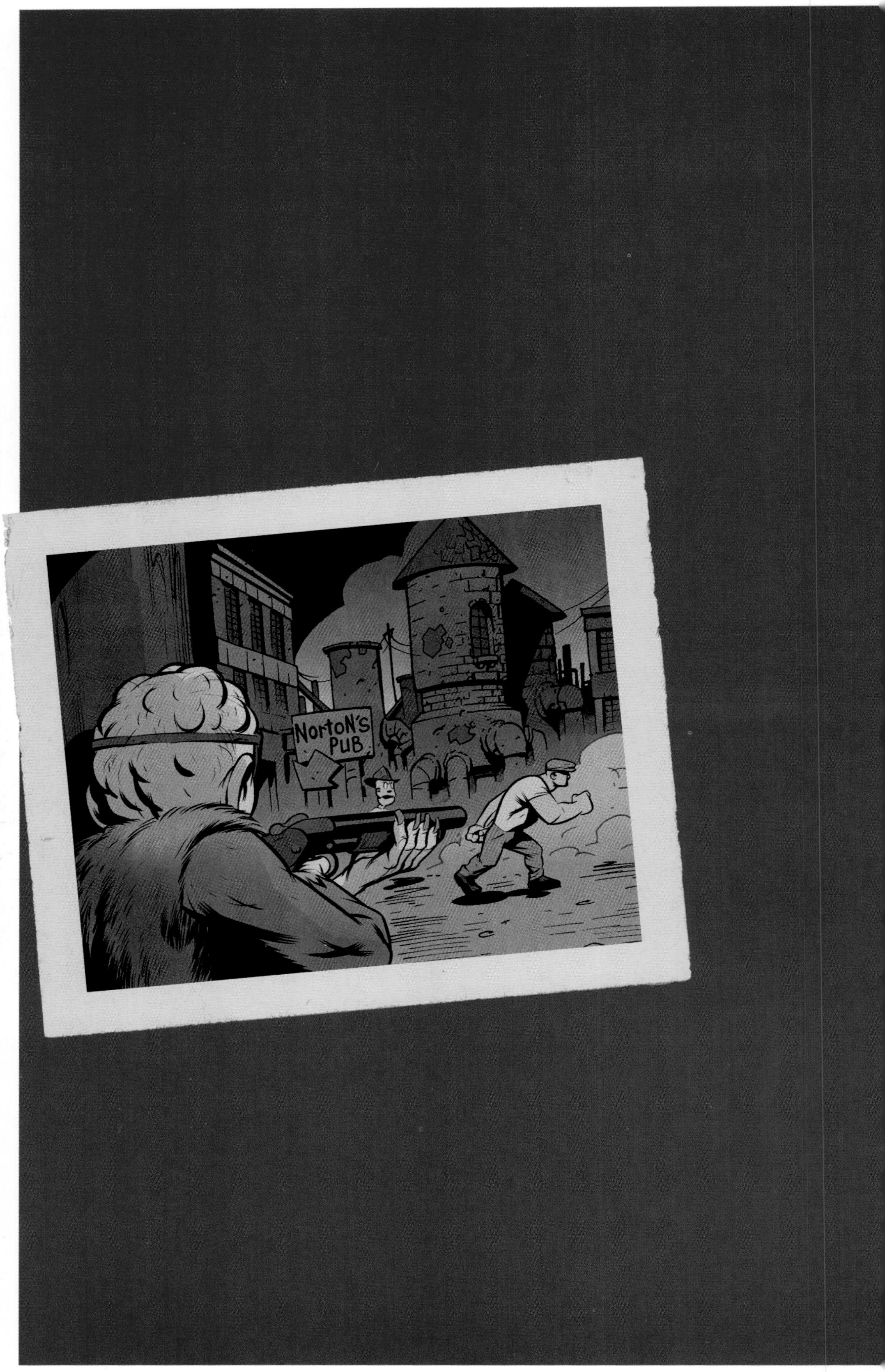
NortoN's PUB

CHAPTER 1

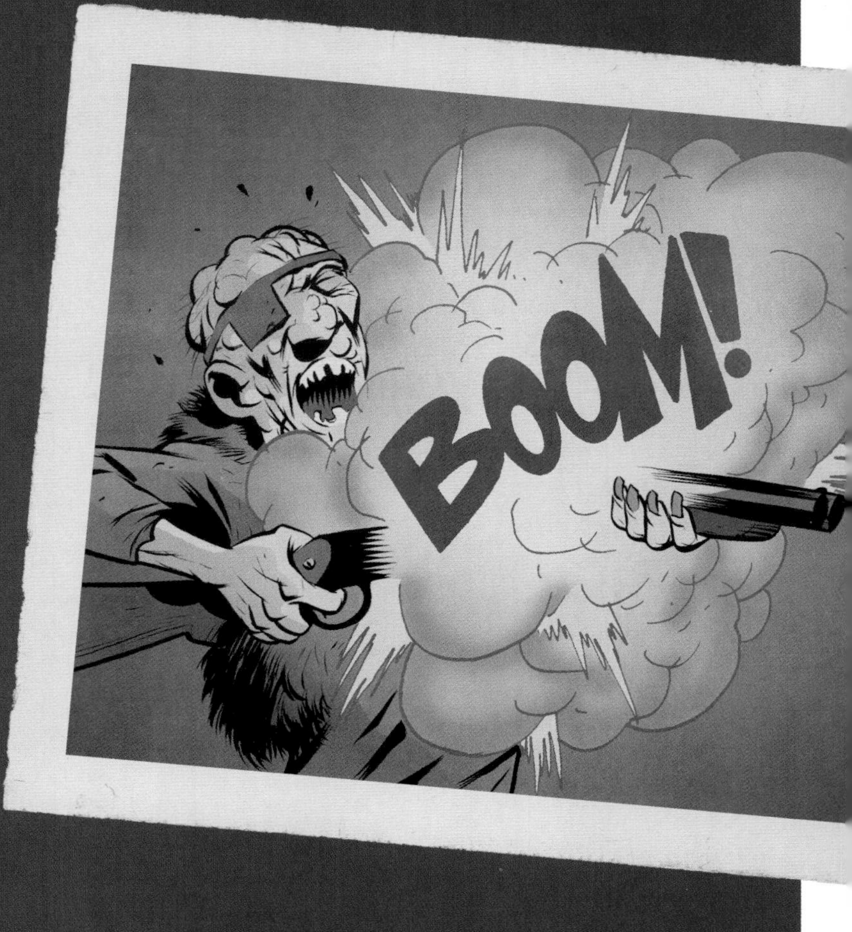
BOOM!

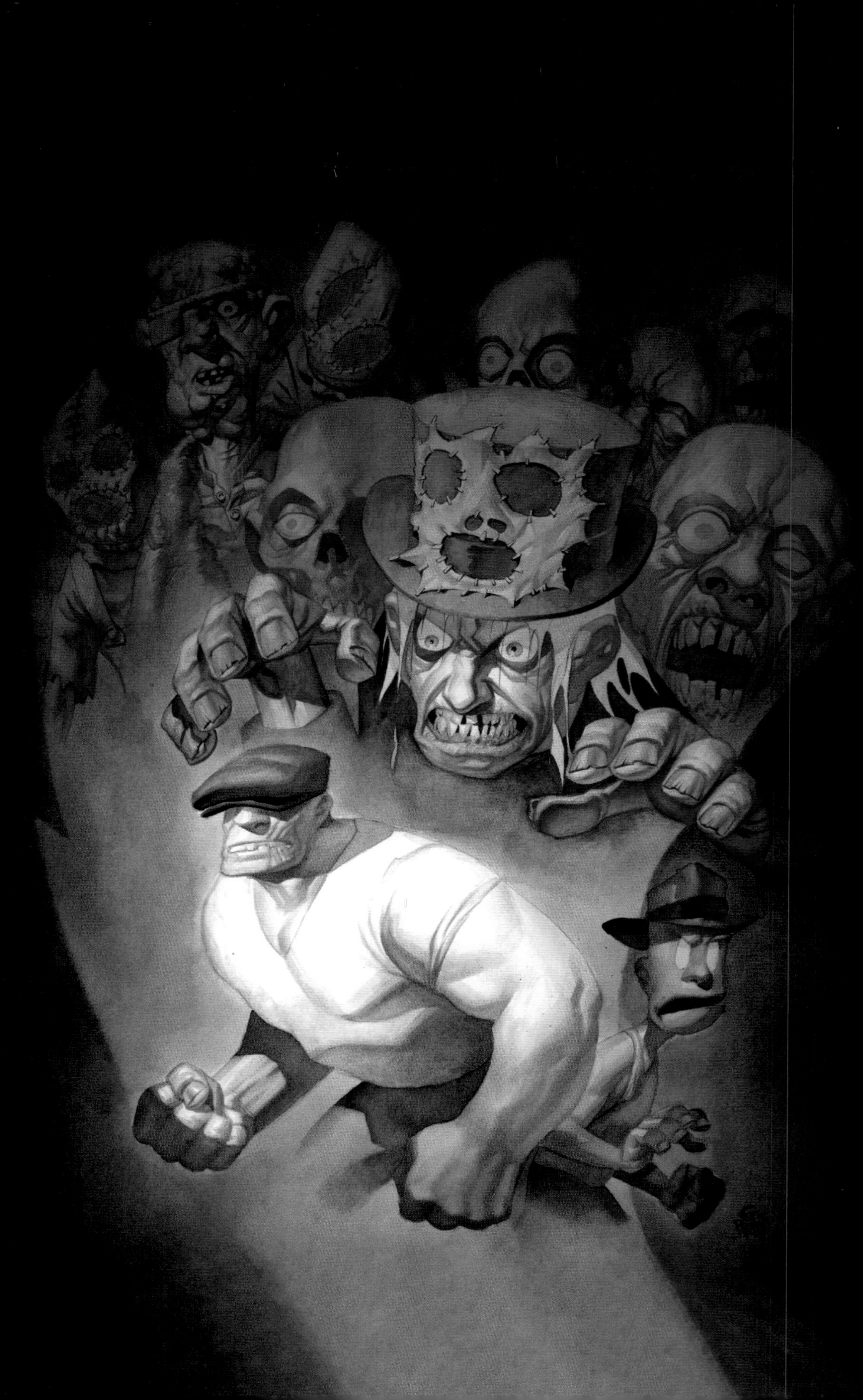

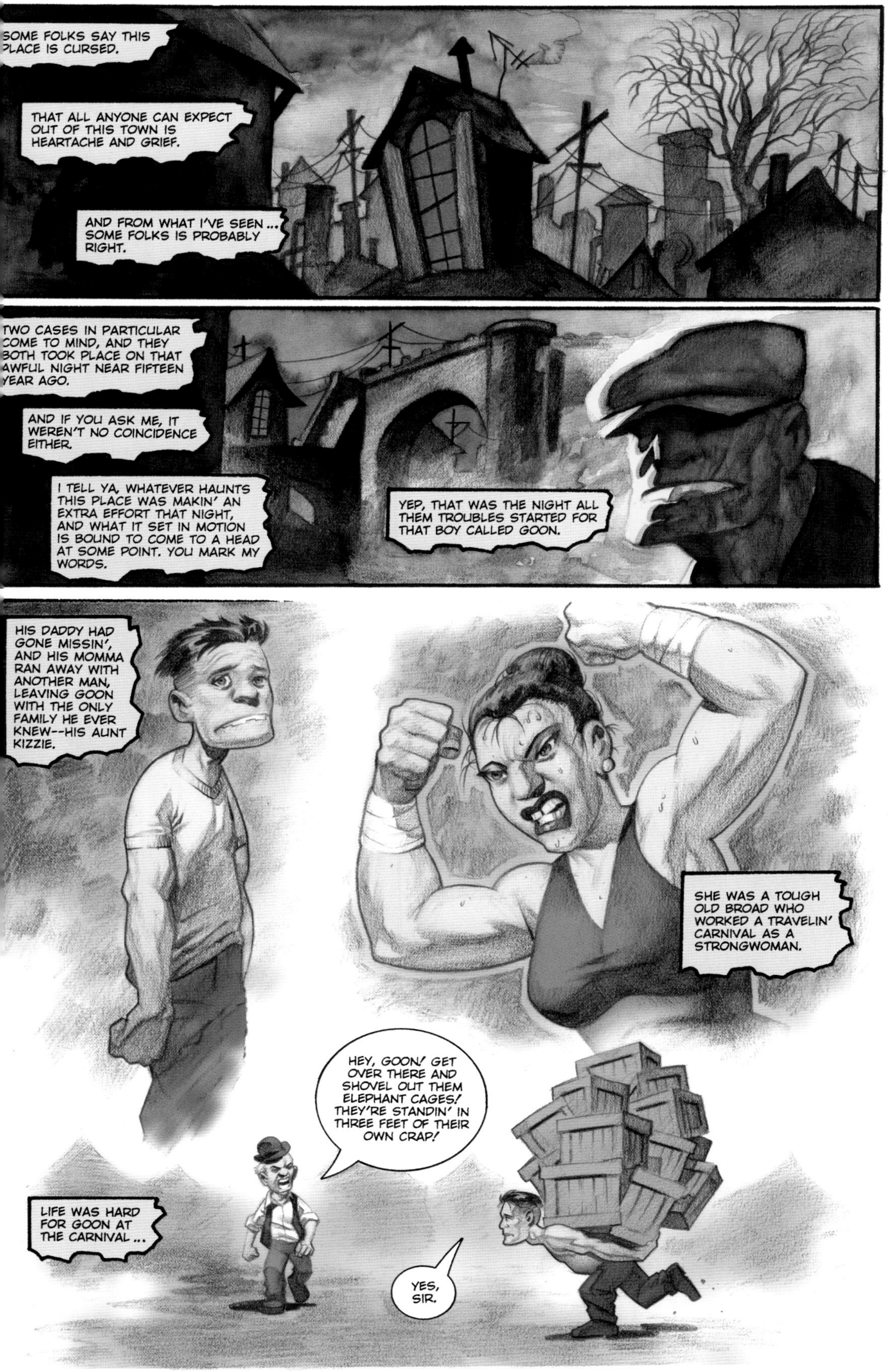
SOME FOLKS SAY THIS PLACE IS CURSED.
THAT ALL ANYONE CAN EXPECT OUT OF THIS TOWN IS HEARTACHE AND GRIEF.
AND FROM WHAT I'VE SEEN ... SOME FOLKS IS PROBABLY RIGHT.
TWO CASES IN PARTICULAR COME TO MIND, AND THEY BOTH TOOK PLACE ON THAT AWFUL NIGHT NEAR FIFTEEN YEAR AGO.
AND IF YOU ASK ME, IT WEREN'T NO COINCIDENCE EITHER.
I TELL YA, WHATEVER HAUNTS THIS PLACE WAS MAKIN' AN EXTRA EFFORT THAT NIGHT, AND WHAT IT SET IN MOTION IS BOUND TO COME TO A HEAD AT SOME POINT. YOU MARK MY WORDS.
YEP, THAT WAS THE NIGHT ALL THEM TROUBLES STARTED FOR THAT BOY CALLED GOON.
HIS DADDY HAD GONE MISSIN', AND HIS MOMMA RAN AWAY WITH ANOTHER MAN, LEAVING GOON WITH THE ONLY FAMILY HE EVER KNEW--HIS AUNT KIZZIE.
SHE WAS A TOUGH OLD BROAD WHO WORKED A TRAVELIN' CARNIVAL AS A STRONGWOMAN.
LIFE WAS HARD FOR GOON AT THE CARNIVAL ...
HEY, GOON! GET OVER THERE AND SHOVEL OUT THEM ELEPHANT CAGES! THEY'RE STANDIN' IN THREE FEET OF THEIR OWN CRAP!
YES, SIR.

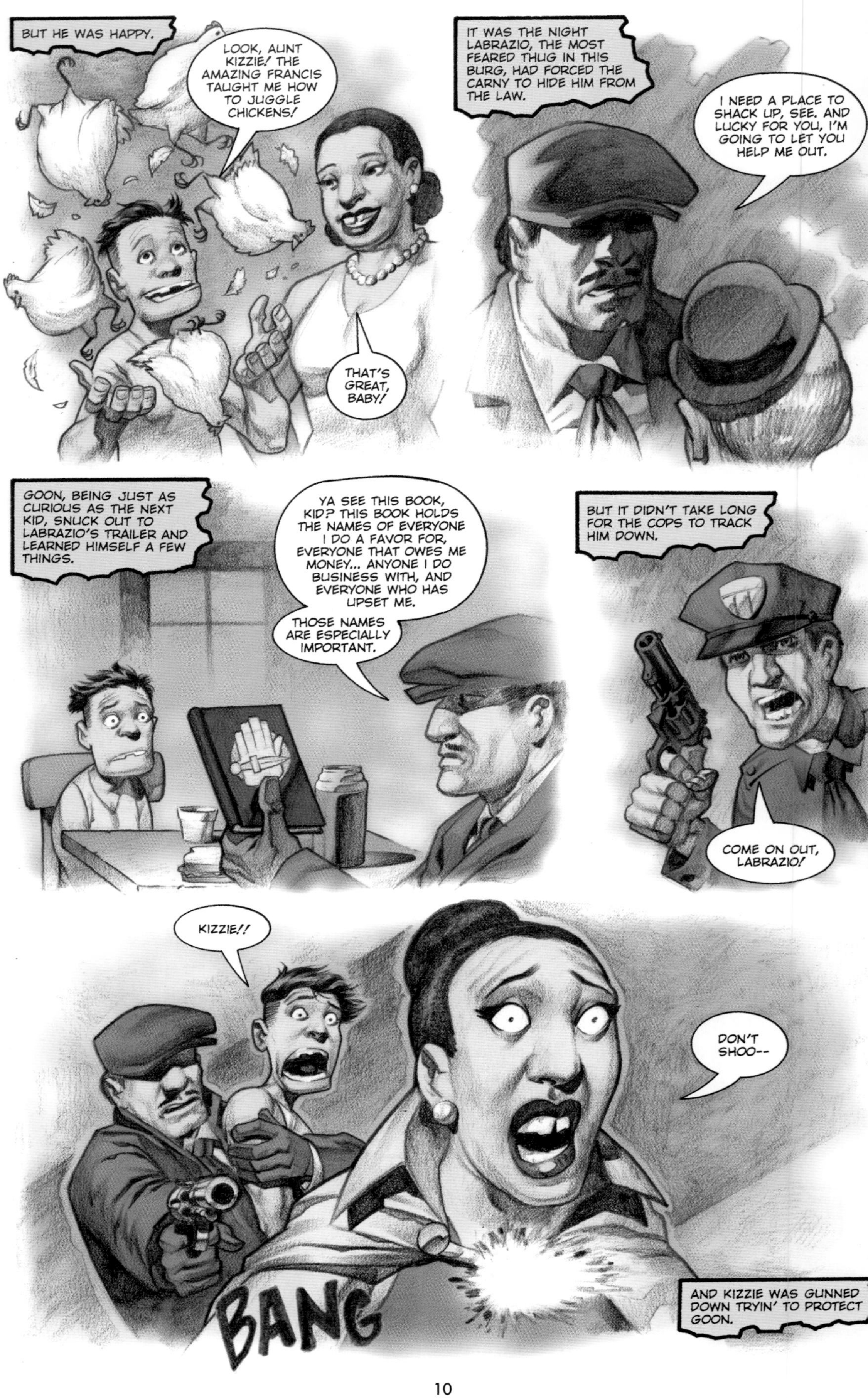

BUT HE WAS HAPPY.
LOOK, AUNT KIZZIE! THE AMAZING FRANCIS TAUGHT ME HOW TO JUGGLE CHICKENS!
THAT'S GREAT, BABY!
IT WAS THE NIGHT LABRAZIO, THE MOST FEARED THUG IN THIS BURG, HAD FORCED THE CARNY TO HIDE HIM FROM THE LAW.
I NEED A PLACE TO SHACK UP, SEE. AND LUCKY FOR YOU, I'M GOING TO LET YOU HELP ME OUT.
GOON, BEING JUST AS CURIOUS AS THE NEXT KID, SNUCK OUT TO LABRAZIO'S TRAILER AND LEARNED HIMSELF A FEW THINGS.
YA SEE THIS BOOK, KID? THIS BOOK HOLDS THE NAMES OF EVERYONE I DO A FAVOR FOR, EVERYONE THAT OWES ME MONEY... ANYONE I DO BUSINESS WITH, AND EVERYONE WHO HAS UPSET ME.
THOSE NAMES ARE ESPECIALLY IMPORTANT.
BUT IT DIDN'T TAKE LONG FOR THE COPS TO TRACK HIM DOWN.
COME ON OUT, LABRAZIO!
KIZZIE!!
DON'T SHOO--
BANG
AND KIZZIE WAS GUNNED DOWN TRYIN' TO PROTECT GOON.

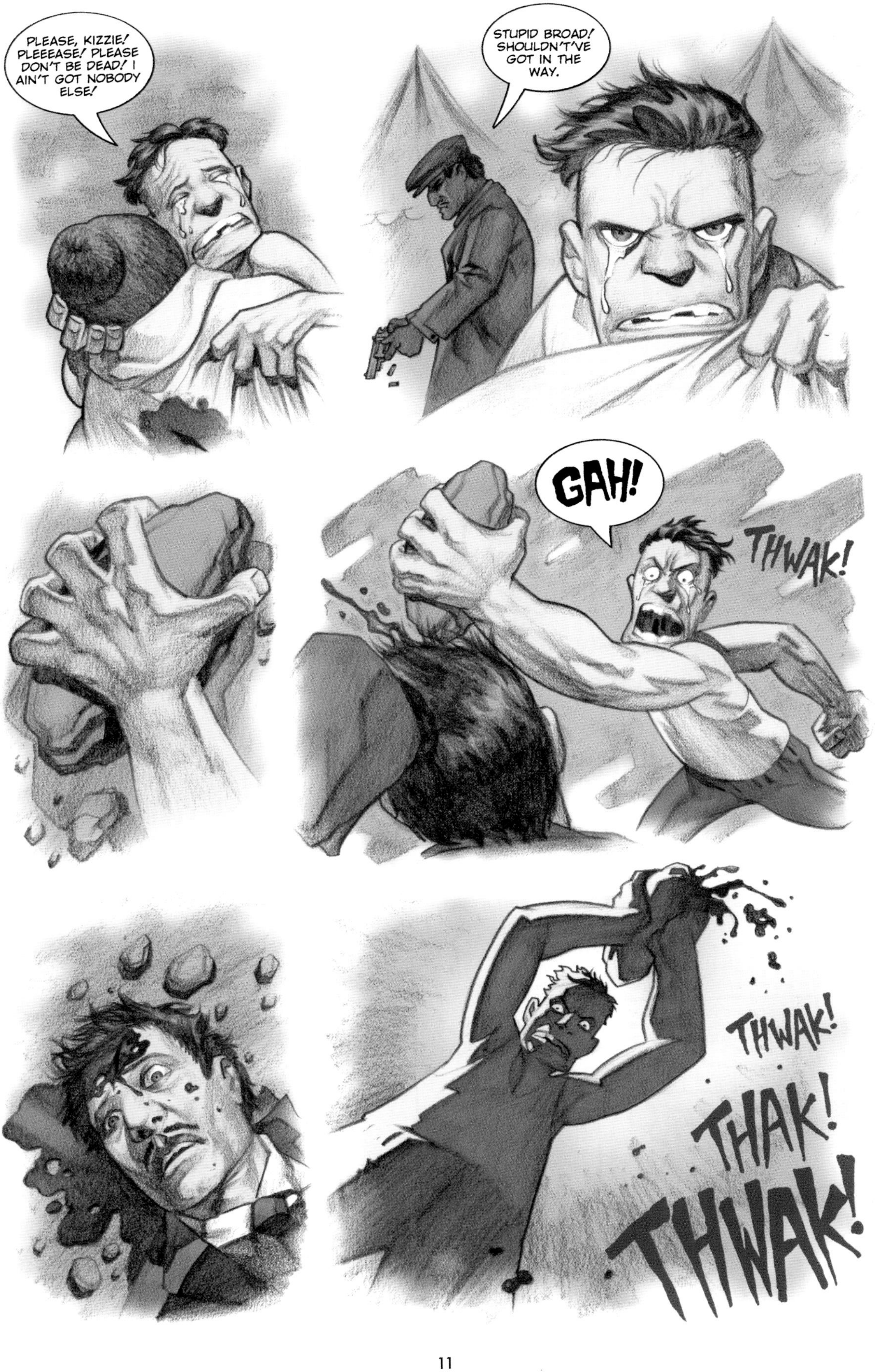
PLEASE, KIZZIE! PLEEEASE! PLEASE DON'T BE DEAD! I AIN'T GOT NOBODY ELSE!
STUPID BROAD! SHOULDN'T'VE GOT IN THE WAY.
GAH!
THWAK!
THWAK!
THAK!
THWAK!

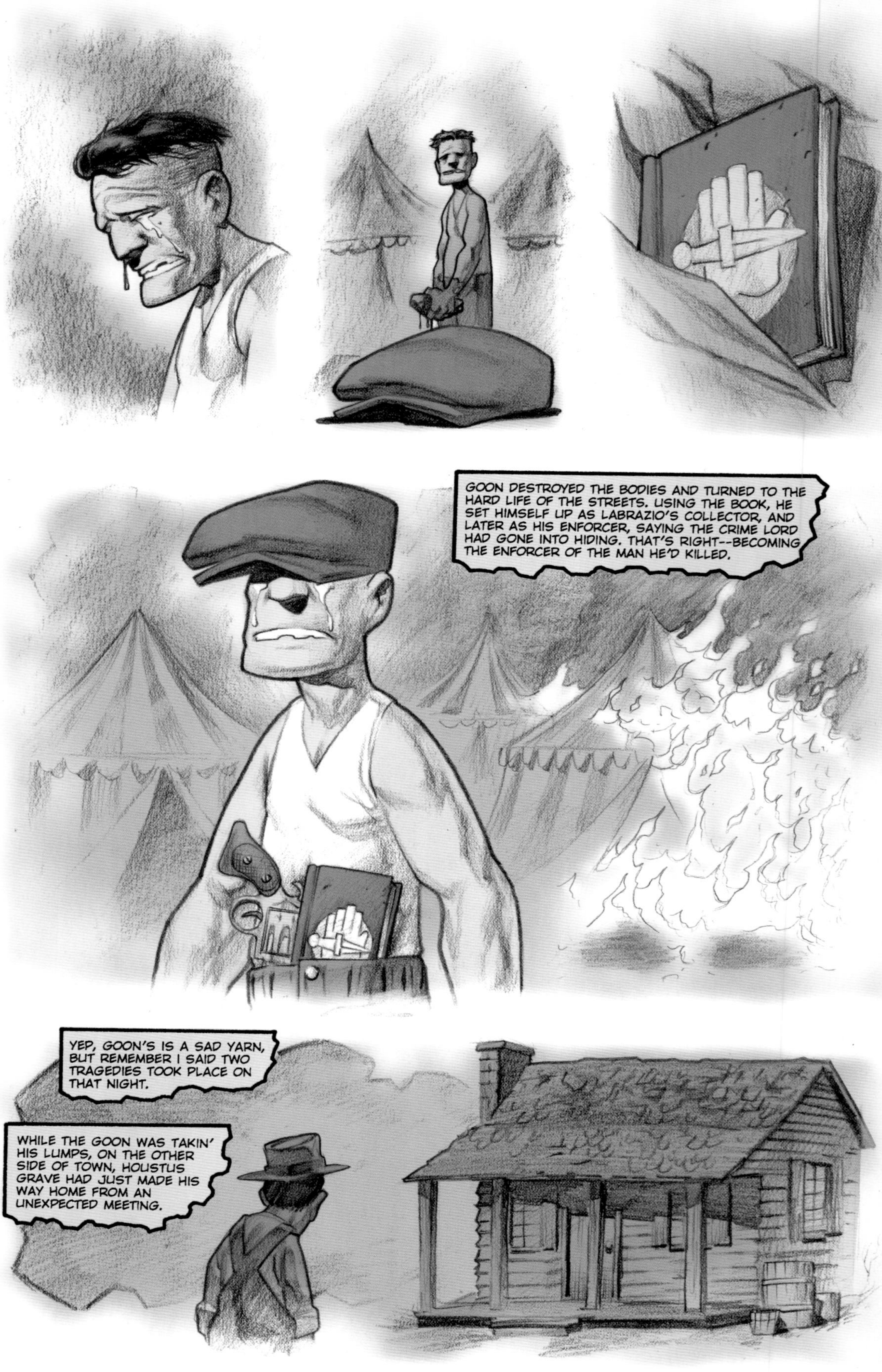
GOON DESTROYED THE BODIES AND TURNED TO THE HARD LIFE OF THE STREETS. USING THE BOOK, HE SET HIMSELF UP AS LABRAZIO'S COLLECTOR, AND LATER AS HIS ENFORCER, SAYING THE CRIME LORD HAD GONE INTO HIDING. THAT'S RIGHT--BECOMING THE ENFORCER OF THE MAN HE'D KILLED.
YEP, GOON'S IS A SAD YARN, BUT REMEMBER I SAID TWO TRAGEDIES TOOK PLACE ON THAT NIGHT.
WHILE THE GOON WAS TAKIN' HIS LUMPS, ON THE OTHER SIDE OF TOWN, HOUSTUS GRAVE HAD JUST MADE HIS WAY HOME FROM AN UNEXPECTED MEETING.

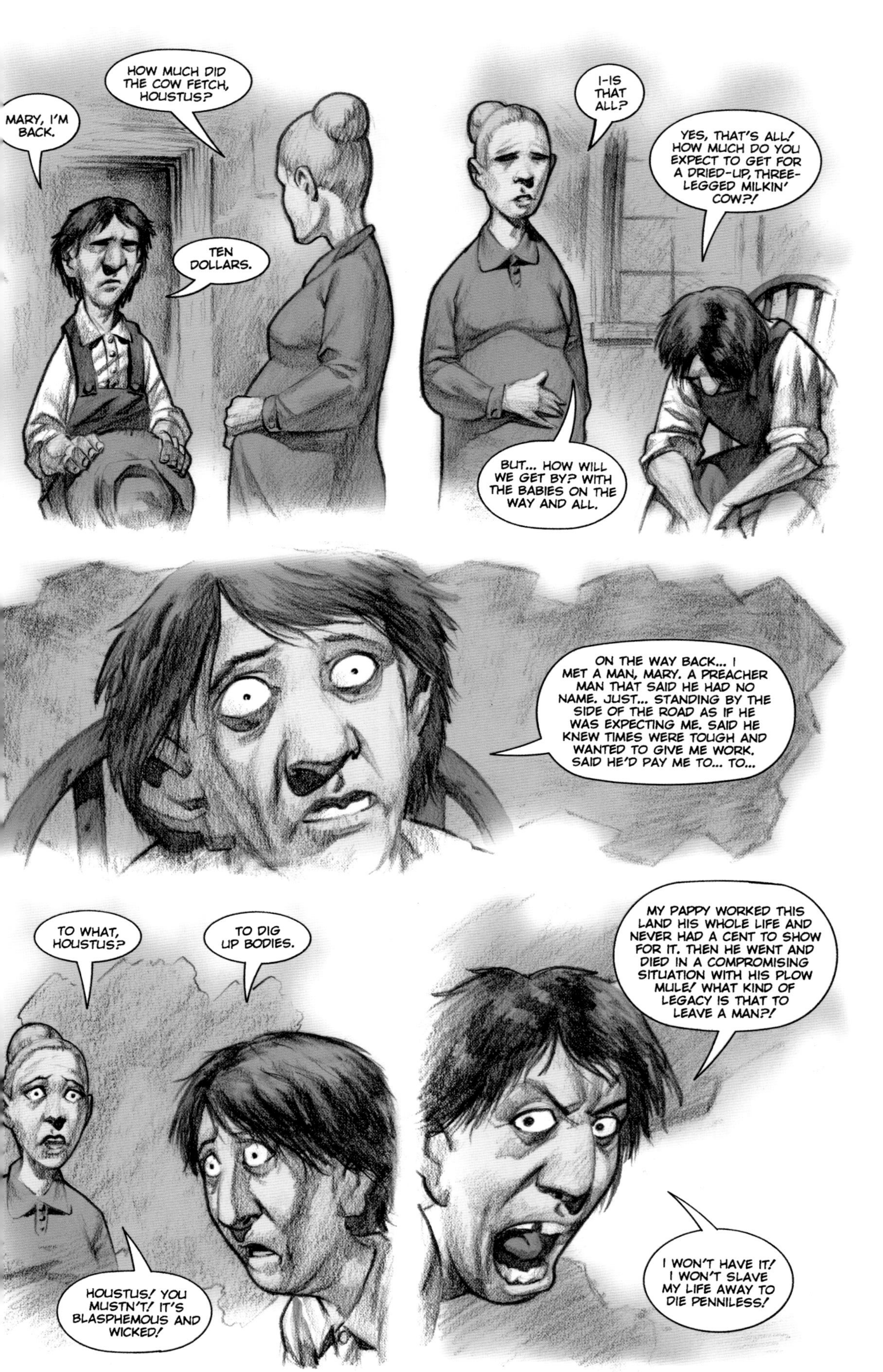
MARY, I'M BACK.
HOW MUCH DID THE COW FETCH, HOUSTUS?
TEN DOLLARS.
I-IS THAT ALL?
YES, THAT'S ALL! HOW MUCH DO YOU EXPECT TO GET FOR A DRIED-UP, THREE-LEGGED MILKIN' COW?!
BUT... HOW WILL WE GET BY? WITH THE BABIES ON THE WAY AND ALL.
ON THE WAY BACK... I MET A MAN, MARY. A PREACHER MAN THAT SAID HE HAD NO NAME. JUST... STANDING BY THE SIDE OF THE ROAD AS IF HE WAS EXPECTING ME. SAID HE KNEW TIMES WERE TOUGH AND WANTED TO GIVE ME WORK. SAID HE'D PAY ME TO... TO...
TO WHAT, HOUSTUS?
TO DIG UP BODIES.
HOUSTUS! YOU MUSTN'T! IT'S BLASPHEMOUS AND WICKED!
MY PAPPY WORKED THIS LAND HIS WHOLE LIFE AND NEVER HAD A CENT TO SHOW FOR IT. THEN HE WENT AND DIED IN A COMPROMISING SITUATION WITH HIS PLOW MULE! WHAT KIND OF LEGACY IS THAT TO LEAVE A MAN?!
I WON'T HAVE IT! I WON'T SLAVE MY LIFE AWAY TO DIE PENNILESS!

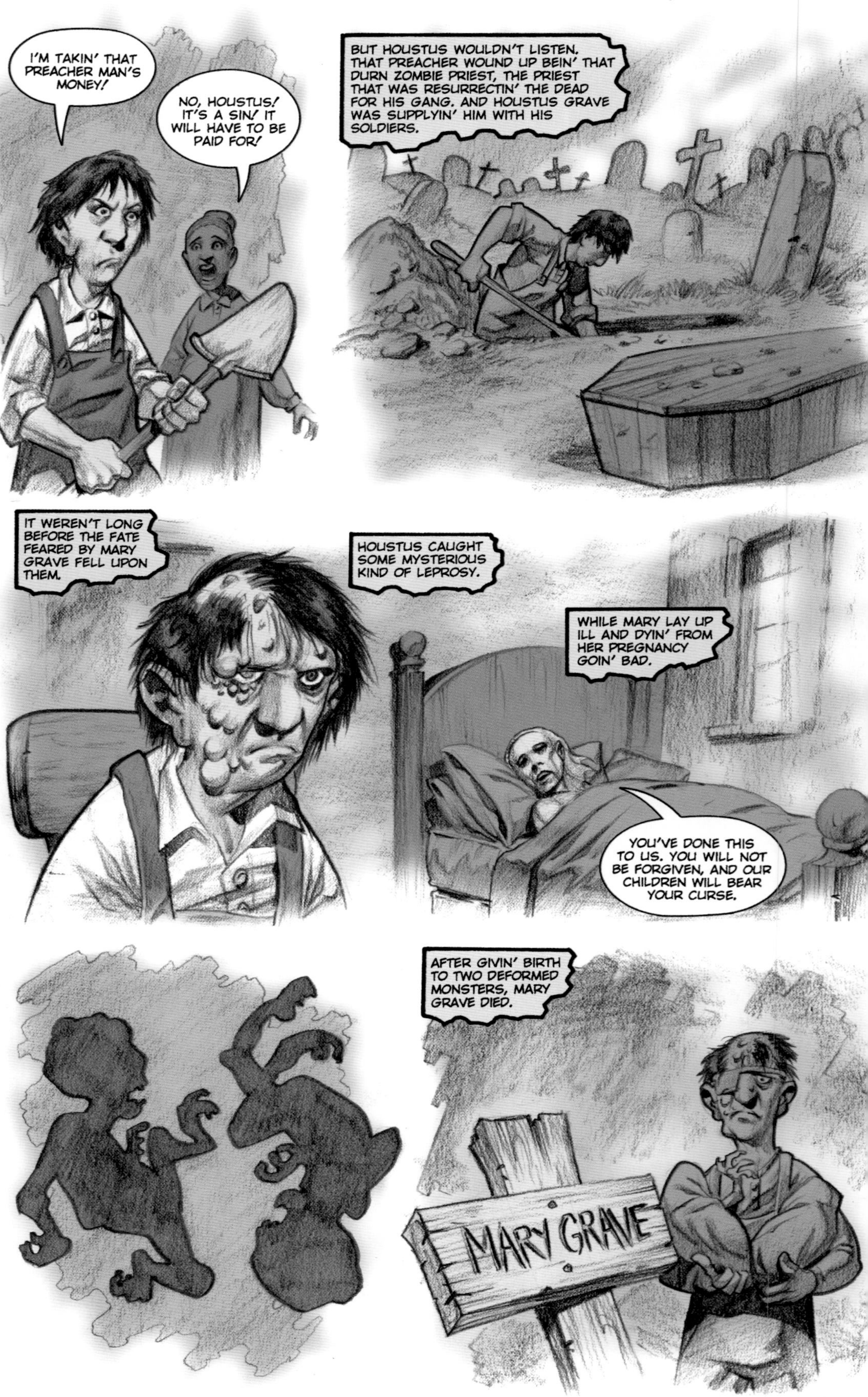
I'M TAKIN' THAT PREACHER MAN'S MONEY!
NO, HOUSTUS! IT'S A SIN! IT WILL HAVE TO BE PAID FOR!
BUT HOUSTUS WOULDN'T LISTEN. THAT PREACHER WOUND UP BEIN' THAT DURN ZOMBIE PRIEST, THE PRIEST THAT WAS RESURRECTIN' THE DEAD FOR HIS GANG. AND HOUSTUS GRAVE WAS SUPPLYIN' HIM WITH HIS SOLDIERS.
IT WEREN'T LONG BEFORE THE FATE FEARED BY MARY GRAVE FELL UPON THEM.
HOUSTUS CAUGHT SOME MYSTERIOUS KIND OF LEPROSY.
WHILE MARY LAY UP ILL AND DYIN' FROM HER PREGNANCY GOIN' BAD.
YOU'VE DONE THIS TO US. YOU WILL NOT BE FORGIVEN, AND OUR CHILDREN WILL BEAR YOUR CURSE.
AFTER GIVIN' BIRTH TO TWO DEFORMED MONSTERS, MARY GRAVE DIED.
MARY GRAVE

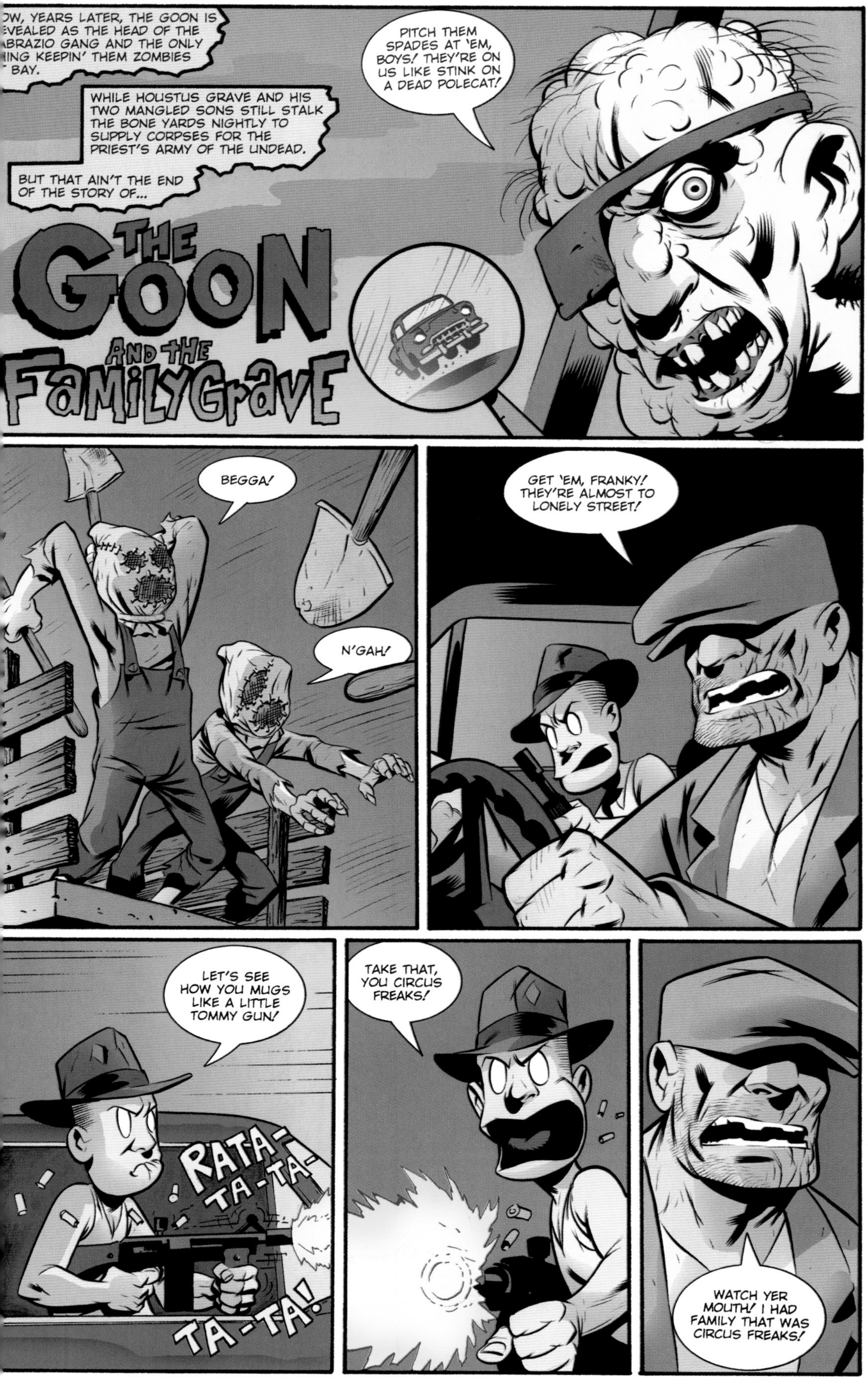

OW, YEARS LATER, THE GOON IS EVEALED AS THE HEAD OF THE BRAZIO GANG AND THE ONLY HING KEEPIN' THEM ZOMBIES BAY.
WHILE HOUSTUS GRAVE AND HIS TWO MANGLED SONS STILL STALK THE BONE YARDS NIGHTLY TO SUPPLY CORPSES FOR THE PRIEST'S ARMY OF THE UNDEAD.
BUT THAT AIN'T THE END OF THE STORY OF...
THE GOON AND THE FAMILY GRAVE
PITCH THEM SPADES AT 'EM, BOYS! THEY'RE ON US LIKE STINK ON A DEAD POLECAT!
BEGGA!
N'GAH!
GET 'EM, FRANKY! THEY'RE ALMOST TO LONELY STREET!
LET'S SEE HOW YOU MUGS LIKE A LITTLE TOMMY GUN!
RATA-TA-TA-TA-TA!
TAKE THAT, YOU CIRCUS FREAKS!
WATCH YER MOUTH! I HAD FAMILY THAT WAS CIRCUS FREAKS!

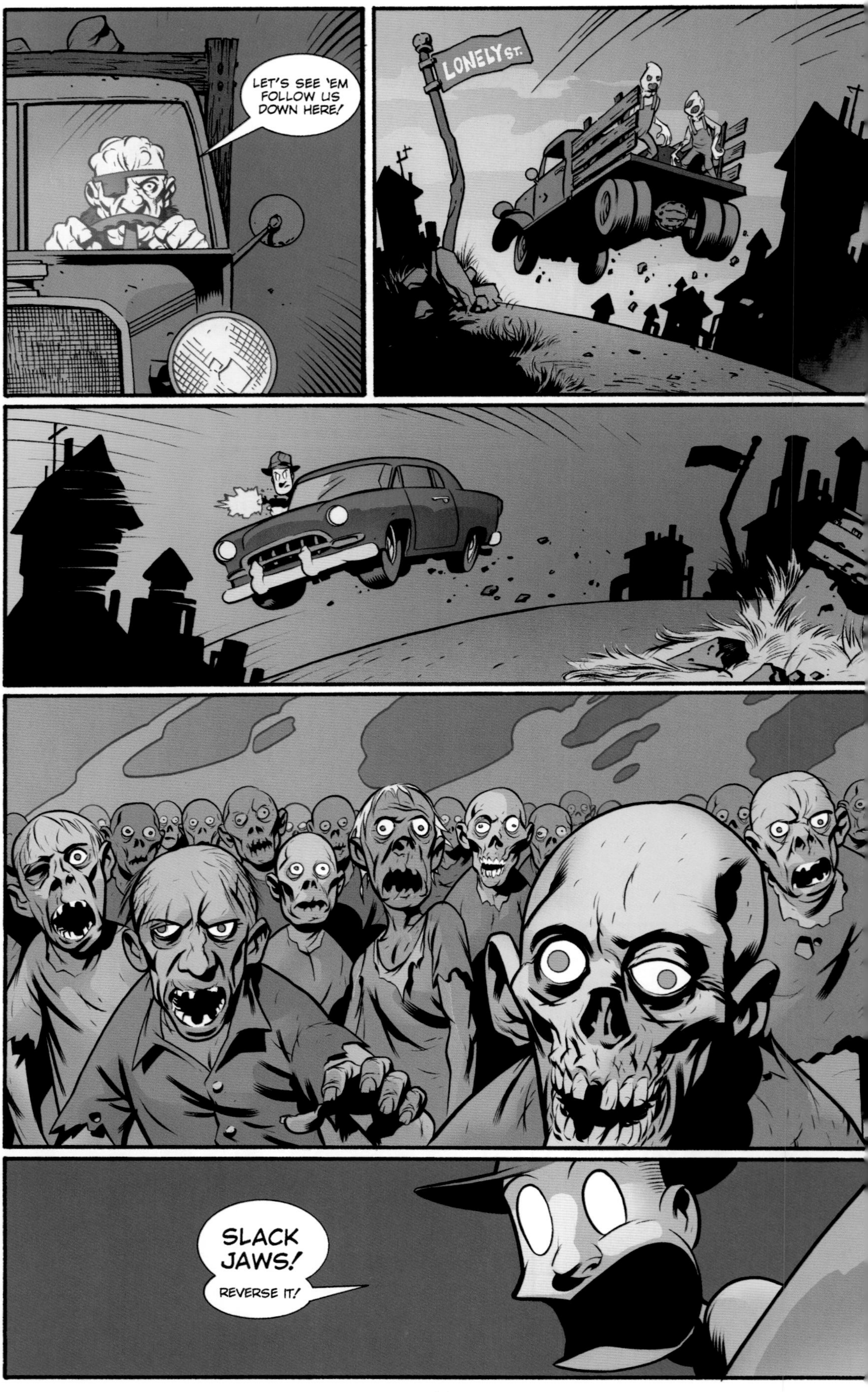
LET'S SEE 'EM FOLLOW US DOWN HERE!
LONELY ST.
SLACK JAWS!
REVERSE IT!

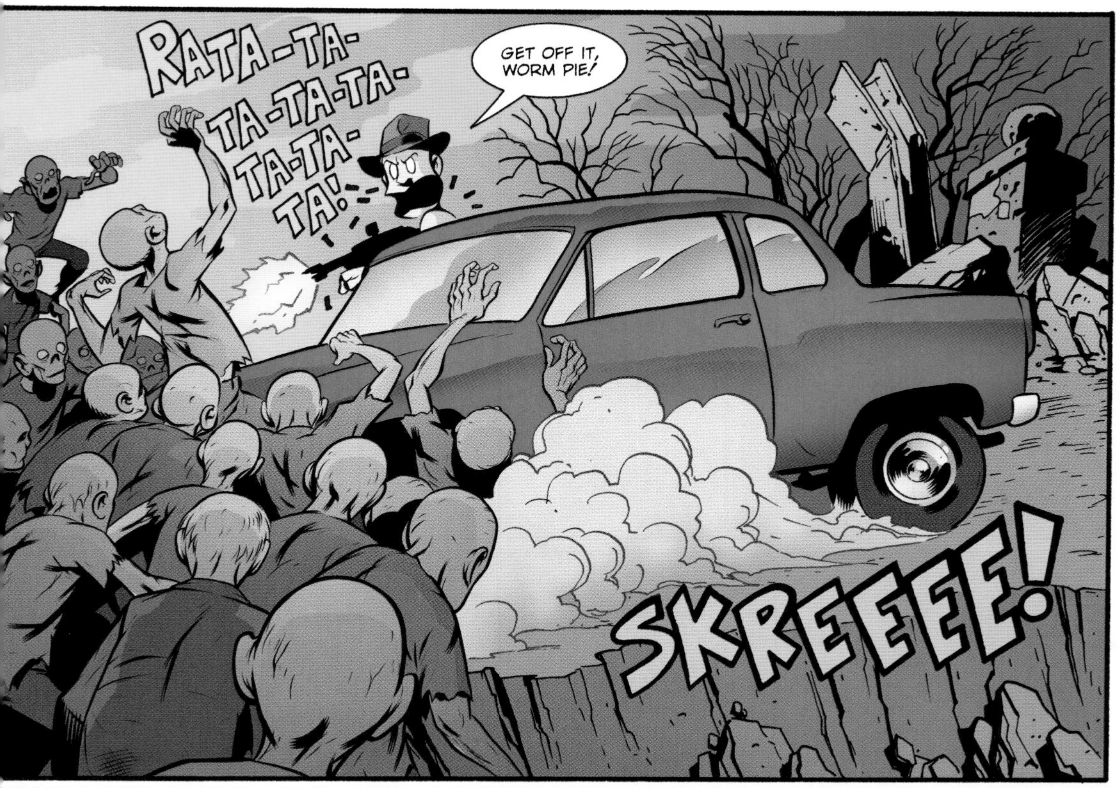
RATA-TA-TA-TA-TA-TA-TA-TA!
GET OFF IT, WORM PIE!
SKREEEE!

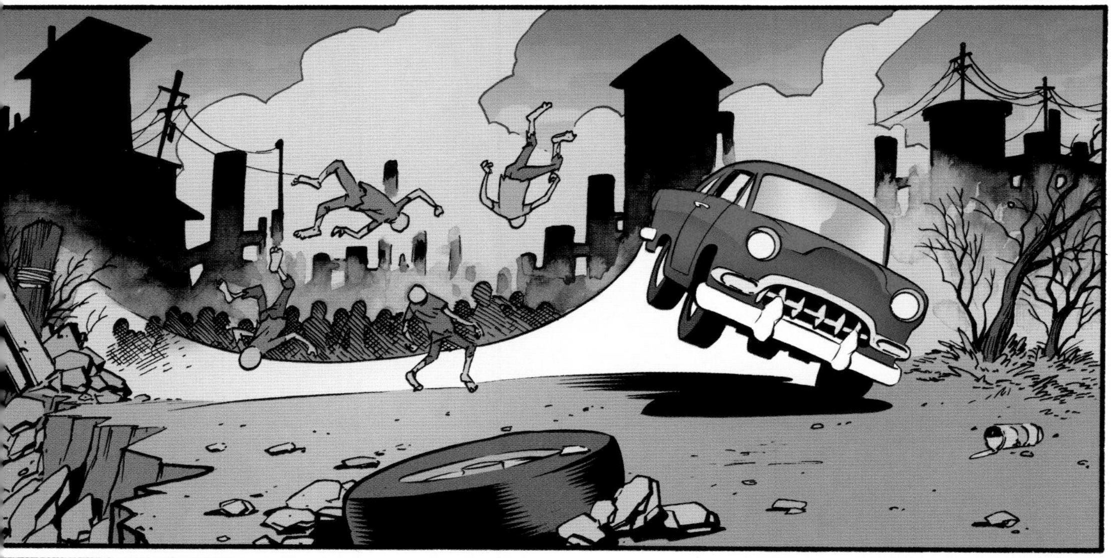

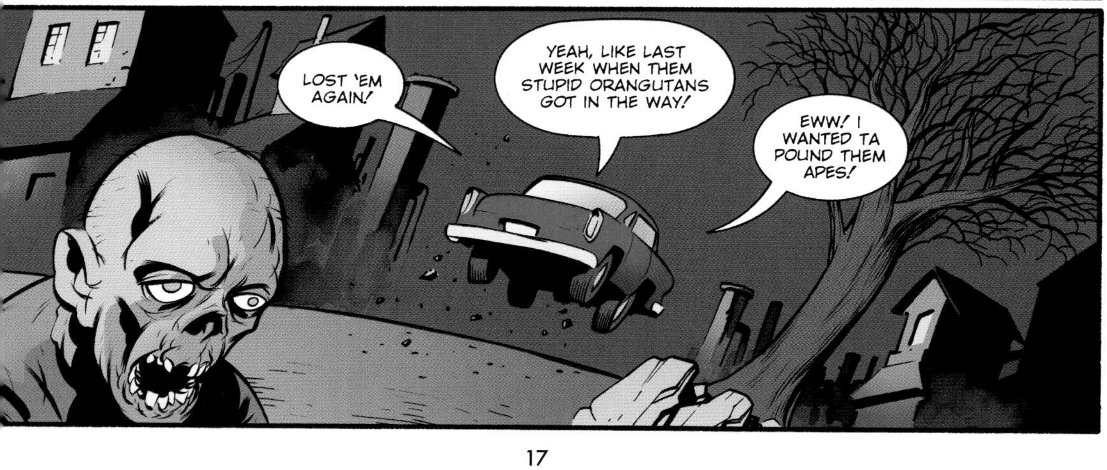
LOST 'EM AGAIN!
YEAH, LIKE LAST WEEK WHEN THEM STUPID ORANGUTANS GOT IN THE WAY!
EWW! I WANTED TA POUND THEM APES!

DOESN'T IT LOOK GOOD, BUZZARD? WOULDN'T YOU LIKE JUST A LITTLE BITE?

EEH-EEH--I WOULDN'T TAKE SO MUCH AS A SUGAR CUBE FROM YER HAND, YOU SKIRT-WEARIN' MAGGOT!

SIR, GRAVE IS HERE.

IT'S ABOUT TIME! I NEEDED REINFORCEMENTS THREE WEEKS AGO!

SAY, WHO'S HE?

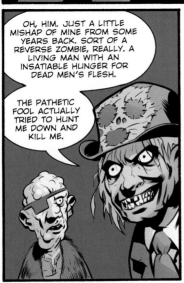

OH, HIM. JUST A LITTLE MISHAP OF MINE FROM SOME YEARS BACK. SORT OF A REVERSE ZOMBIE, REALLY. A LIVING MAN WITH AN INSATIABLE HUNGER FOR DEAD MEN'S FLESH.

THE PATHETIC FOOL ACTUALLY TRIED TO HUNT ME DOWN AND KILL ME.

NOW, I'M STARVING HIM. JUST FOR CURIOSITY. JUST TO SEE HOW LONG HE CAN LAST. WHAT'S IT BEEN, BUZZARD, TWO MONTHS? APPARENTLY THE ACCIDENT HAS MADE HIM INCREDIBLY RESILIENT.

I GOT YER RESILIENT RIGHT HERE, YOU BOW-LEGGED, PRISSY LITTLE FAIRY MARY!

I'M GONNA SKIN YOU AND WEAR YER MAW AS A PARTY HAT!

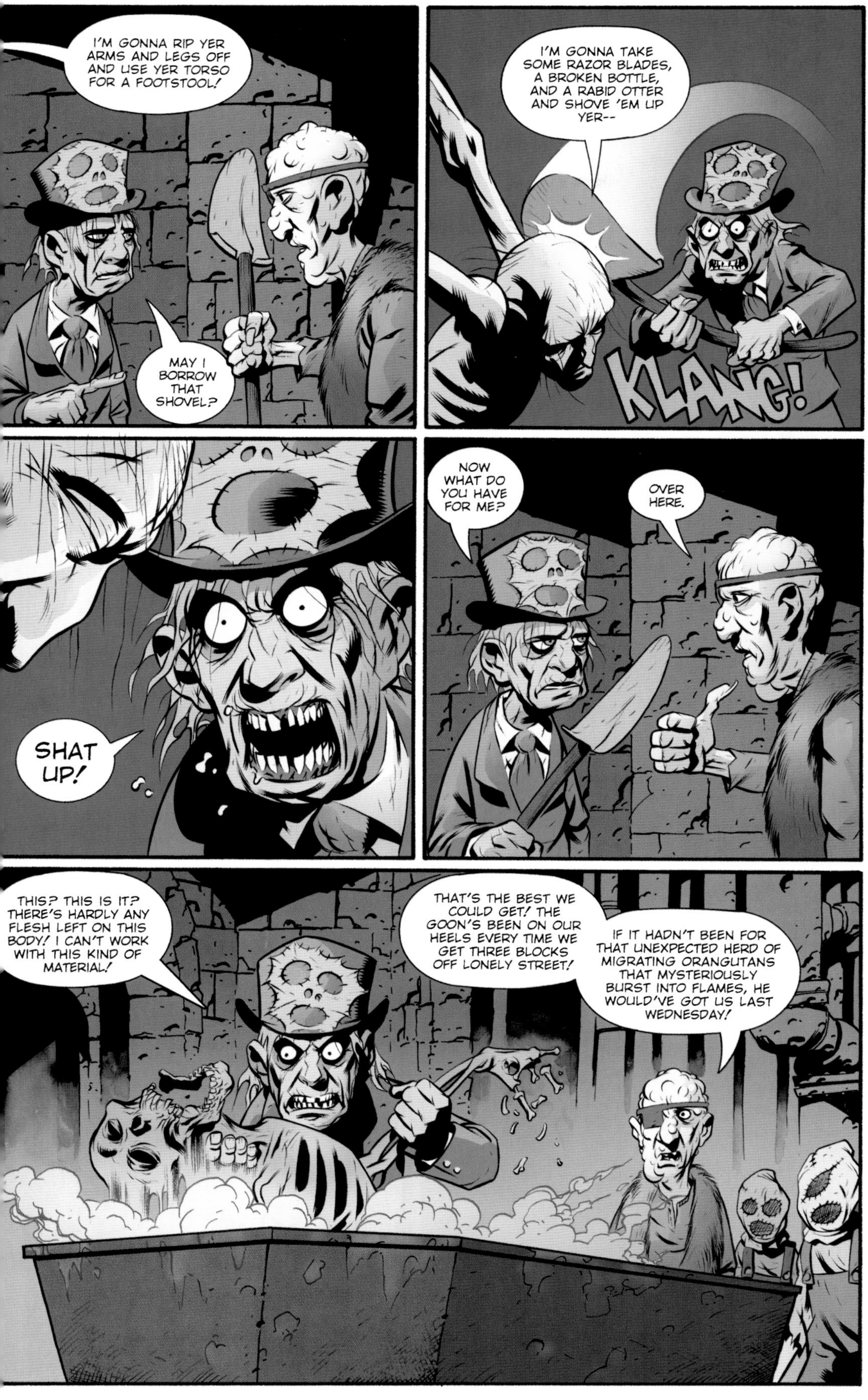
I'M GONNA RIP YER ARMS AND LEGS OFF AND USE YER TORSO FOR A FOOTSTOOL!
MAY I BORROW THAT SHOVEL?
I'M GONNA TAKE SOME RAZOR BLADES, A BROKEN BOTTLE, AND A RABID OTTER AND SHOVE 'EM UP YER--
KLANG!
SHAT UP!
NOW WHAT DO YOU HAVE FOR ME?
OVER HERE.
THIS? THIS IS IT? THERE'S HARDLY ANY FLESH LEFT ON THIS BODY! I CAN'T WORK WITH THIS KIND OF MATERIAL!
THAT'S THE BEST WE COULD GET! THE GOON'S BEEN ON OUR HEELS EVERY TIME WE GET THREE BLOCKS OFF LONELY STREET!
IF IT HADN'T BEEN FOR THAT UNEXPECTED HERD OF MIGRATING ORANGUTANS THAT MYSTERIOUSLY BURST INTO FLAMES, HE WOULD'VE GOT US LAST WEDNESDAY!

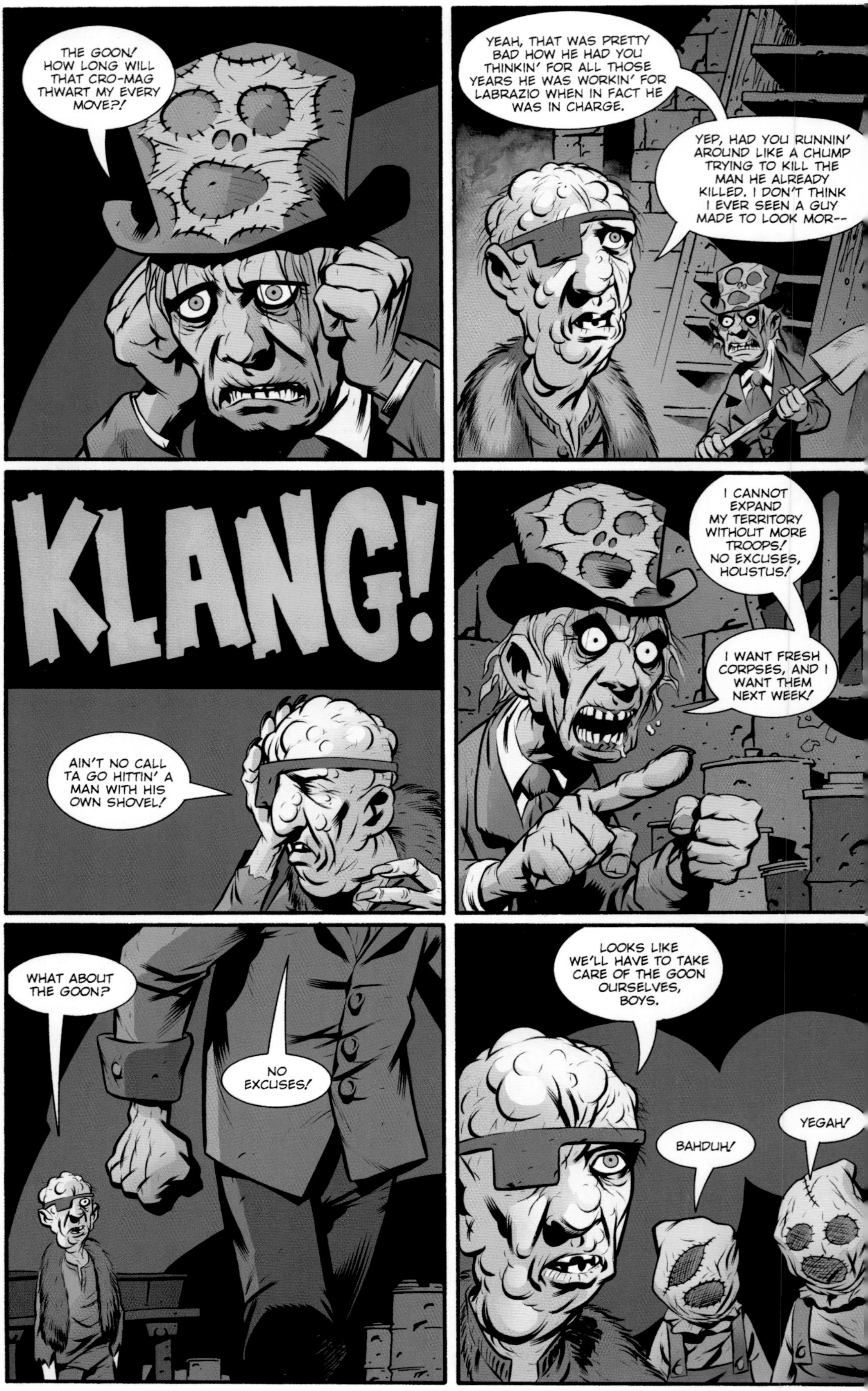
THE GOON! HOW LONG WILL THAT CRO-MAG THWART MY EVERY MOVE?!
YEAH, THAT WAS PRETTY BAD HOW HE HAD YOU THINKIN' FOR ALL THOSE YEARS HE WAS WORKIN' FOR LABRAZIO WHEN IN FACT HE WAS IN CHARGE.
YEP, HAD YOU RUNNIN' AROUND LIKE A CHUMP TRYING TO KILL THE MAN HE ALREADY KILLED. I DON'T THINK I EVER SEEN A GUY MADE TO LOOK MOR--
KLANG!
AIN'T NO CALL TA GO HITTIN' A MAN WITH HIS OWN SHOVEL!
I CANNOT EXPAND MY TERRITORY WITHOUT MORE TROOPS! NO EXCUSES, HOUSTUS!
I WANT FRESH CORPSES, AND I WANT THEM NEXT WEEK!
WHAT ABOUT THE GOON?
NO EXCUSES!
LOOKS LIKE WE'LL HAVE TO TAKE CARE OF THE GOON OURSELVES, BOYS.
BAHDUH!
YEGAH!

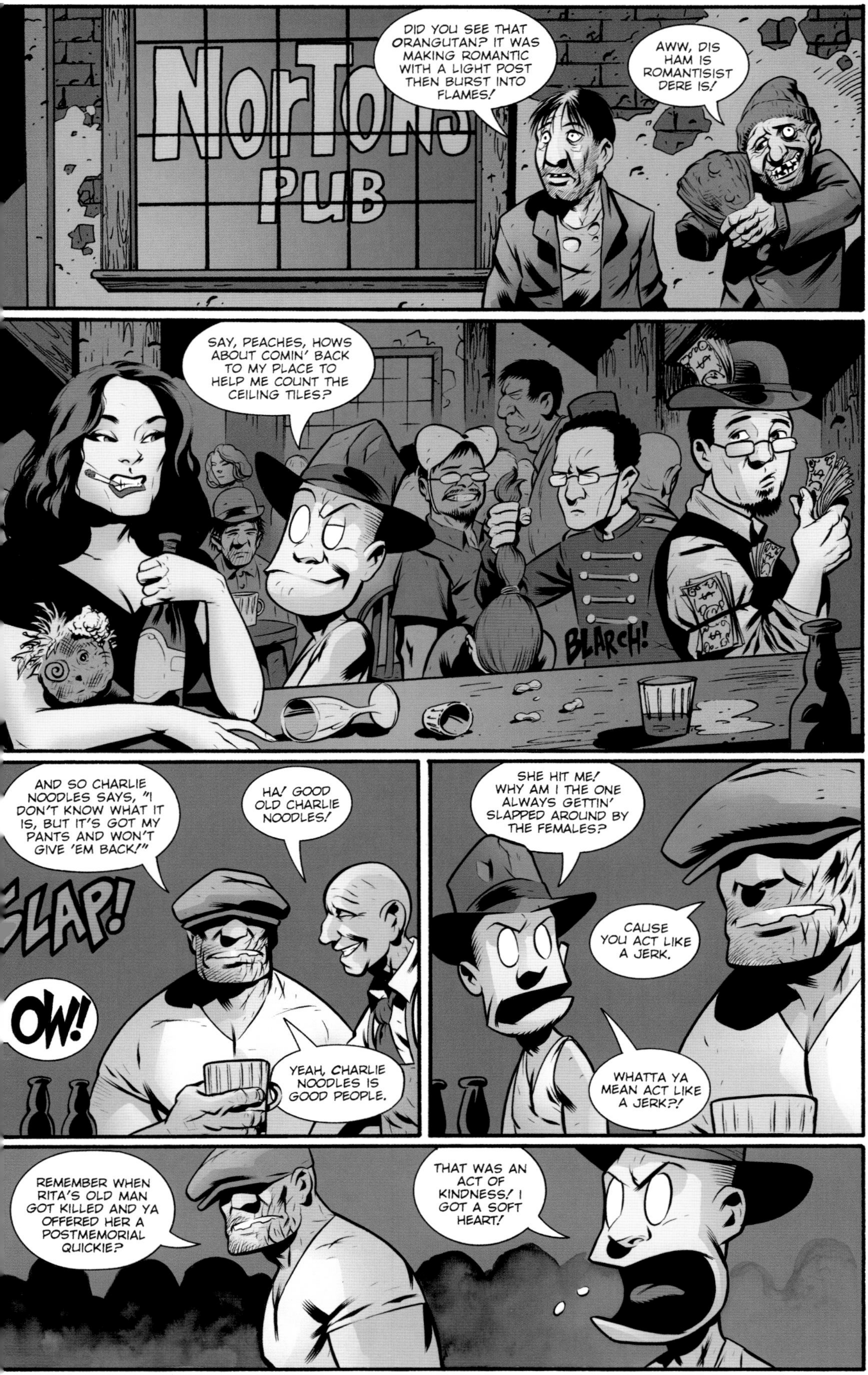
NorTons PUB
DID YOU SEE THAT ORANGUTAN? IT WAS MAKING ROMANTIC WITH A LIGHT POST THEN BURST INTO FLAMES!
AWW, DIS HAM IS ROMANTISIST DERE IS!
SAY, PEACHES, HOWS ABOUT COMIN' BACK TO MY PLACE TO HELP ME COUNT THE CEILING TILES?
BLARCH!
AND SO CHARLIE NOODLES SAYS, "I DON'T KNOW WHAT IT IS, BUT IT'S GOT MY PANTS AND WON'T GIVE 'EM BACK!"
HA! GOOD OLD CHARLIE NOODLES!
SLAP!
OW!
YEAH, CHARLIE NOODLES IS GOOD PEOPLE.
SHE HIT ME! WHY AM I THE ONE ALWAYS GETTIN' SLAPPED AROUND BY THE FEMALES?
CAUSE YOU ACT LIKE A JERK.
WHATTA YA MEAN ACT LIKE A JERK?!
REMEMBER WHEN RITA'S OLD MAN GOT KILLED AND YA OFFERED HER A POSTMEMORIAL QUICKIE?
THAT WAS AN ACT OF KINDNESS! I GOT A SOFT HEART!

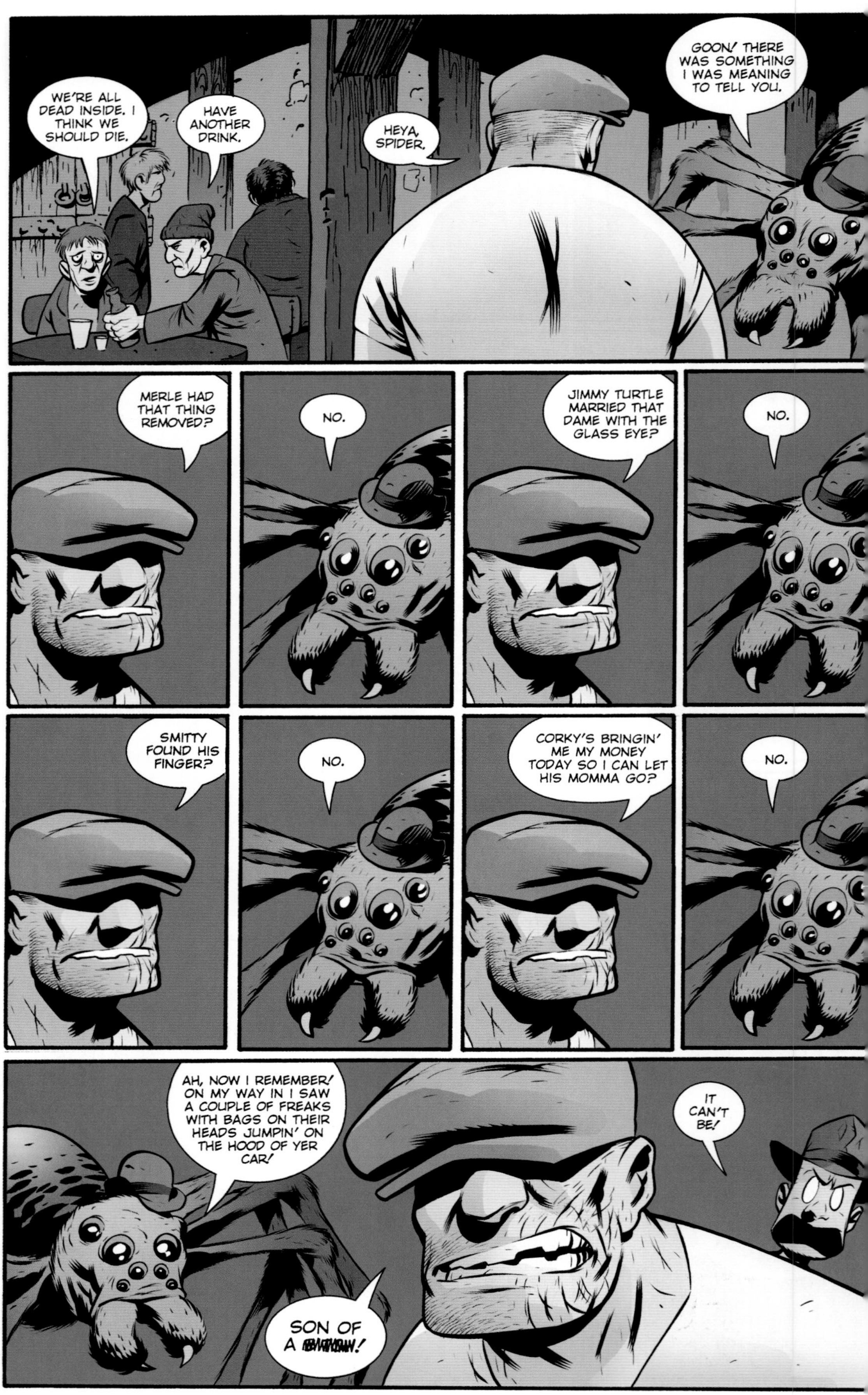
WE'RE ALL DEAD INSIDE. I THINK WE SHOULD DIE.
HAVE ANOTHER DRINK.
HEYA, SPIDER.
GOON! THERE WAS SOMETHING I WAS MEANING TO TELL YOU.
MERLE HAD THAT THING REMOVED?
NO.
JIMMY TURTLE MARRIED THAT DAME WITH THE GLASS EYE?
NO.
SMITTY FOUND HIS FINGER?
NO.
CORKY'S BRINGIN' ME MY MONEY TODAY SO I CAN LET HIS MOMMA GO?
NO.
AH, NOW I REMEMBER! ON MY WAY IN I SAW A COUPLE OF FREAKS WITH BAGS ON THEIR HEADS JUMPIN' ON THE HOOD OF YER CAR!
IT CAN'T BE!
SON OF A

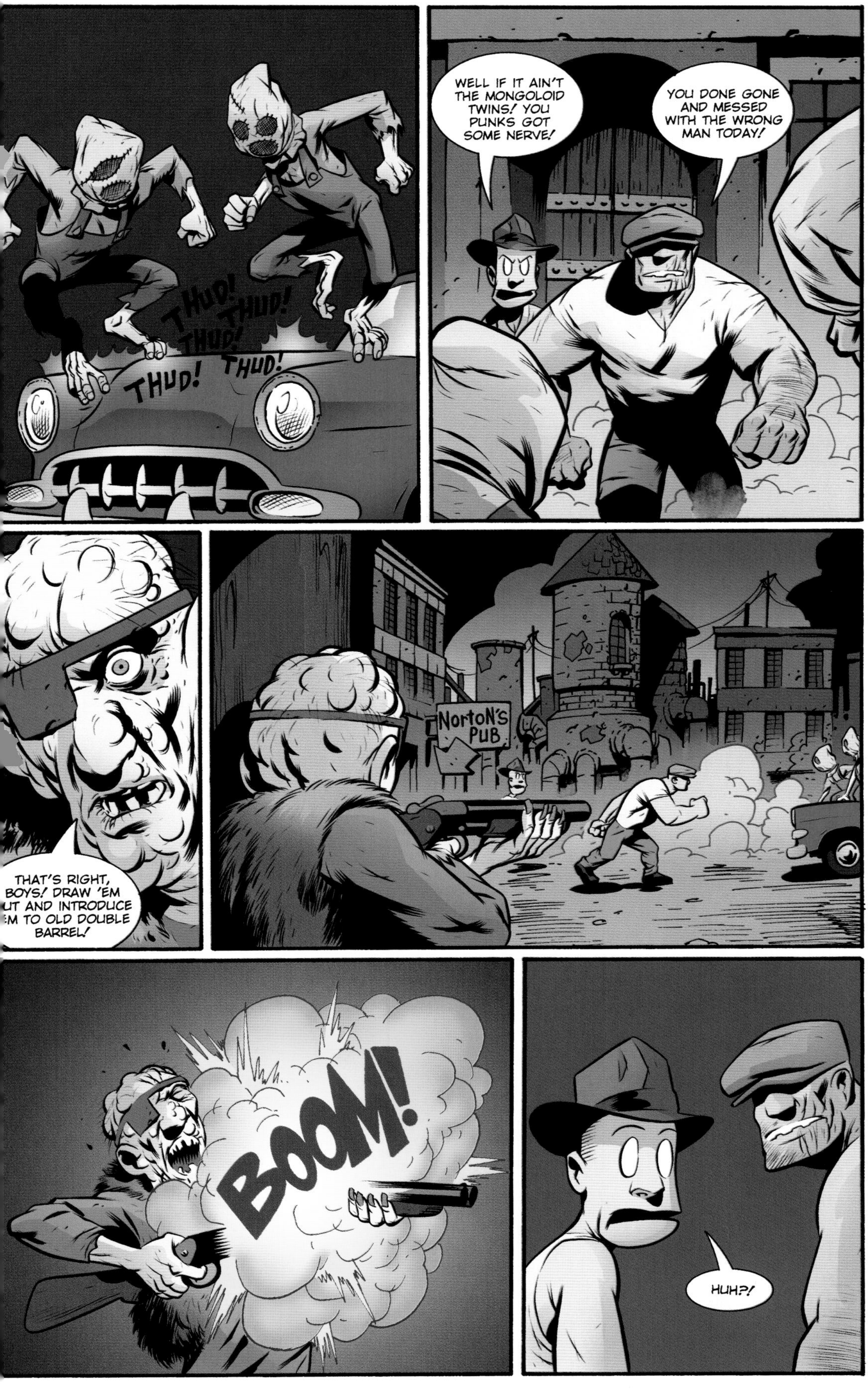

THUD! THUD! THUD! THUD! THUD!
WELL IF IT AIN'T THE MONGOLOID TWINS! YOU PUNKS GOT SOME NERVE!
YOU DONE GONE AND MESSED WITH THE WRONG MAN TODAY!
THAT'S RIGHT, BOYS! DRAW 'EM UT AND INTRODUCE EM TO OLD DOUBLE BARREL!
NortoN'S PUB
BOOM!
HUH?!

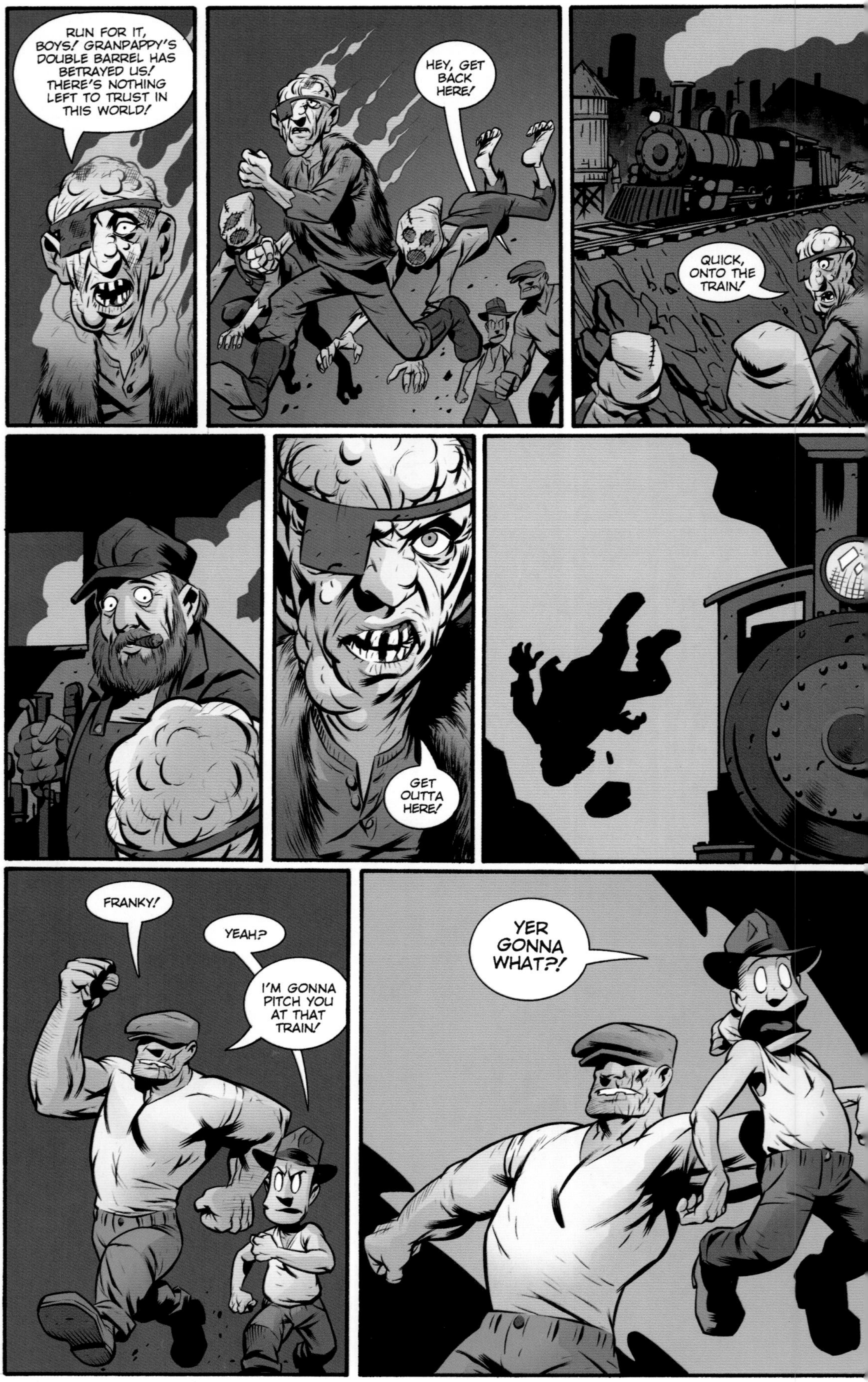
RUN FOR IT, BOYS! GRANPAPPY'S DOUBLE BARREL HAS BETRAYED US! THERE'S NOTHING LEFT TO TRUST IN THIS WORLD!
HEY, GET BACK HERE!
QUICK, ONTO THE TRAIN!
GET OUTTA HERE!
FRANKY!
YEAH?
I'M GONNA PITCH YOU AT THAT TRAIN!
YER GONNA WHAT?!

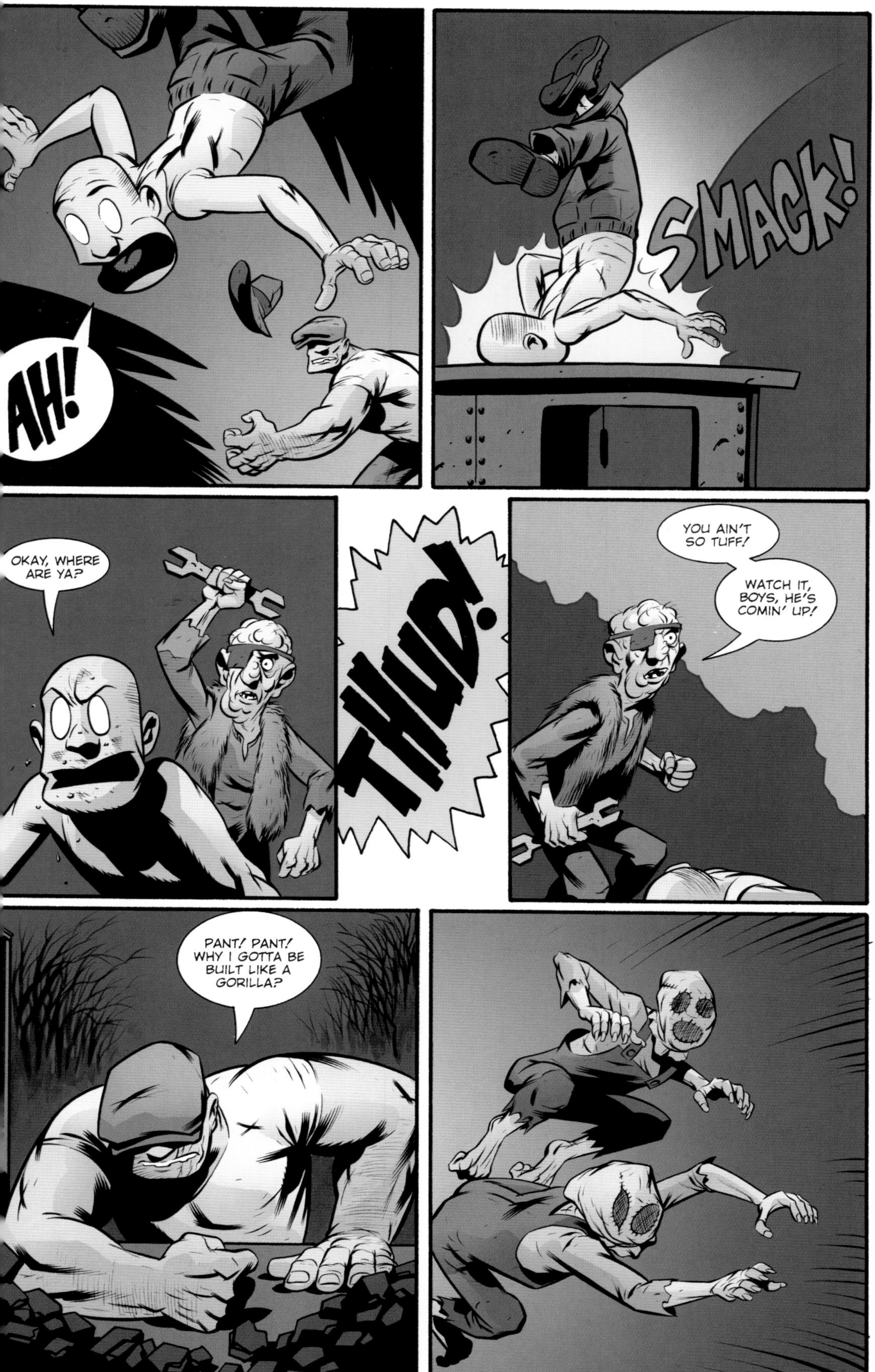
AH!
SMACK!
OKAY, WHERE ARE YA?
THUD!
YOU AIN'T SO TUFF!
WATCH IT, BOYS, HE'S COMIN' UP!
PANT! PANT! WHY I GOTTA BE BUILT LIKE A GORILLA?

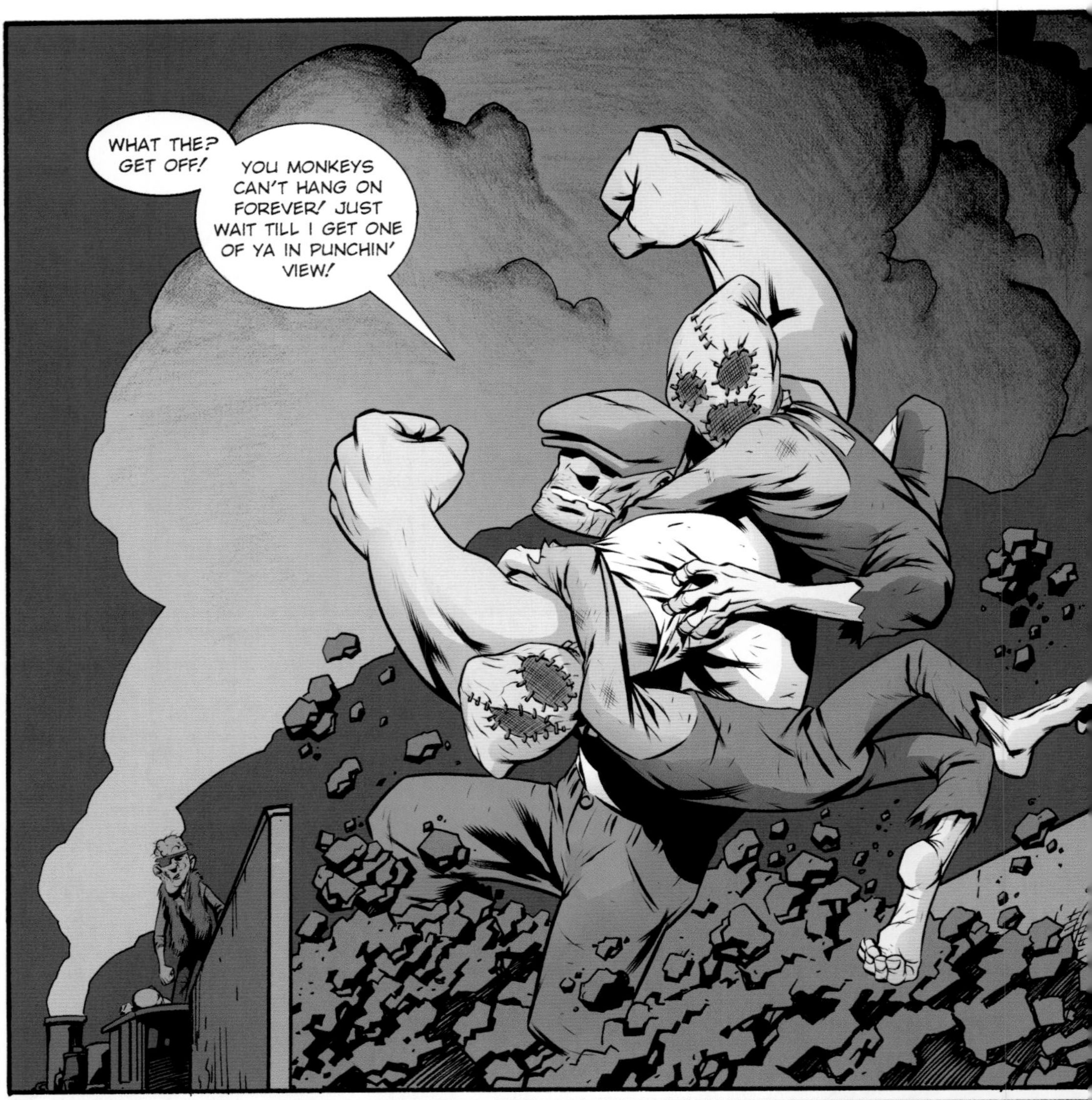
WHAT THE? GET OFF!
YOU MONKEYS CAN'T HANG ON FOREVER! JUST WAIT TILL I GET ONE OF YA IN PUNCHIN' VIEW!

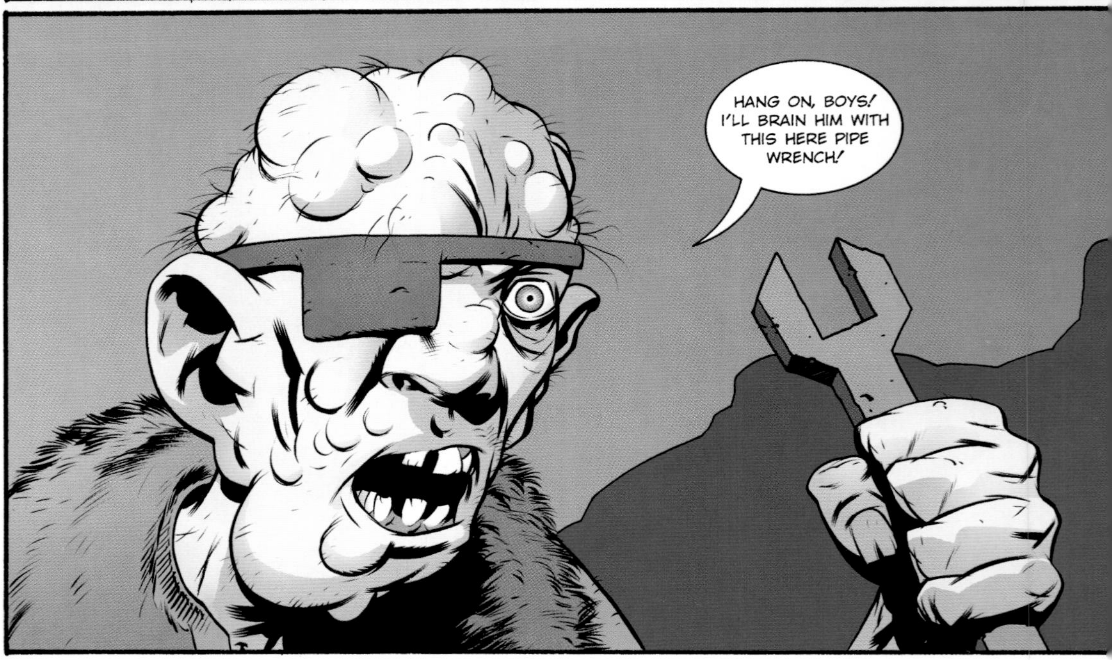
HANG ON, BOYS! I'LL BRAIN HIM WITH THIS HERE PIPE WRENCH!

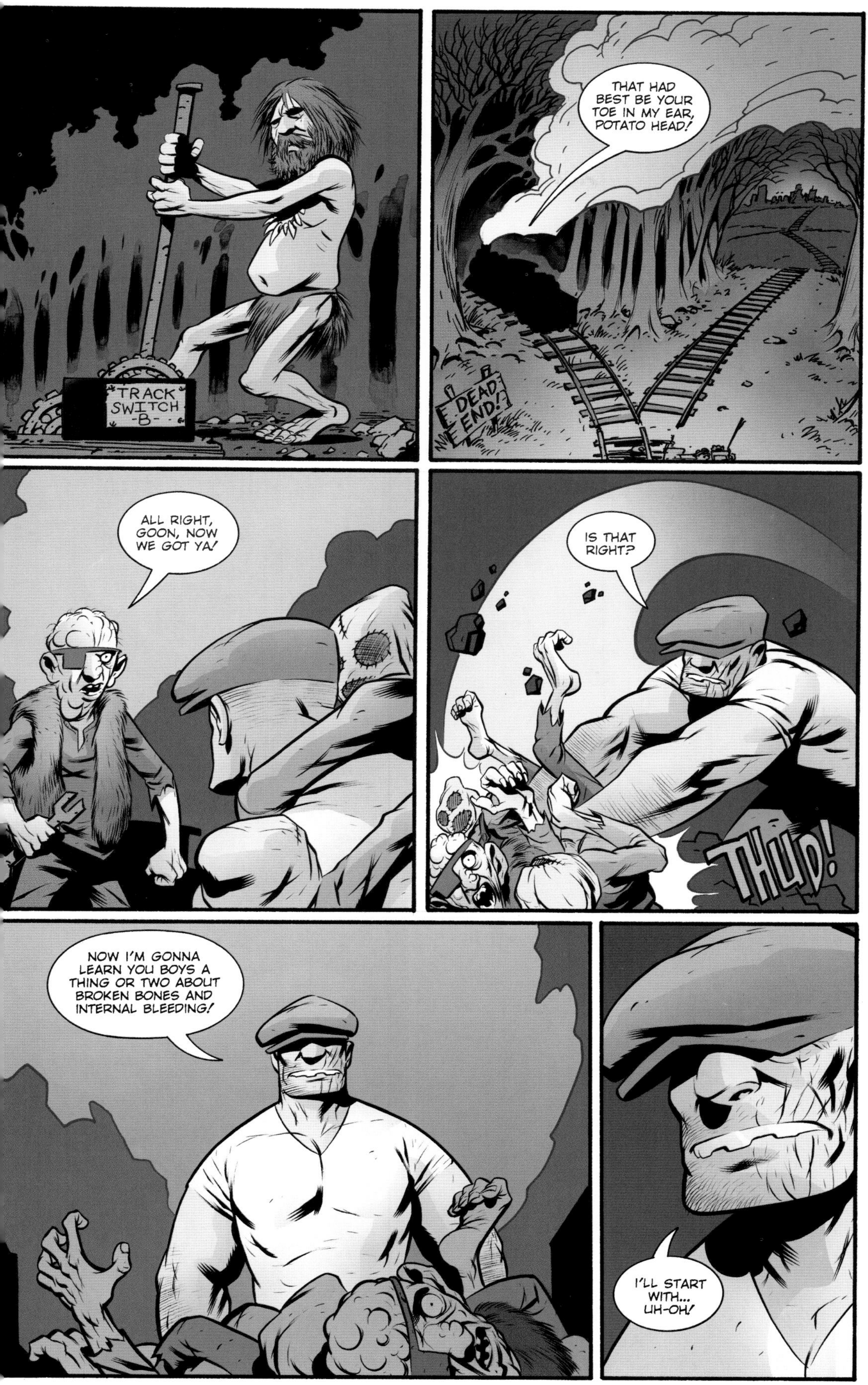
TRACK
SWITCH
-B-
THAT HAD BEST BE YOUR TOE IN MY EAR, POTATO HEAD!
DEAD END!
ALL RIGHT, GOON, NOW WE GOT YA!
IS THAT RIGHT?
THUD!
NOW I'M GONNA LEARN YOU BOYS A THING OR TWO ABOUT BROKEN BONES AND INTERNAL BLEEDING!
I'LL START WITH... UH-OH!

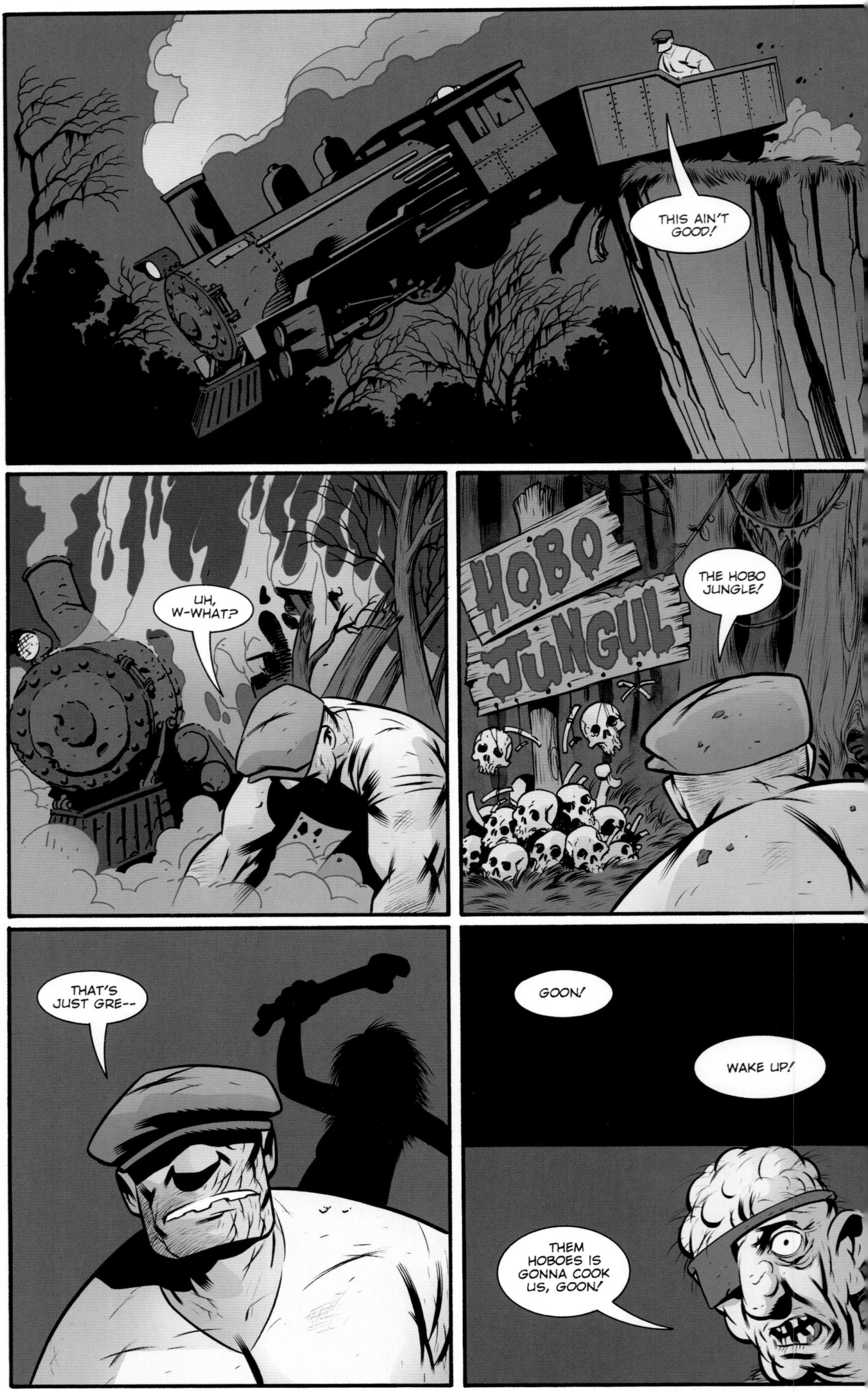
THIS AIN'T GOOD!
UH, W-WHAT?
HOBO JUNGUL
THE HOBO JUNGLE!
THAT'S JUST GRE--
GOON!
WAKE UP!
THEM HOBOES IS GONNA COOK US, GOON!

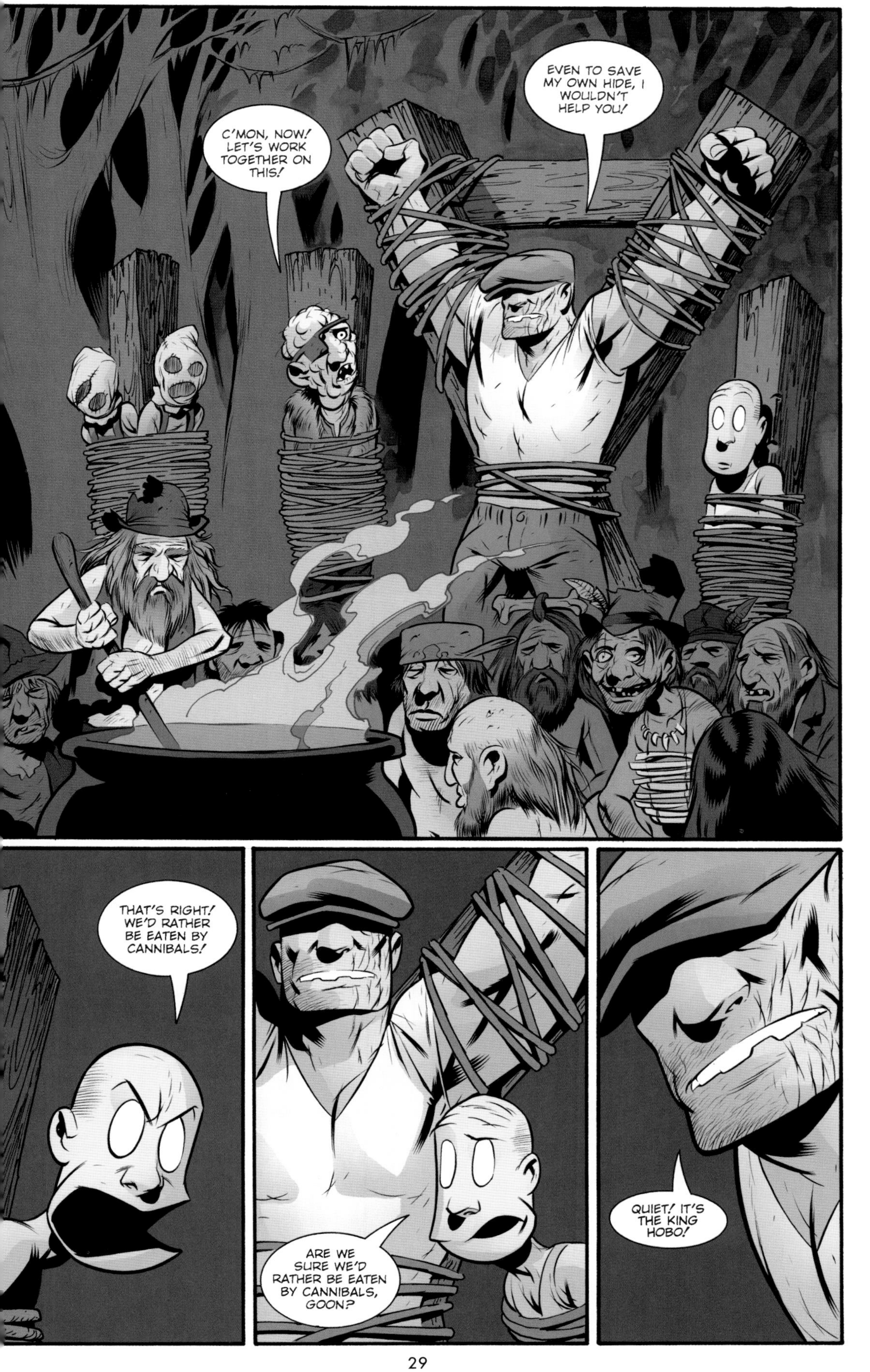
C'MON, NOW! LET'S WORK TOGETHER ON THIS!
EVEN TO SAVE MY OWN HIDE, I WOULDN'T HELP YOU!
THAT'S RIGHT! WE'D RATHER BE EATEN BY CANNIBALS!
ARE WE SURE WE'D RATHER BE EATEN BY CANNIBALS, GOON?
QUIET! IT'S THE KING HOBO!

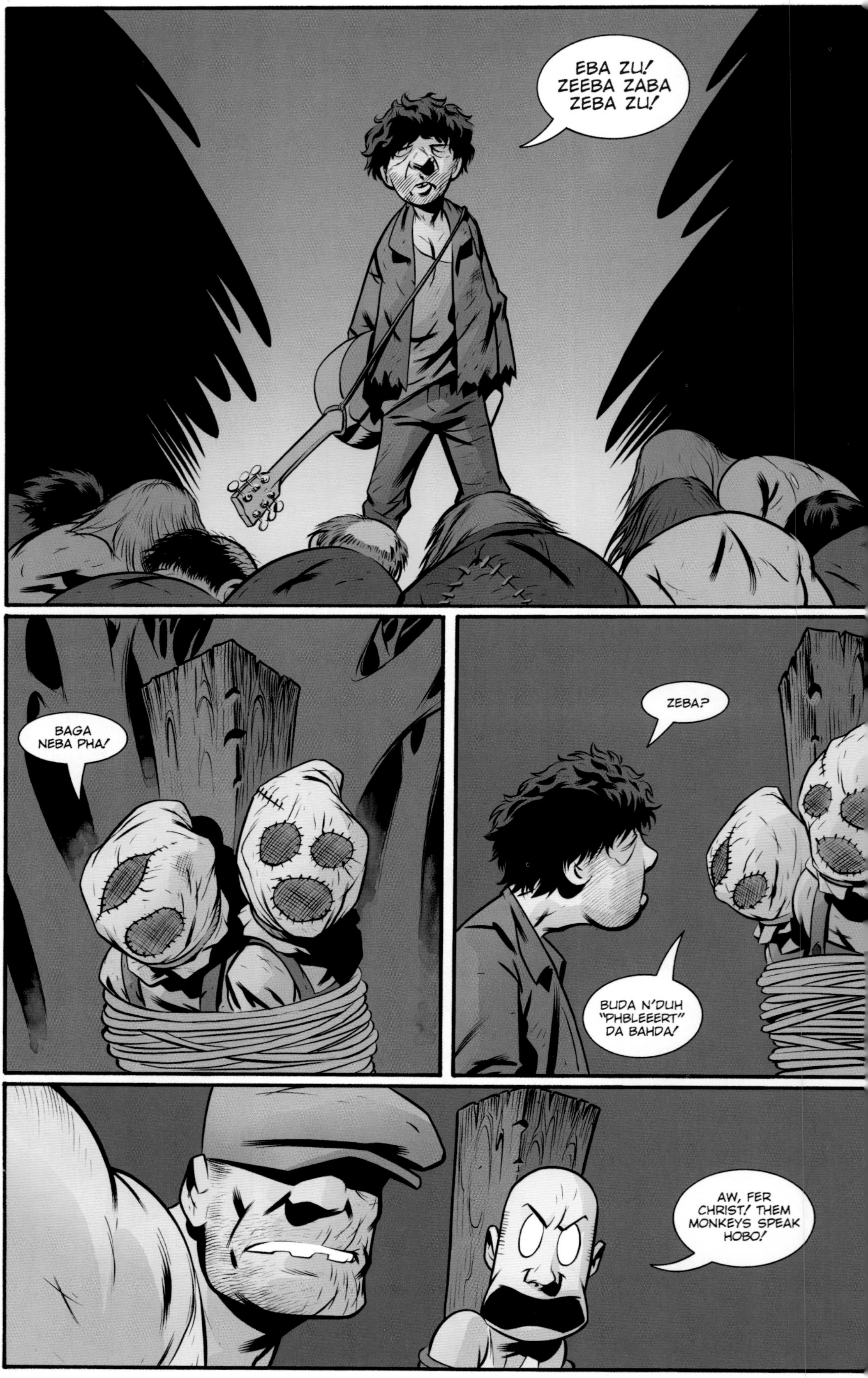
EBA ZU! ZEEBA ZABA ZEBA ZU!
BAGA NEBA PHA!
ZEBA?
BUDA N'DUH "PHBLEEERT" DA BAHDA!
AW, FER CHRIST! THEM MONKEYS SPEAK HOBO!

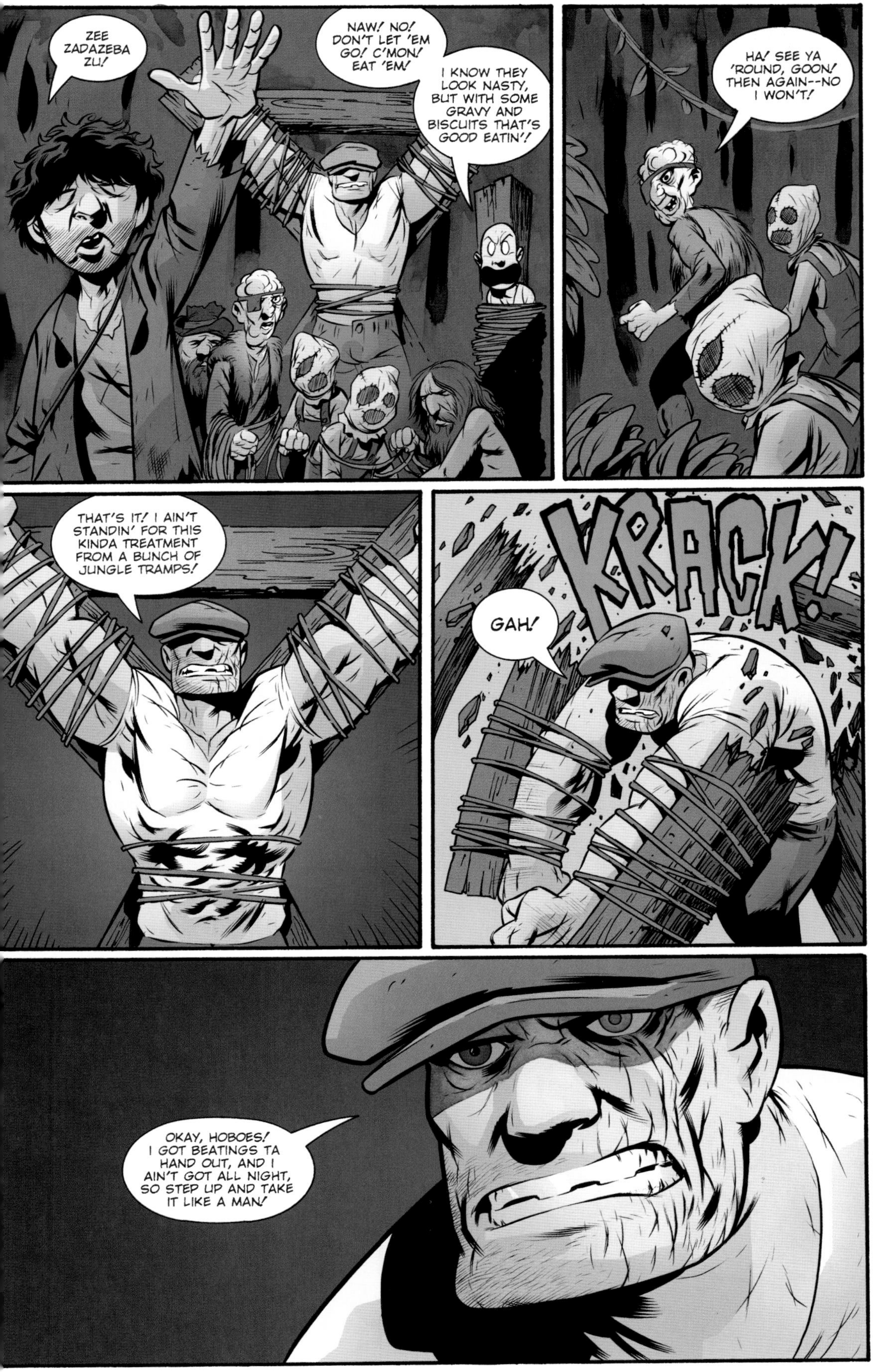
ZEE ZADAZEBA ZU!
NAW! NO! DON'T LET 'EM GO! C'MON! EAT 'EM!
I KNOW THEY LOOK NASTY, BUT WITH SOME GRAVY AND BISCUITS THAT'S GOOD EATIN'!
HA! SEE YA 'ROUND, GOON! THEN AGAIN--NO I WON'T!
THAT'S IT! I AIN'T STANDIN' FOR THIS KINDA TREATMENT FROM A BUNCH OF JUNGLE TRAMPS!
KRACK!
GAH!
OKAY, HOBOES! I GOT BEATINGS TA HAND OUT, AND I AIN'T GOT ALL NIGHT, SO STEP UP AND TAKE IT LIKE A MAN!

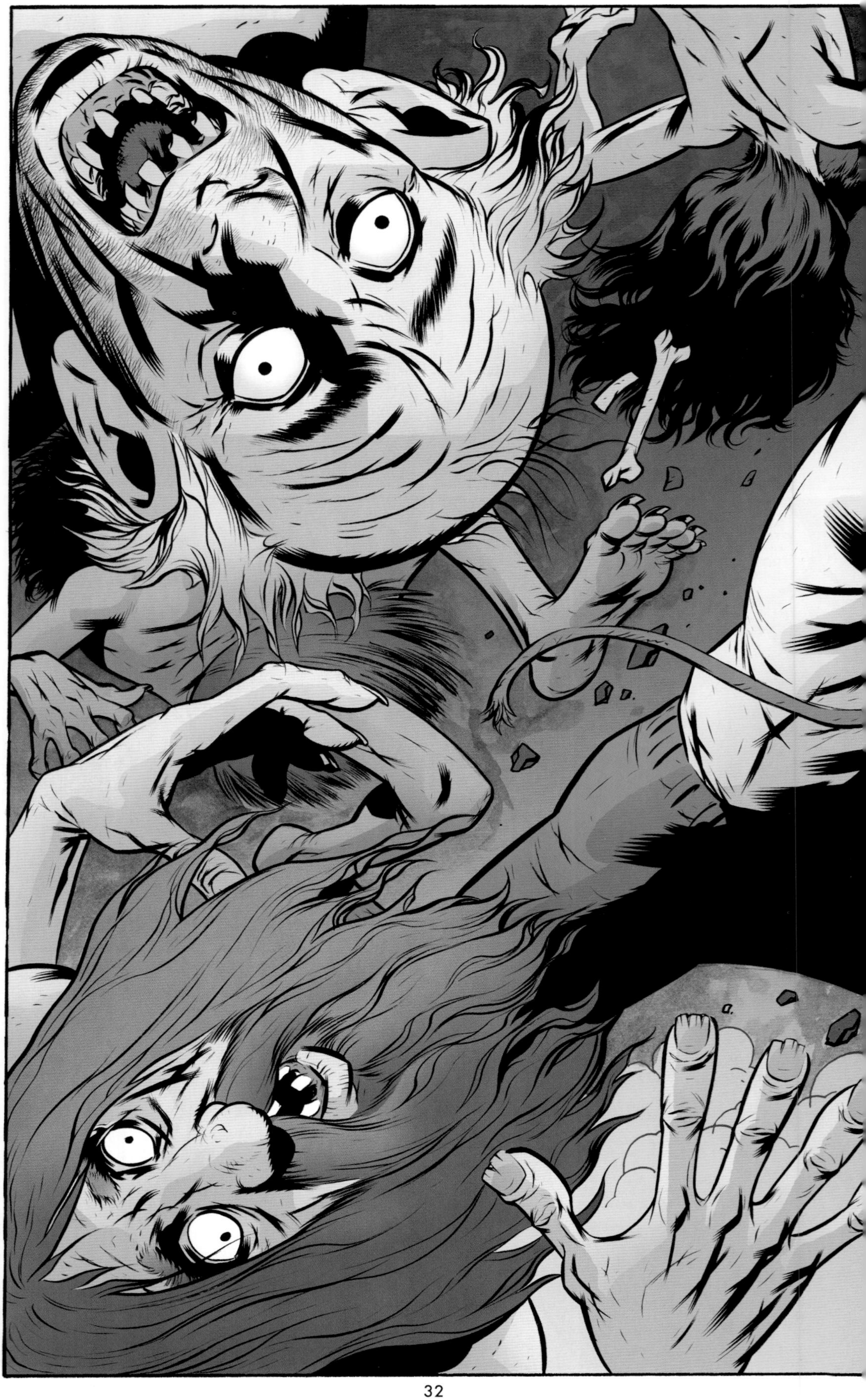

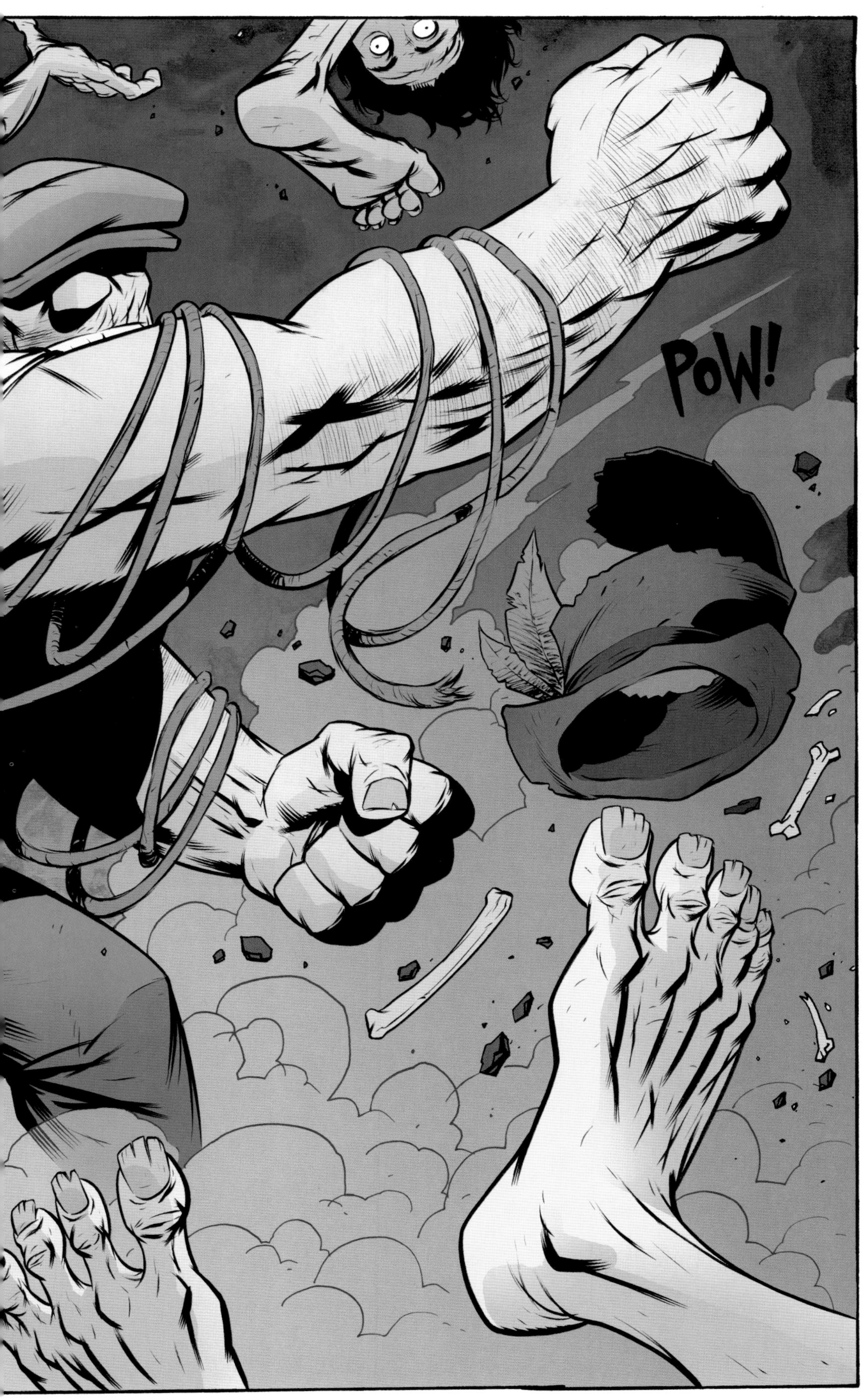
POW!

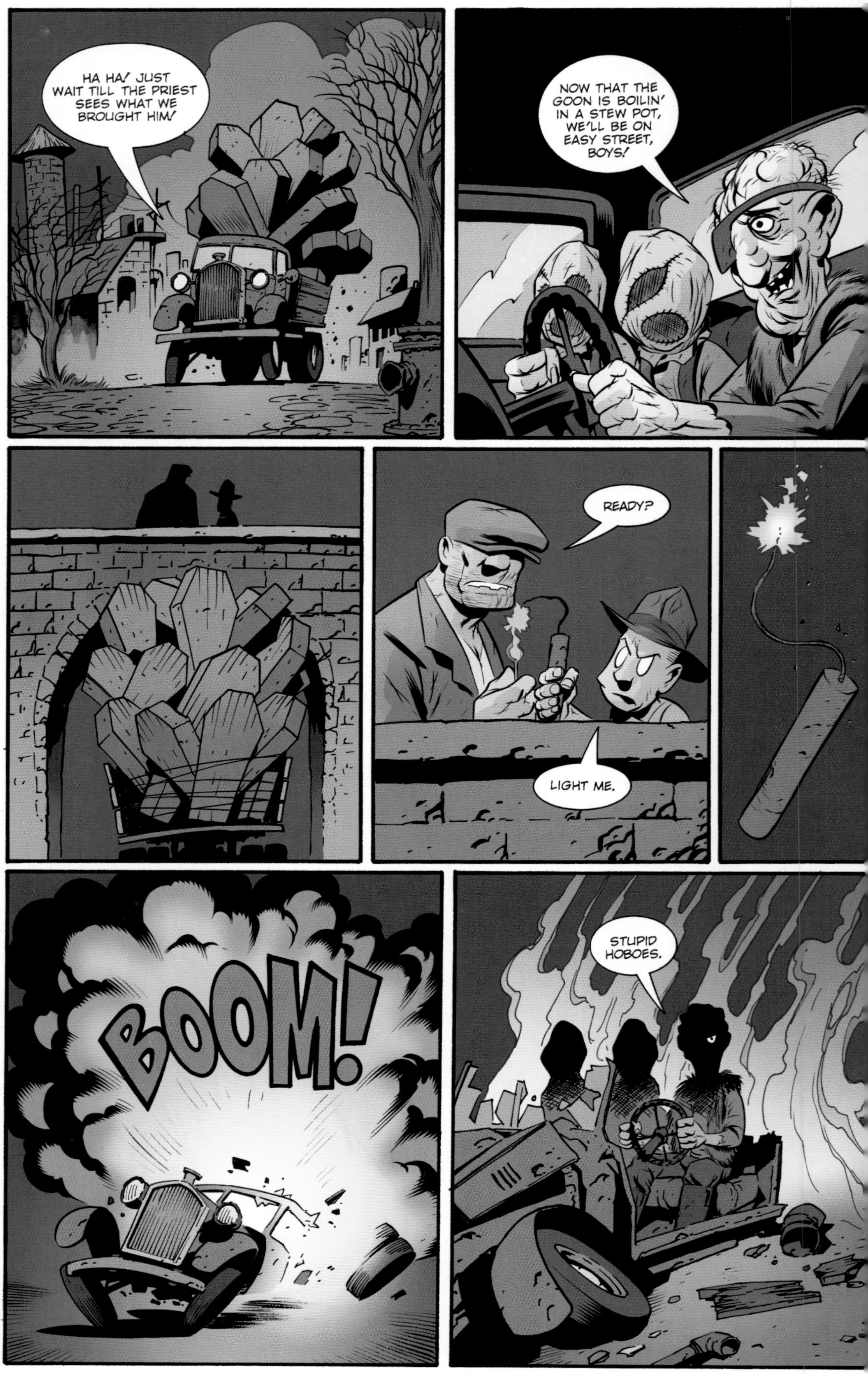
HA HA! JUST WAIT TILL THE PRIEST SEES WHAT WE BROUGHT HIM!
NOW THAT THE GOON IS BOILIN' IN A STEW POT, WE'LL BE ON EASY STREET, BOYS!
READY?
LIGHT ME.
BOOM!
STUPID HOBOES.

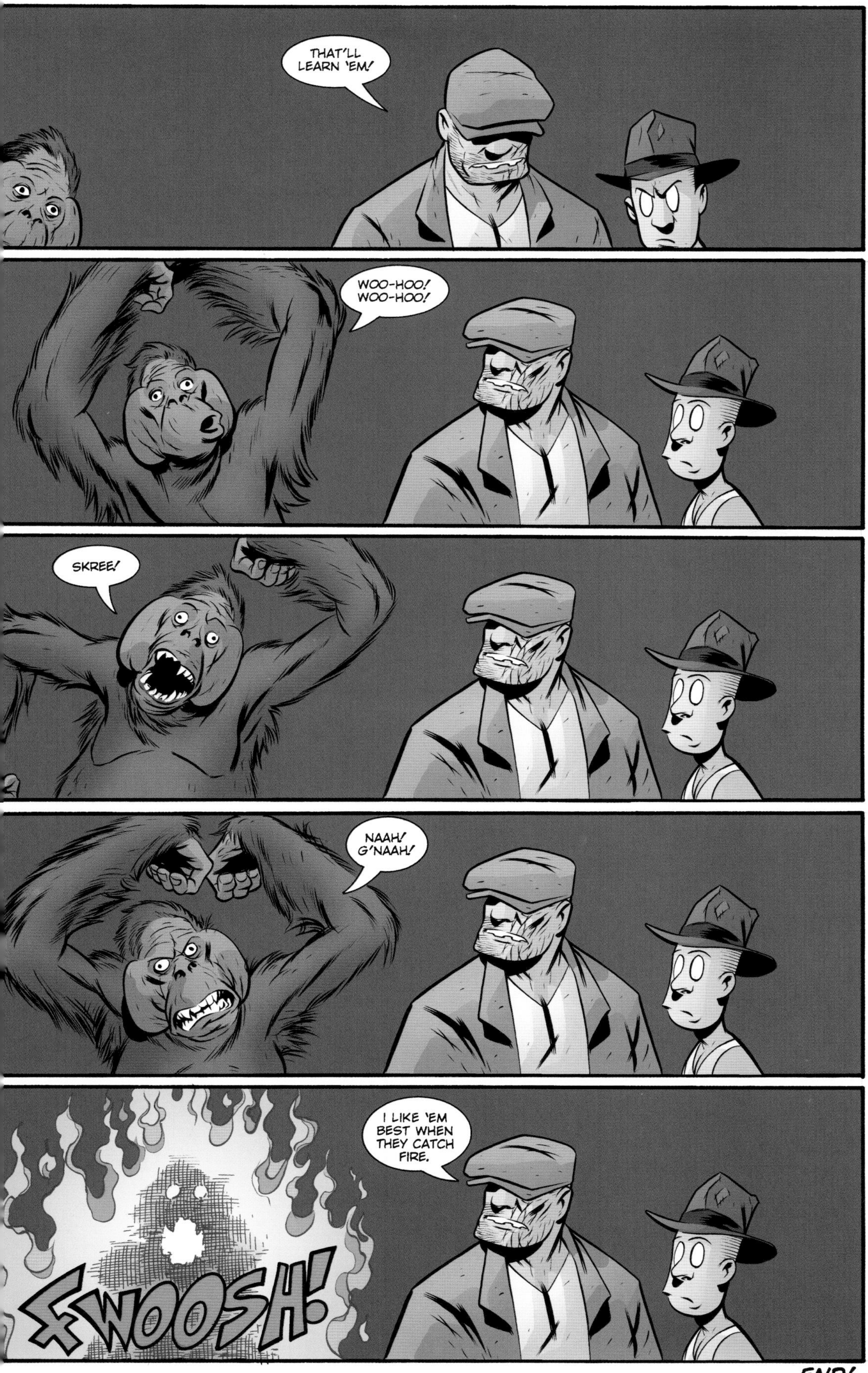
THAT'LL LEARN 'EM!
WOO-HOO! WOO-HOO!
SKREE!
NAAH! G'NAAH!
I LIKE 'EM BEST WHEN THEY CATCH FIRE.
FWOOSH!

END!

CHAPTER 2

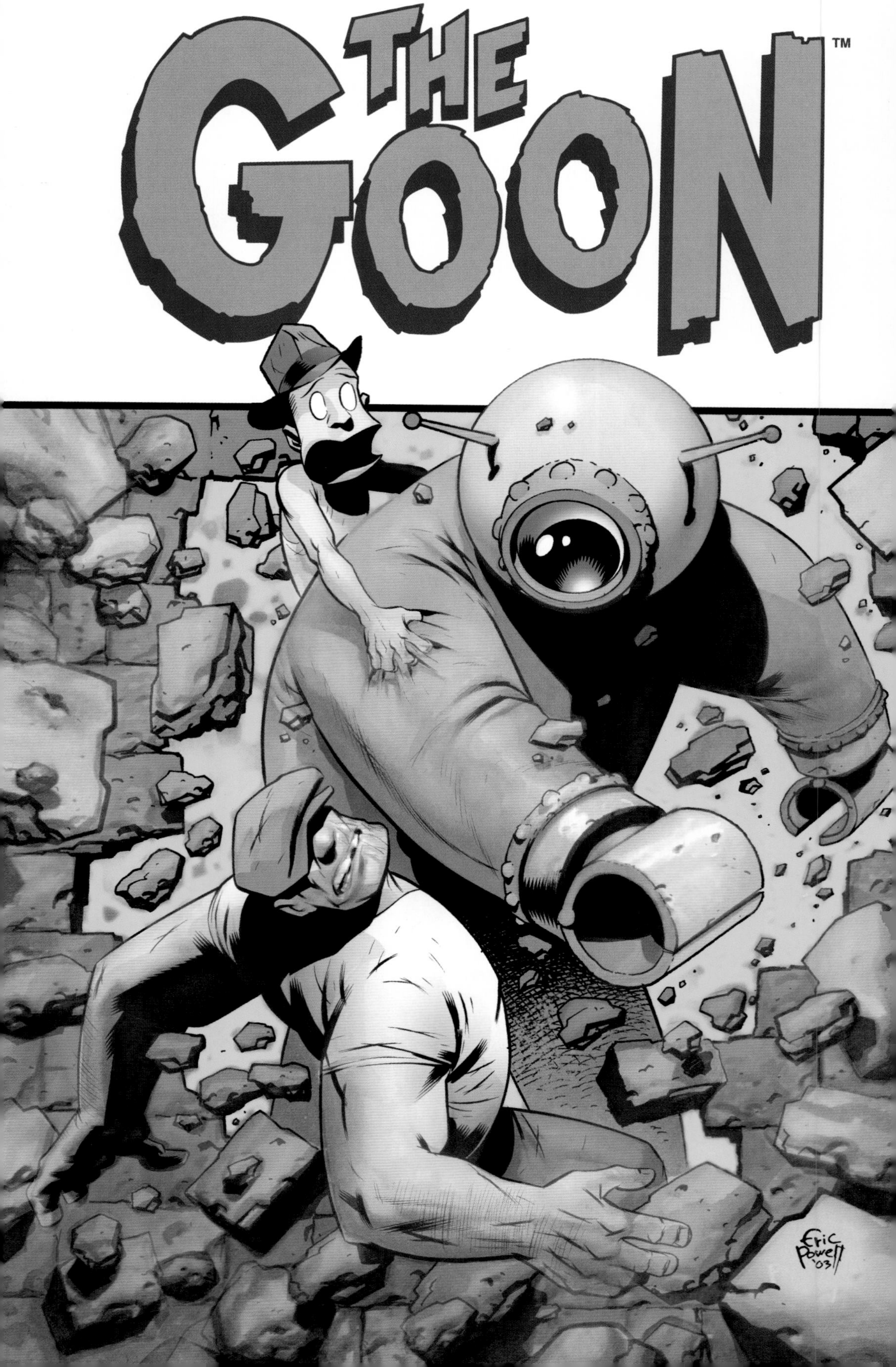
THE GOON™
Eric Powell '03

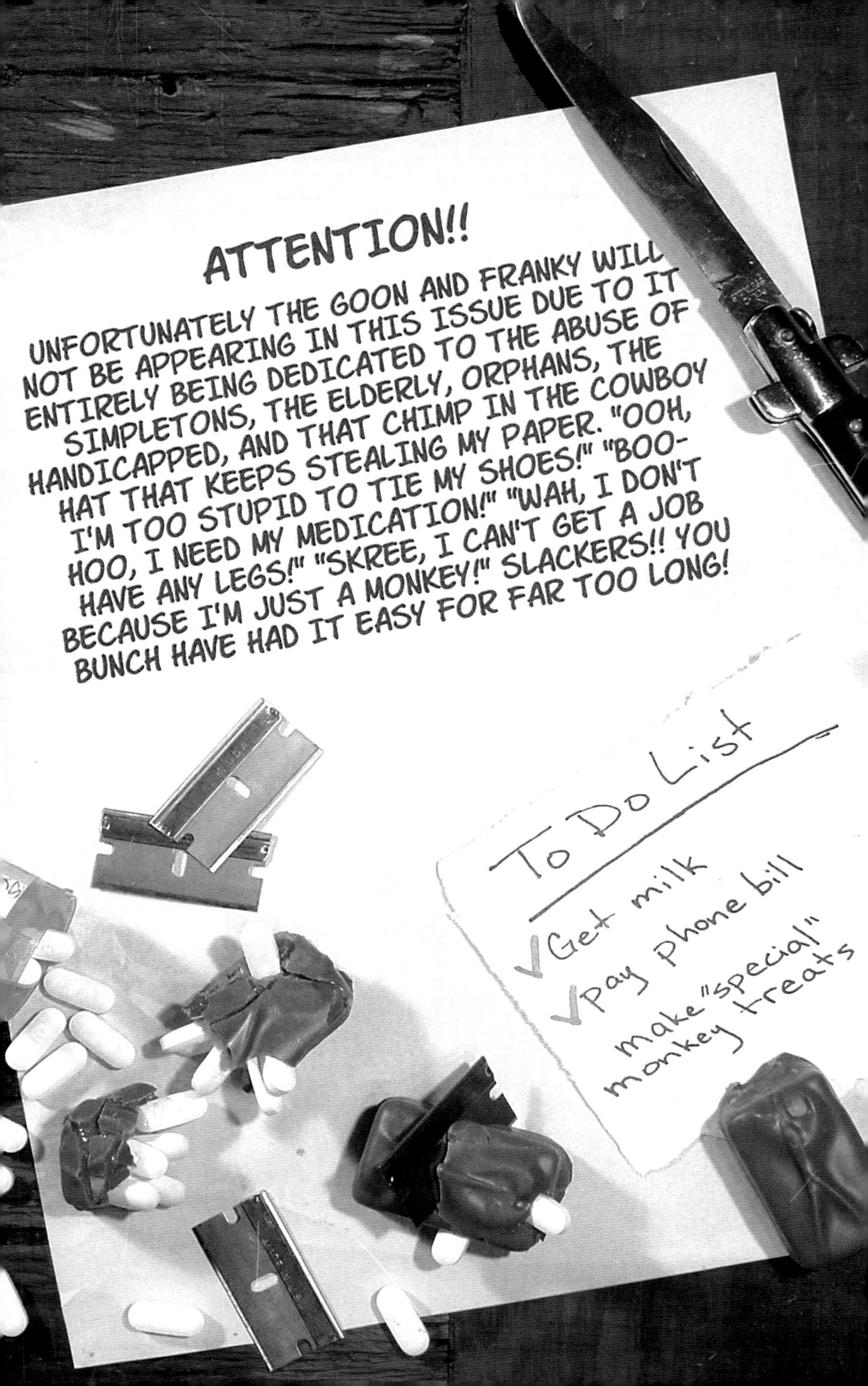
ATTENTION!!
UNFORTUNATELY THE GOON AND FRANKY WILL NOT BE APPEARING IN THIS ISSUE DUE TO IT ENTIRELY BEING DEDICATED TO THE ABUSE OF SIMPLETONS, THE ELDERLY, ORPHANS, THE HANDICAPPED, AND THAT CHIMP IN THE COWBOY HAT THAT KEEPS STEALING MY PAPER. "OOH, I'M TOO STUPID TO TIE MY SHOES!" "BOO-HOO, I NEED MY MEDICATION!" "WAH, I DON'T HAVE ANY LEGS!" "SKREE, I CAN'T GET A JOB BECAUSE I'M JUST A MONKEY!" SLACKERS!! YOU BUNCH HAVE HAD IT EASY FOR FAR TOO LONG!
To Do List
Get milk
pay phone bill
make "special" monkey treats

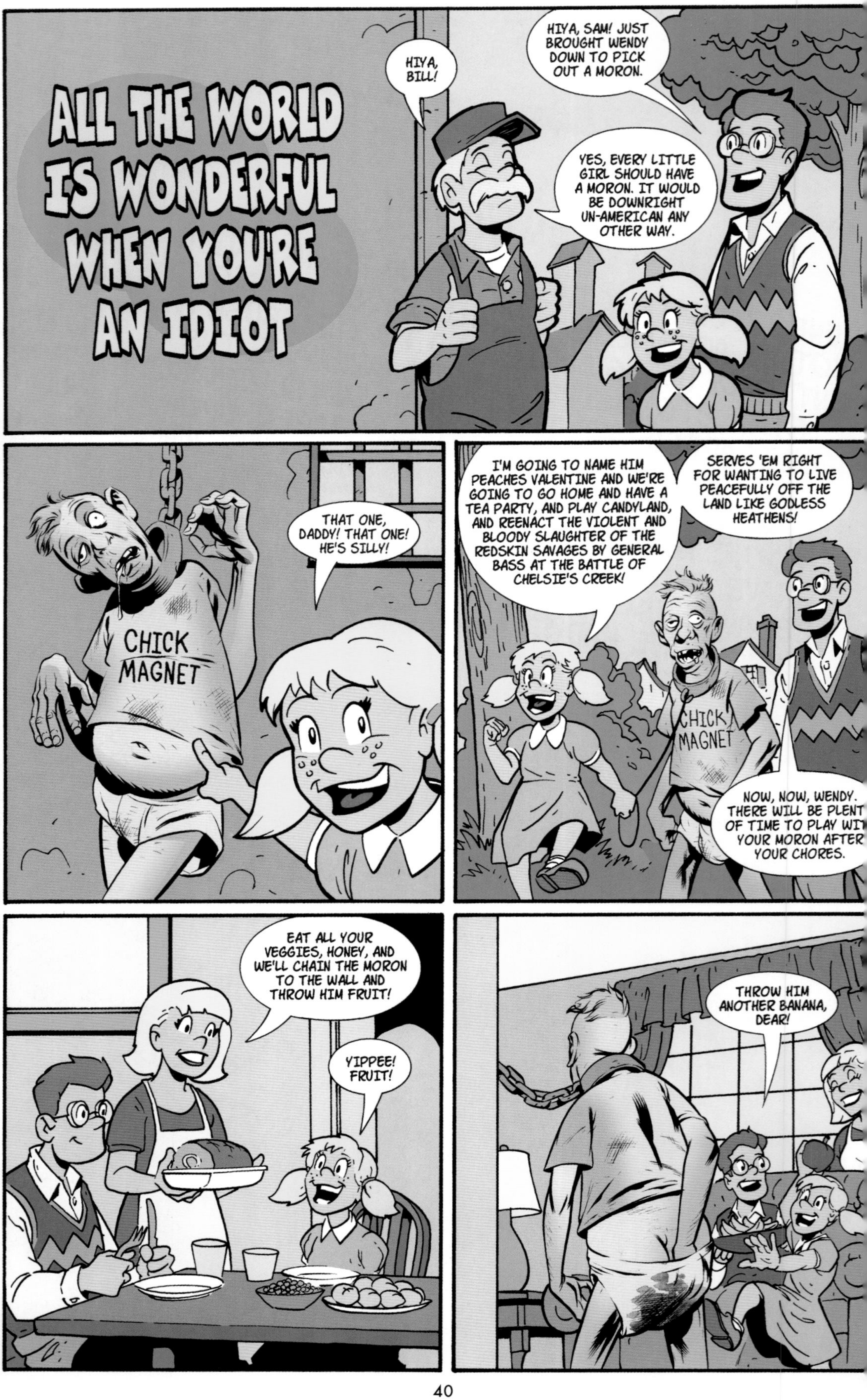
ALL THE WORLD IS WONDERFUL WHEN YOU'RE AN IDIOT
HIYA, BILL!
HIYA, SAM! JUST BROUGHT WENDY DOWN TO PICK OUT A MORON.
YES, EVERY LITTLE GIRL SHOULD HAVE A MORON. IT WOULD BE DOWNRIGHT UN-AMERICAN ANY OTHER WAY.
CHICK MAGNET
THAT ONE, DADDY! THAT ONE! HE'S SILLY!
I'M GOING TO NAME HIM PEACHES VALENTINE AND WE'RE GOING TO GO HOME AND HAVE A TEA PARTY, AND PLAY CANDYLAND, AND REENACT THE VIOLENT AND BLOODY SLAUGHTER OF THE REDSKIN SAVAGES BY GENERAL BASS AT THE BATTLE OF CHELSIE'S CREEK!
SERVES 'EM RIGHT FOR WANTING TO LIVE PEACEFULLY OFF THE LAND LIKE GODLESS HEATHENS!
CHICK MAGNET
NOW, NOW, WENDY. THERE WILL BE PLENT OF TIME TO PLAY WI YOUR MORON AFTER YOUR CHORES.
EAT ALL YOUR VEGGIES, HONEY, AND WE'LL CHAIN THE MORON TO THE WALL AND THROW HIM FRUIT!
YIPPEE! FRUIT!
THROW HIM ANOTHER BANANA, DEAR!

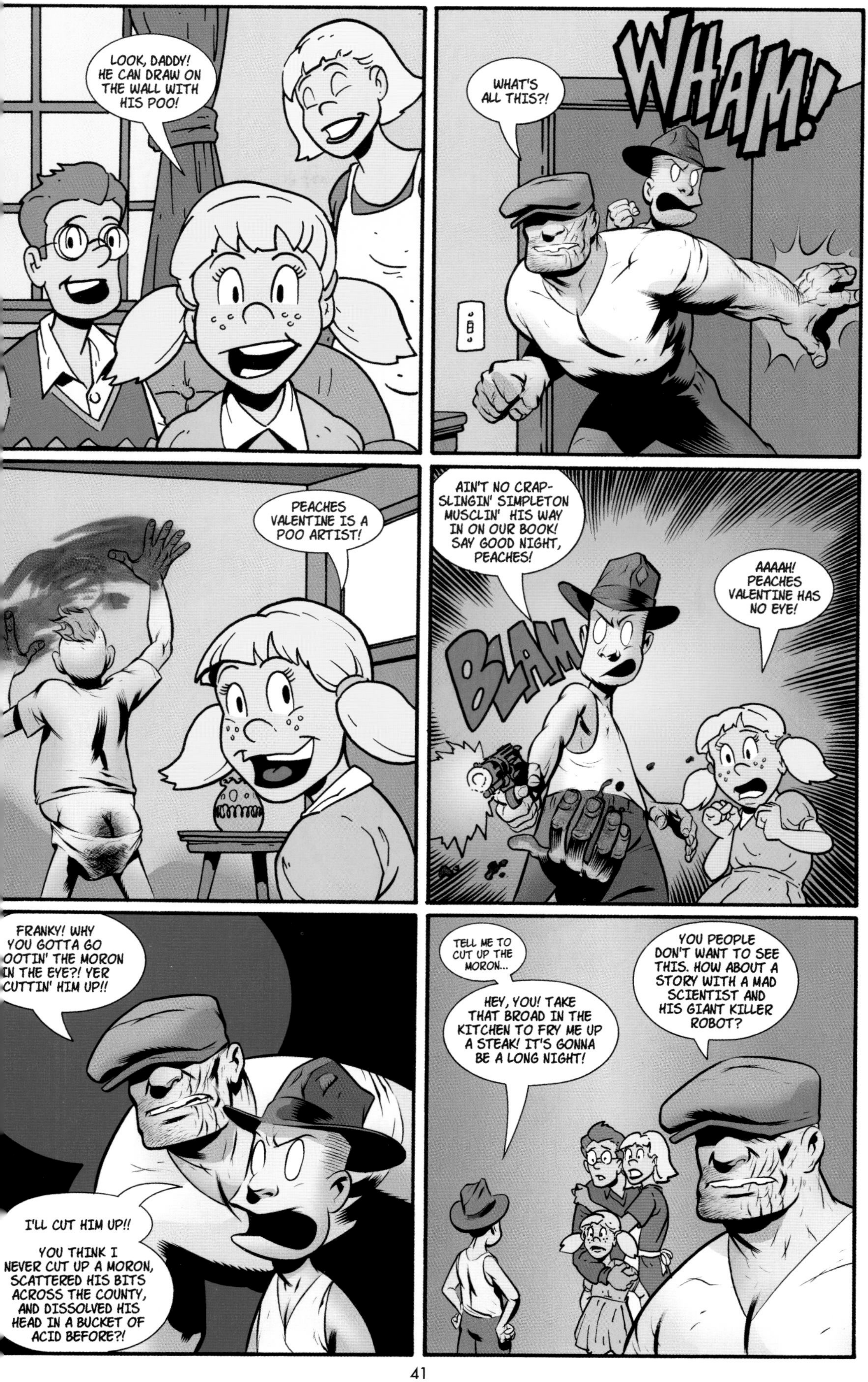
LOOK, DADDY! HE CAN DRAW ON THE WALL WITH HIS POO!
WHAT'S ALL THIS?!
WHAM!
PEACHES VALENTINE IS A POO ARTIST!
AIN'T NO CRAP-SLINGIN' SIMPLETON MUSCLIN' HIS WAY IN ON OUR BOOK! SAY GOOD NIGHT, PEACHES!
BLAM
AAAAH! PEACHES VALENTINE HAS NO EYE!
FRANKY! WHY YOU GOTTA GO OOTIN' THE MORON IN THE EYE?! YER CUTTIN' HIM UP!!
I'LL CUT HIM UP!!
YOU THINK I NEVER CUT UP A MORON, SCATTERED HIS BITS ACROSS THE COUNTY, AND DISSOLVED HIS HEAD IN A BUCKET OF ACID BEFORE?!
TELL ME TO CUT UP THE MORON...
HEY, YOU! TAKE THAT BROAD IN THE KITCHEN TO FRY ME UP A STEAK! IT'S GONNA BE A LONG NIGHT!
YOU PEOPLE DON'T WANT TO SEE THIS. HOW ABOUT A STORY WITH A MAD SCIENTIST AND HIS GIANT KILLER ROBOT?

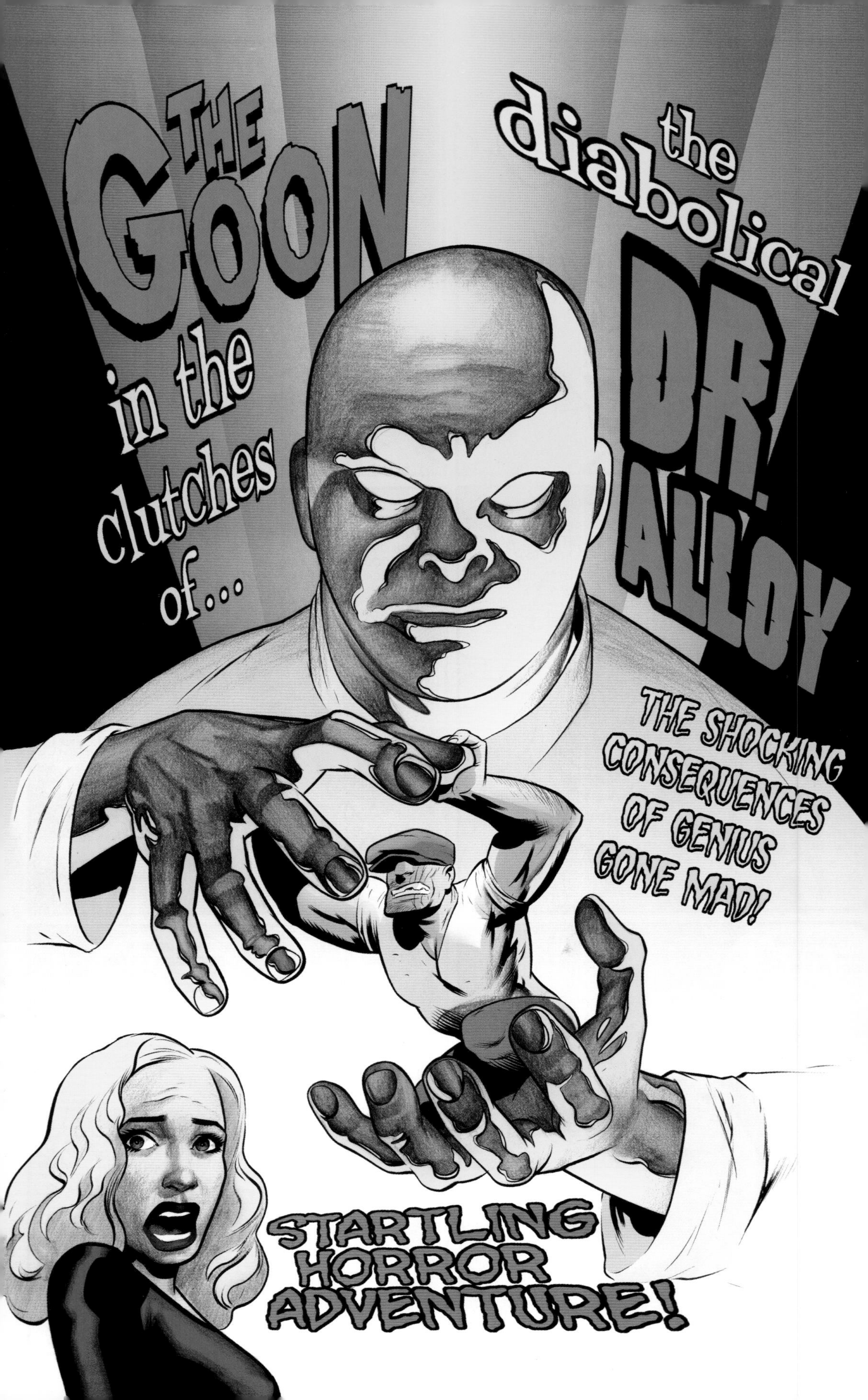
THE GOON
in the clutches of...
the diabolical DR. ALLOY
THE SHOCKING CONSEQUENCES OF GENIUS GONE MAD!
STARTLING HORROR ADVENTURE!

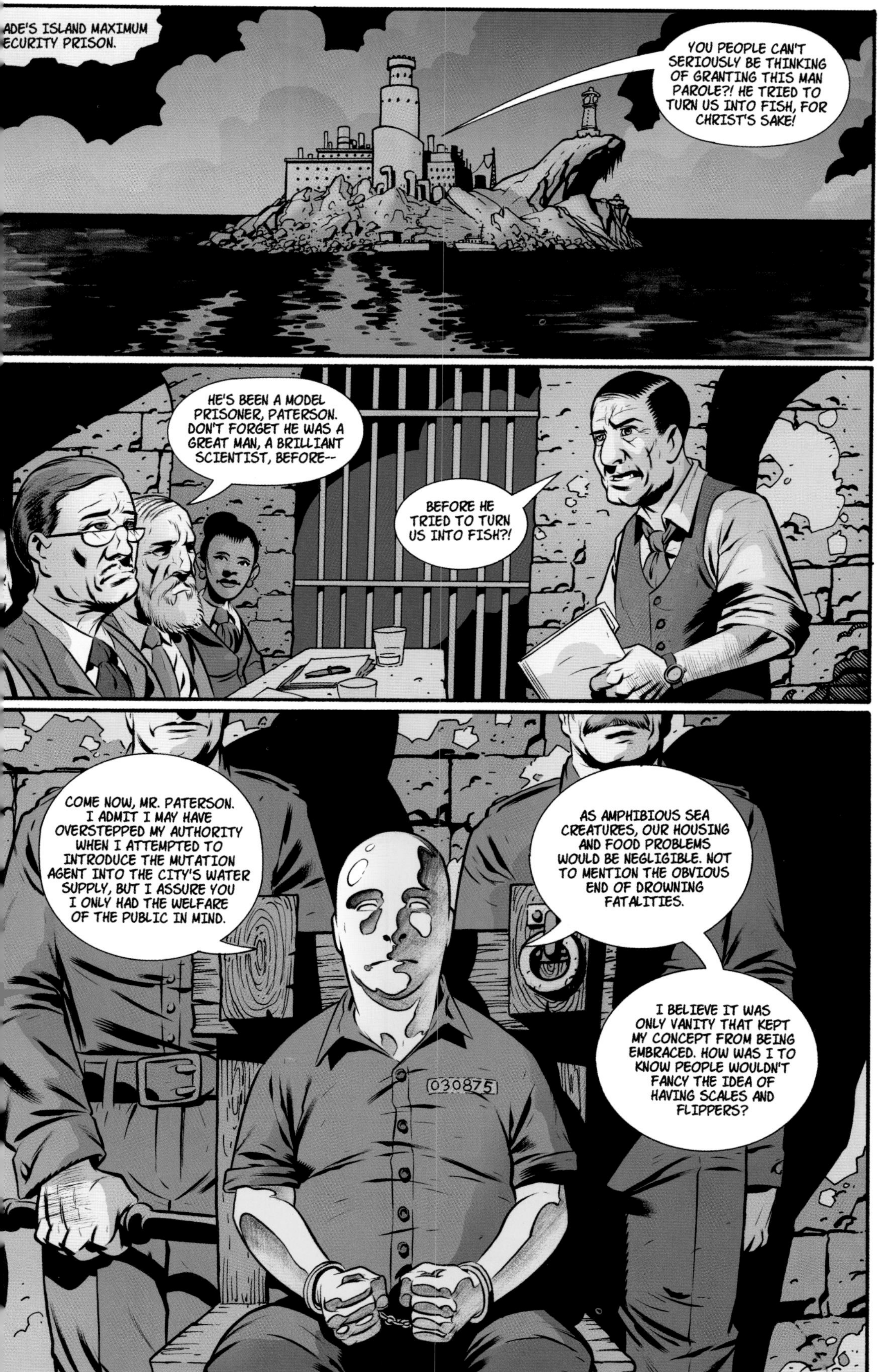
ADE'S ISLAND MAXIMUM ECURITY PRISON.
YOU PEOPLE CAN'T SERIOUSLY BE THINKING OF GRANTING THIS MAN PAROLE?! HE TRIED TO TURN US INTO FISH, FOR CHRIST'S SAKE!
HE'S BEEN A MODEL PRISONER, PATERSON. DON'T FORGET HE WAS A GREAT MAN, A BRILLIANT SCIENTIST, BEFORE--
BEFORE HE TRIED TO TURN US INTO FISH?!
COME NOW, MR. PATERSON. I ADMIT I MAY HAVE OVERSTEPPED MY AUTHORITY WHEN I ATTEMPTED TO INTRODUCE THE MUTATION AGENT INTO THE CITY'S WATER SUPPLY, BUT I ASSURE YOU I ONLY HAD THE WELFARE OF THE PUBLIC IN MIND.
030875
AS AMPHIBIOUS SEA CREATURES, OUR HOUSING AND FOOD PROBLEMS WOULD BE NEGLIGIBLE. NOT TO MENTION THE OBVIOUS END OF DROWNING FATALITIES.
I BELIEVE IT WAS ONLY VANITY THAT KEPT MY CONCEPT FROM BEING EMBRACED. HOW WAS I TO KNOW PEOPLE WOULDN'T FANCY THE IDEA OF HAVING SCALES AND FLIPPERS?

ARE YOU HEARING THIS?!

THIS MAN IS DERANGED! JUST LOOK AT HIM! WHAT KIND OF SICK MIND WOULD DO THAT TO HIMSELF?!

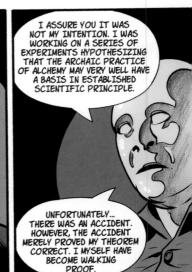

I ASSURE YOU IT WAS NOT MY INTENTION. I WAS WORKING ON A SERIES OF EXPERIMENTS HYPOTHESIZING THAT THE ARCHAIC PRACTICE OF ALCHEMY MAY VERY WELL HAVE A BASIS IN ESTABLISHED SCIENTIFIC PRINCIPLE.

UNFORTUNATELY... THERE WAS AN ACCIDENT. HOWEVER, THE ACCIDENT MERELY PROVED MY THEOREM CORRECT. I MYSELF HAVE BECOME WALKING PROOF.

HE'S GOT A POINT THERE, PATERSON.

WHAT'S THE MATTER WITH YOU PEOPLE?!! HAVE YOU FORGOTTEN THE KILLER ROBOT?!!

THAT WAS NOT MY FAULT. I WAS AS HORRIFIED AS YOU BY THE CARNAGE AT THAT PET SHOP. OH, THOSE POOR, POOR CHINCHILLAS.

YOU SEE, I HAD ORDERED A THIRTY-THREE-HUNDRED-VOLT X-C CONDENSER FROM THE MANUFACTURER. THEY SENT A TWENTY-FIVE-HUNDRED-VOLT INTEROCITOR. THE TWO ARE NEARLY INDISTINGUISHABLE TO THE NAKED EYE.

OF COURSE BRUNO-- ORIGINALLY DESIGNED AS A WINDOW WASHER--WOULD MALFUNCTION WITH AN IMPROPER INTEROCITOR INSTALLED! I ASSURE YOU THAT I WROTE A VERY STRONGLY WORDED LETTER TO THAT MANUFACTURER, AND I SHAN'T BE USING THEM AGAIN!

THERE YOU HAVE IT, PATERSON. JUST AN ACCIDENT.

ACCIDENT?! YOU PUT THIS FREAK BACK OUT ON THE STREET AND WE'LL ALL BE GROWING SECOND HEADS OR SOMETHING!

REALLY, WHY MUST YOU INSIST ON LABELING ME WITH SUCH MONIKERS AS "FREAK" AND "LOONY GUY"? IT'S SO UNPROFESSIONAL.

MAY I SUGGEST THAT IF YOU TOOK A MORE SOPHISTICATED APPROACH WITH YOUR ARGUMENT, YOUR CASE'S VALIDITY MAY SEEM MORE RELEVANT.

SHUT UP, YOU... FREAK! LOONY FREAK!

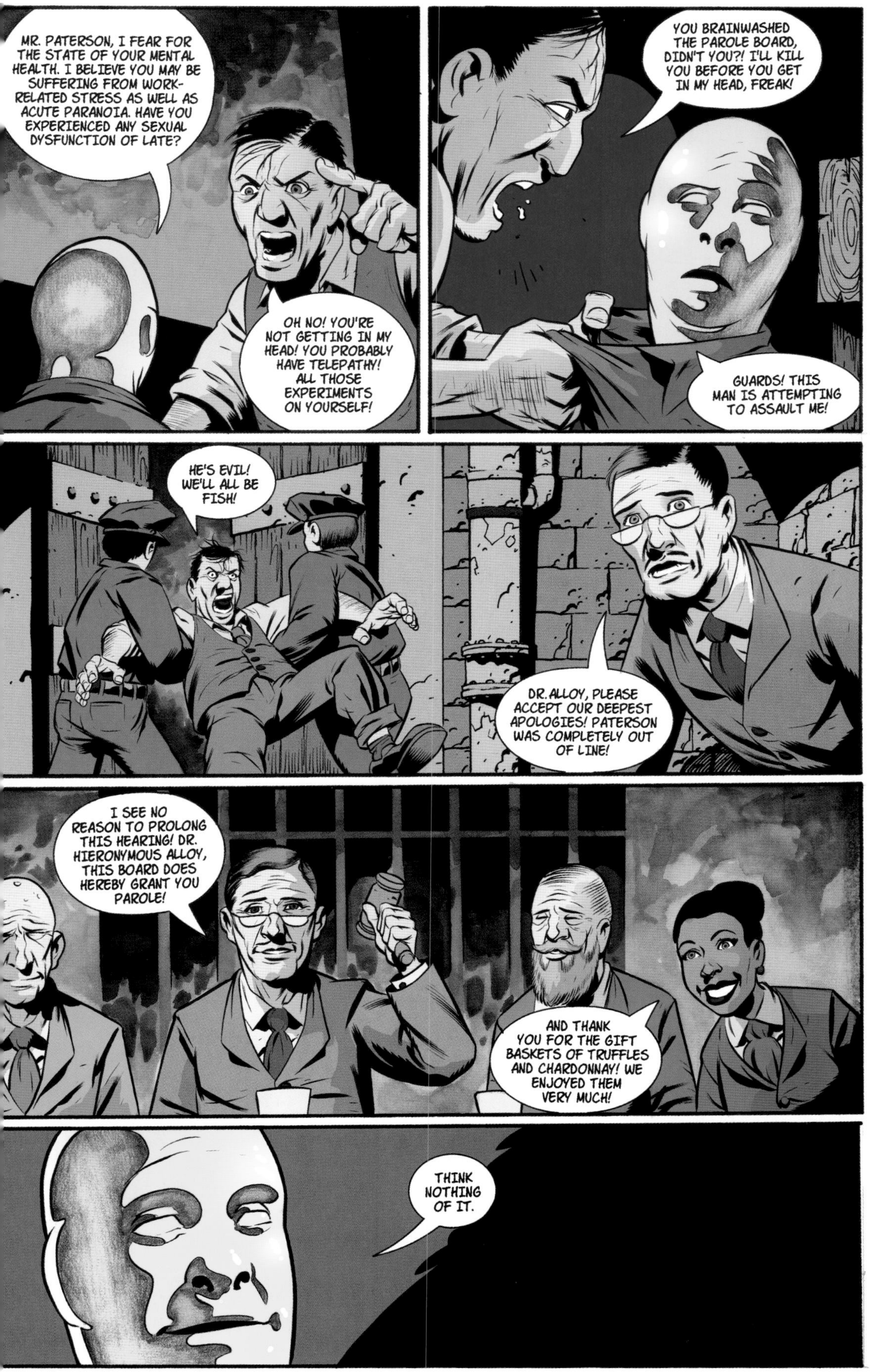
MR. PATERSON, I FEAR FOR THE STATE OF YOUR MENTAL HEALTH. I BELIEVE YOU MAY BE SUFFERING FROM WORK-RELATED STRESS AS WELL AS ACUTE PARANOIA. HAVE YOU EXPERIENCED ANY SEXUAL DYSFUNCTION OF LATE?
OH NO! YOU'RE NOT GETTING IN MY HEAD! YOU PROBABLY HAVE TELEPATHY! ALL THOSE EXPERIMENTS ON YOURSELF!
YOU BRAINWASHED THE PAROLE BOARD, DIDN'T YOU?! I'LL KILL YOU BEFORE YOU GET IN MY HEAD, FREAK!
GUARDS! THIS MAN IS ATTEMPTING TO ASSAULT ME!
HE'S EVIL! WE'LL ALL BE FISH!
DR. ALLOY, PLEASE ACCEPT OUR DEEPEST APOLOGIES! PATERSON WAS COMPLETELY OUT OF LINE!
I SEE NO REASON TO PROLONG THIS HEARING! DR. HIERONYMOUS ALLOY, THIS BOARD DOES HEREBY GRANT YOU PAROLE!
AND THANK YOU FOR THE GIFT BASKETS OF TRUFFLES AND CHARDONNAY! WE ENJOYED THEM VERY MUCH!
THINK NOTHING OF IT.

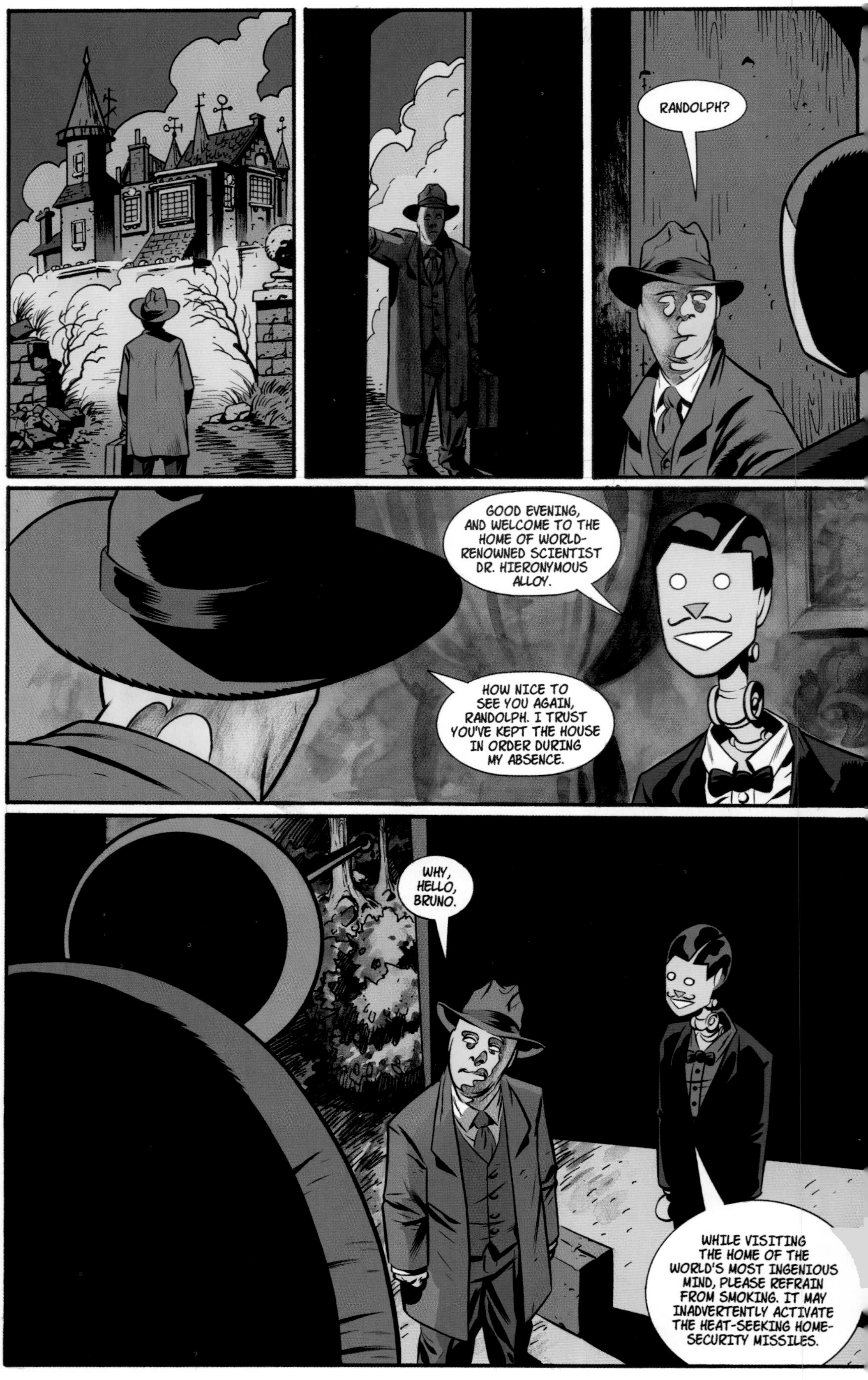
RANDOLPH?
GOOD EVENING, AND WELCOME TO THE HOME OF WORLD-RENOWNED SCIENTIST DR. HIERONYMOUS ALLOY.
HOW NICE TO SEE YOU AGAIN, RANDOLPH. I TRUST YOU'VE KEPT THE HOUSE IN ORDER DURING MY ABSENCE.
WHY, HELLO, BRUNO.
WHILE VISITING THE HOME OF THE WORLD'S MOST INGENIOUS MIND, PLEASE REFRAIN FROM SMOKING. IT MAY INADVERTENTLY ACTIVATE THE HEAT-SEEKING HOME-SECURITY MISSILES.

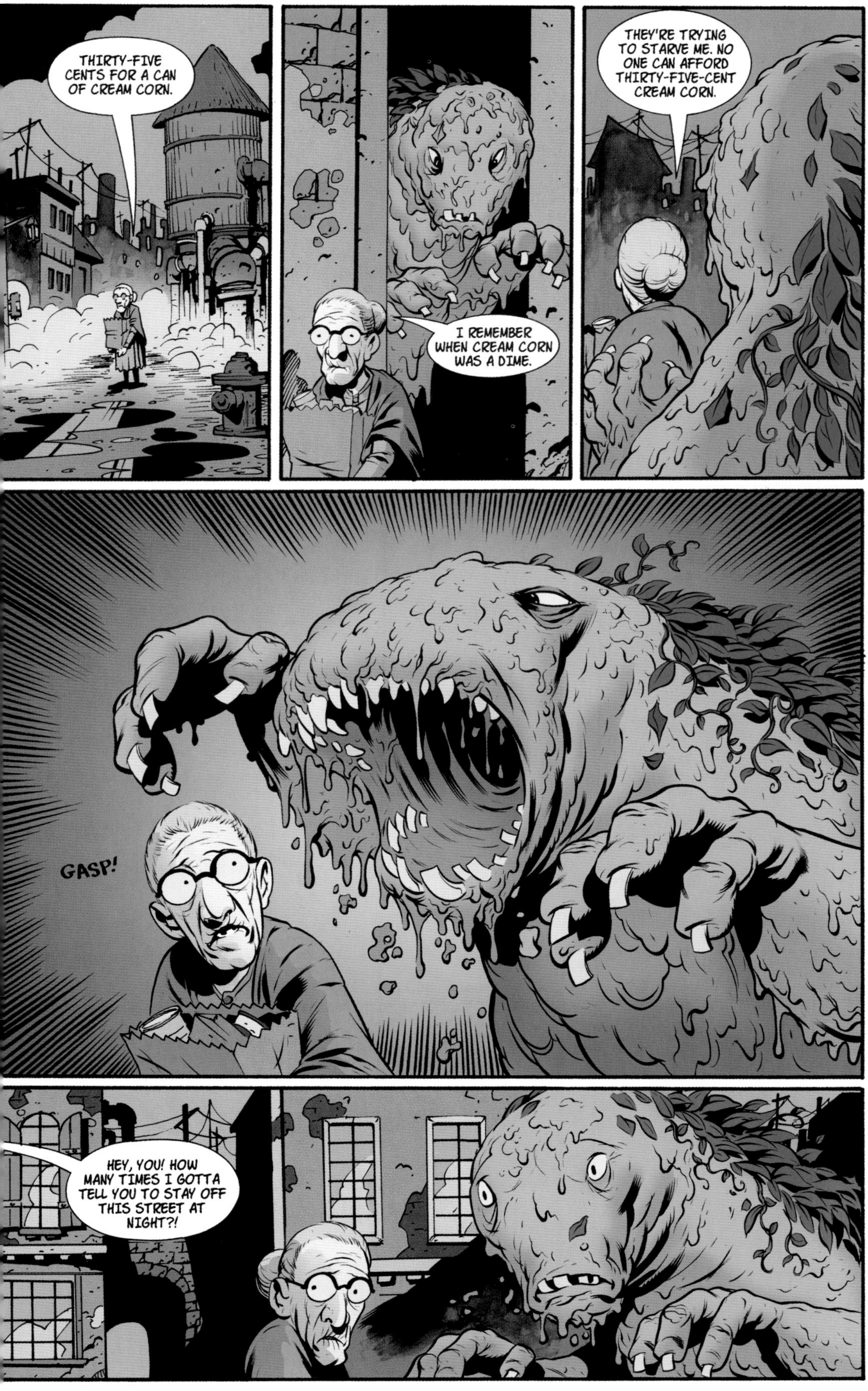
THIRTY-FIVE CENTS FOR A CAN OF CREAM CORN.
I REMEMBER WHEN CREAM CORN WAS A DIME.
THEY'RE TRYING TO STARVE ME. NO ONE CAN AFFORD THIRTY-FIVE-CENT CREAM CORN.
GASP!
HEY, YOU! HOW MANY TIMES I GOTTA TELL YOU TO STAY OFF THIS STREET AT NIGHT?!

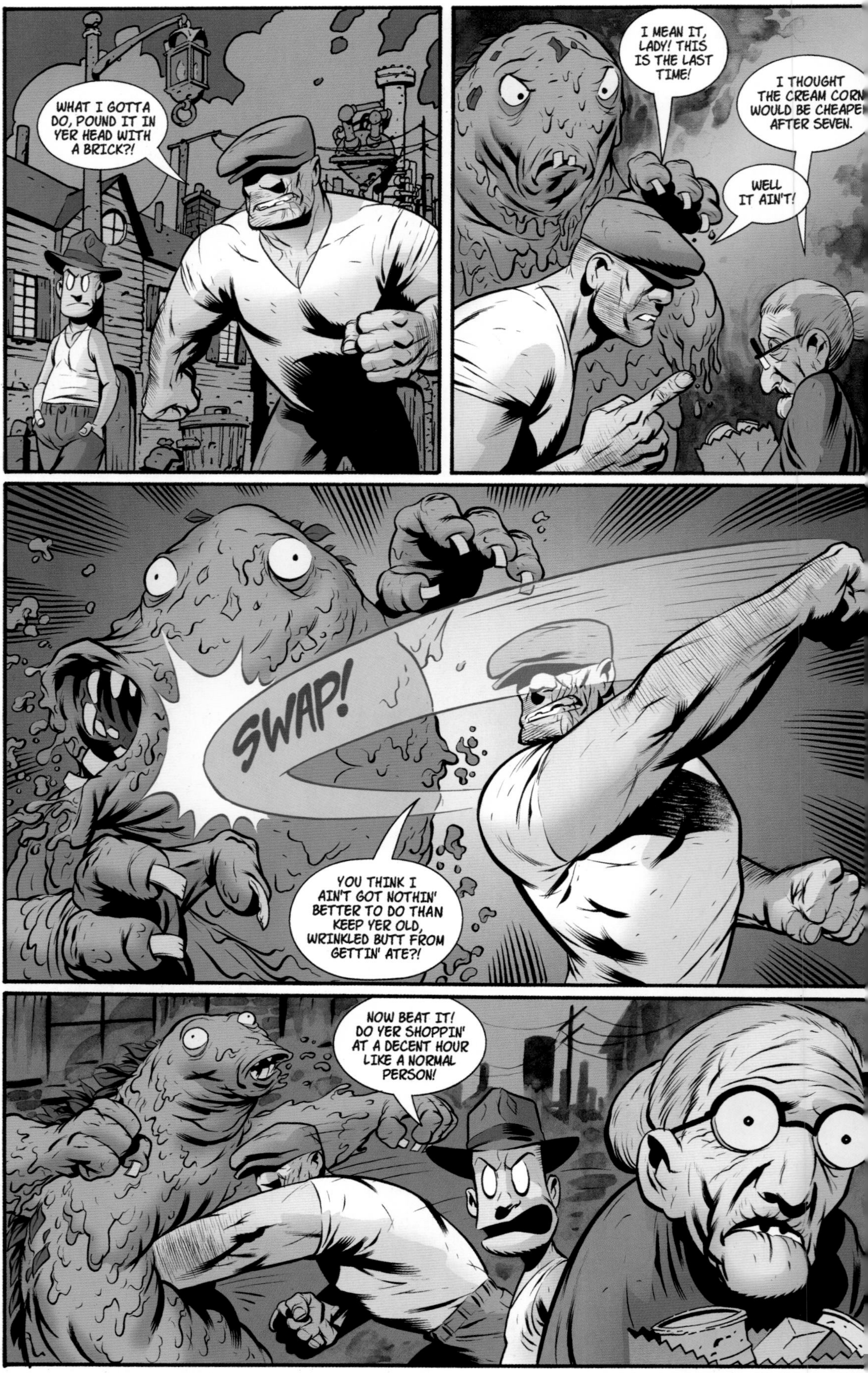
WHAT I GOTTA DO, POUND IT IN YER HEAD WITH A BRICK?!
I MEAN IT, LADY! THIS IS THE LAST TIME!
I THOUGHT THE CREAM CORN WOULD BE CHEAPE AFTER SEVEN.
WELL IT AIN'T!
SWAP!
YOU THINK I AIN'T GOT NOTHIN' BETTER TO DO THAN KEEP YER OLD, WRINKLED BUTT FROM GETTIN' ATE?!
NOW BEAT IT! DO YER SHOPPIN' AT A DECENT HOUR LIKE A NORMAL PERSON!

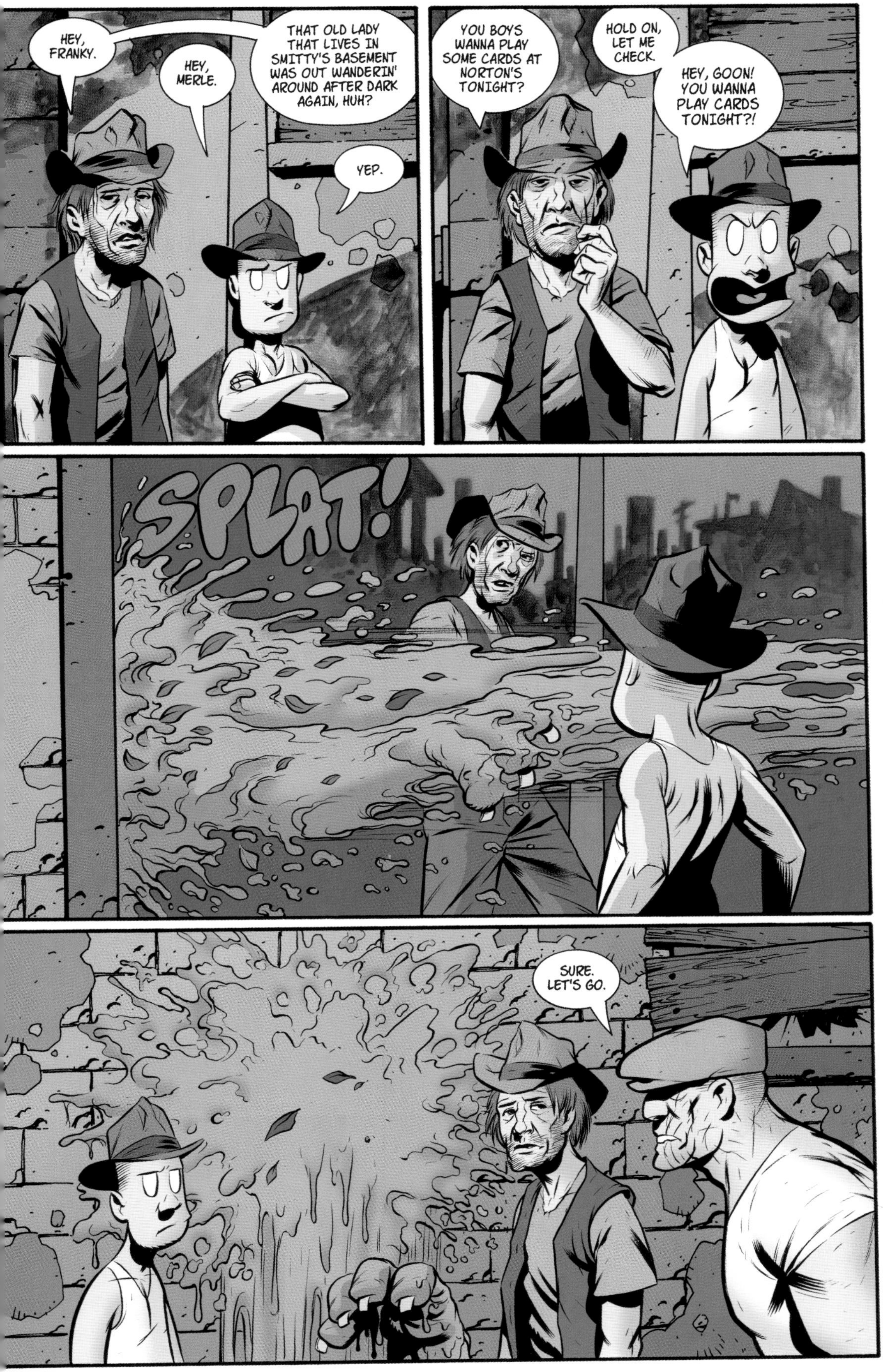
HEY, FRANKY.
HEY, MERLE.
THAT OLD LADY THAT LIVES IN SMITTY'S BASEMENT WAS OUT WANDERIN' AROUND AFTER DARK AGAIN, HUH?
YEP.
YOU BOYS WANNA PLAY SOME CARDS AT NORTON'S TONIGHT?
HOLD ON, LET ME CHECK.
HEY, GOON! YOU WANNA PLAY CARDS TONIGHT?!
SPLAT!
SURE. LET'S GO.

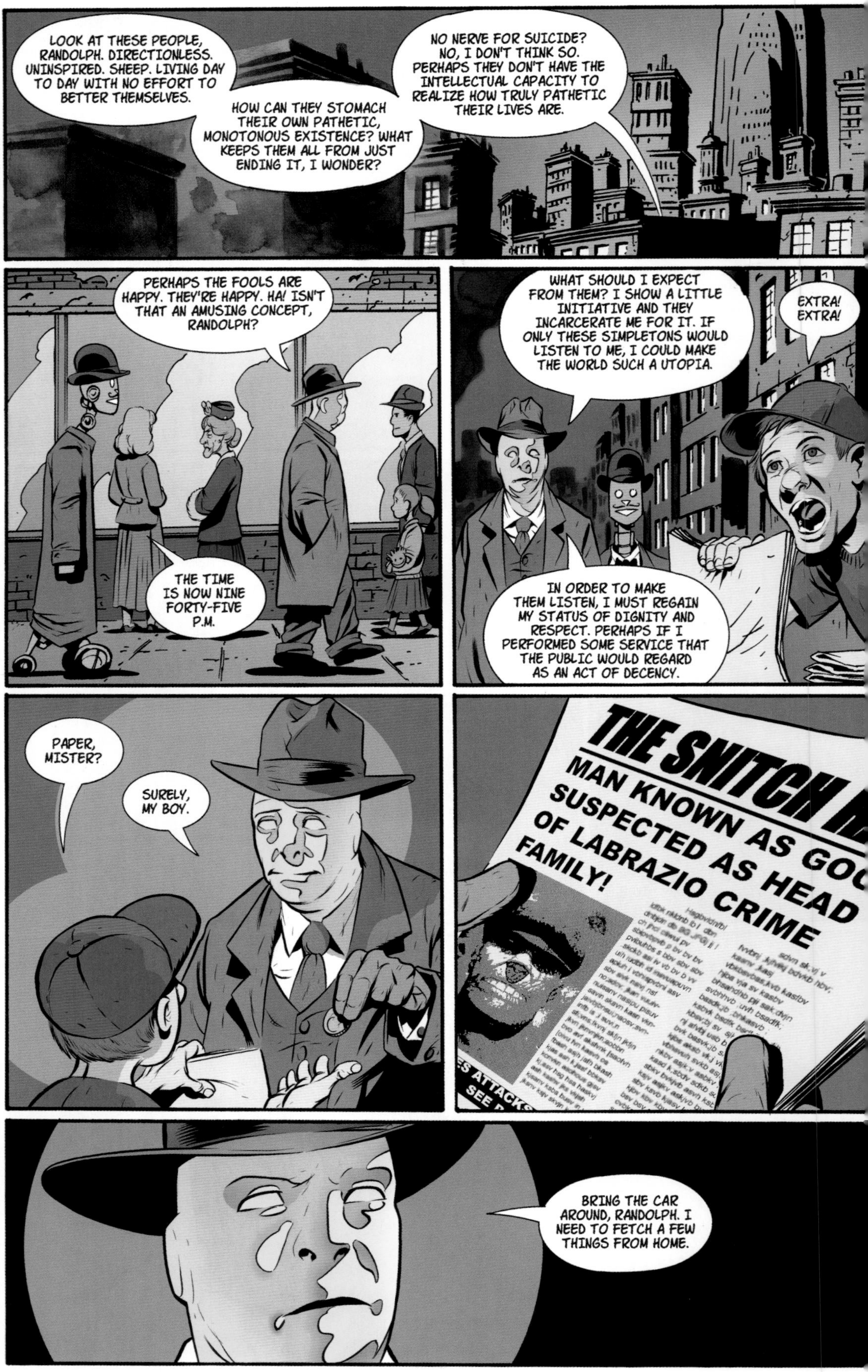
LOOK AT THESE PEOPLE, RANDOLPH. DIRECTIONLESS. UNINSPIRED. SHEEP. LIVING DAY TO DAY WITH NO EFFORT TO BETTER THEMSELVES.
HOW CAN THEY STOMACH THEIR OWN PATHETIC, MONOTONOUS EXISTENCE? WHAT KEEPS THEM ALL FROM JUST ENDING IT, I WONDER?
NO NERVE FOR SUICIDE? NO, I DON'T THINK SO. PERHAPS THEY DON'T HAVE THE INTELLECTUAL CAPACITY TO REALIZE HOW TRULY PATHETIC THEIR LIVES ARE.
PERHAPS THE FOOLS ARE HAPPY. THEY'RE HAPPY. HA! ISN'T THAT AN AMUSING CONCEPT, RANDOLPH?
THE TIME IS NOW NINE FORTY-FIVE P.M.
WHAT SHOULD I EXPECT FROM THEM? I SHOW A LITTLE INITIATIVE AND THEY INCARCERATE ME FOR IT. IF ONLY THESE SIMPLETONS WOULD LISTEN TO ME, I COULD MAKE THE WORLD SUCH A UTOPIA.
EXTRA! EXTRA!
IN ORDER TO MAKE THEM LISTEN, I MUST REGAIN MY STATUS OF DIGNITY AND RESPECT. PERHAPS IF I PERFORMED SOME SERVICE THAT THE PUBLIC WOULD REGARD AS AN ACT OF DECENCY.
PAPER, MISTER?
SURELY, MY BOY.
THE SNITCH
MAN KNOWN AS GOO
SUSPECTED AS HEAD
OF LABRAZIO CRIME
FAMILY!
BRING THE CAR AROUND, RANDOLPH. I NEED TO FETCH A FEW THINGS FROM HOME.

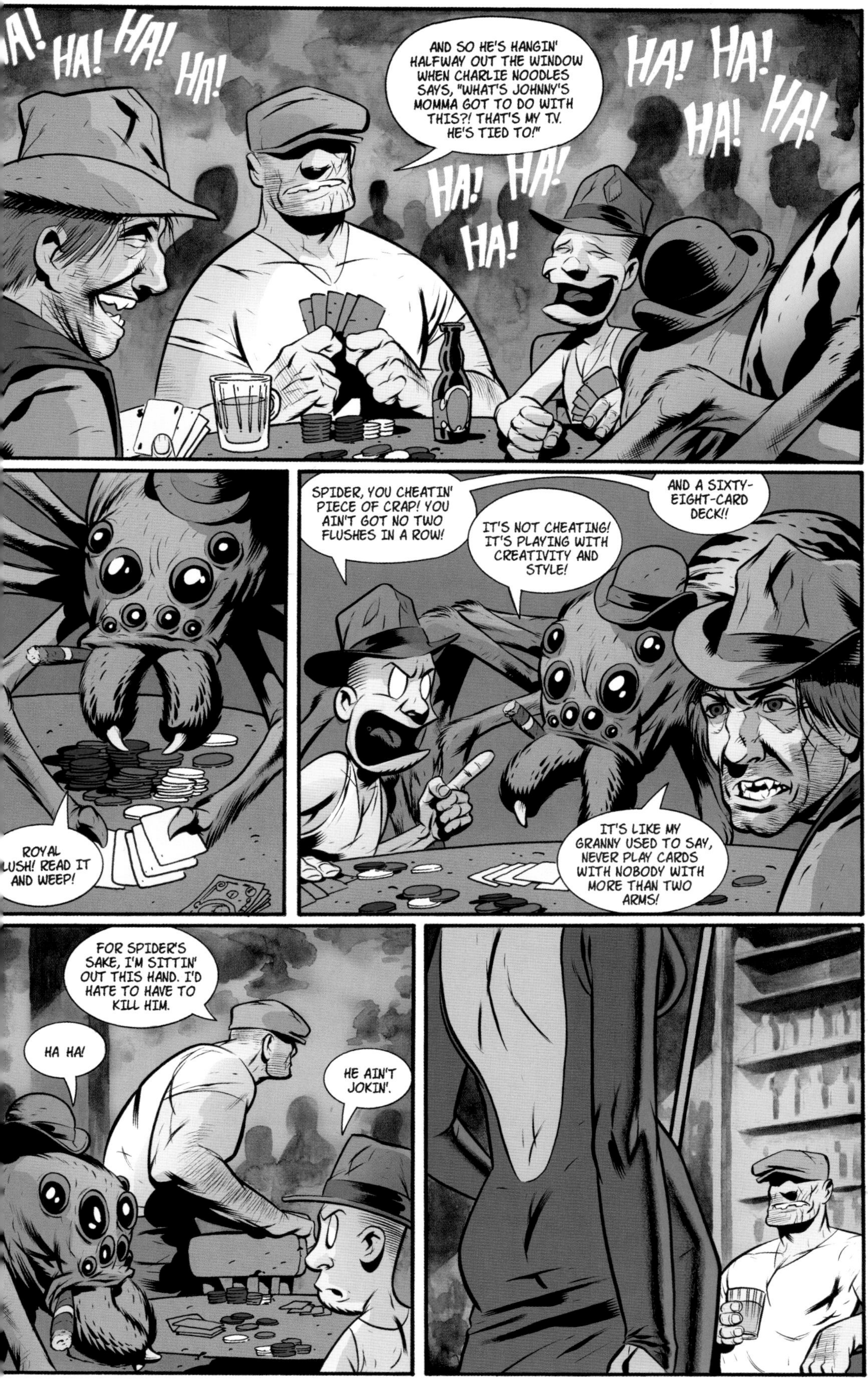
HA! HA! HA! HA!
AND SO HE'S HANGIN' HALFWAY OUT THE WINDOW WHEN CHARLIE NOODLES SAYS, "WHAT'S JOHNNY'S MOMMA GOT TO DO WITH THIS?! THAT'S MY T.V. HE'S TIED TO!"
HA! HA! HA! HA!
HA! HA! HA!
ROYAL LUSH! READ IT AND WEEP!
SPIDER, YOU CHEATIN' PIECE OF CRAP! YOU AIN'T GOT NO TWO FLUSHES IN A ROW!
AND A SIXTY-EIGHT-CARD DECK!!
IT'S NOT CHEATING! IT'S PLAYING WITH CREATIVITY AND STYLE!
IT'S LIKE MY GRANNY USED TO SAY, NEVER PLAY CARDS WITH NOBODY WITH MORE THAN TWO ARMS!
FOR SPIDER'S SAKE, I'M SITTIN' OUT THIS HAND. I'D HATE TO HAVE TO KILL HIM.
HA HA!
HE AIN'T JOKIN'.

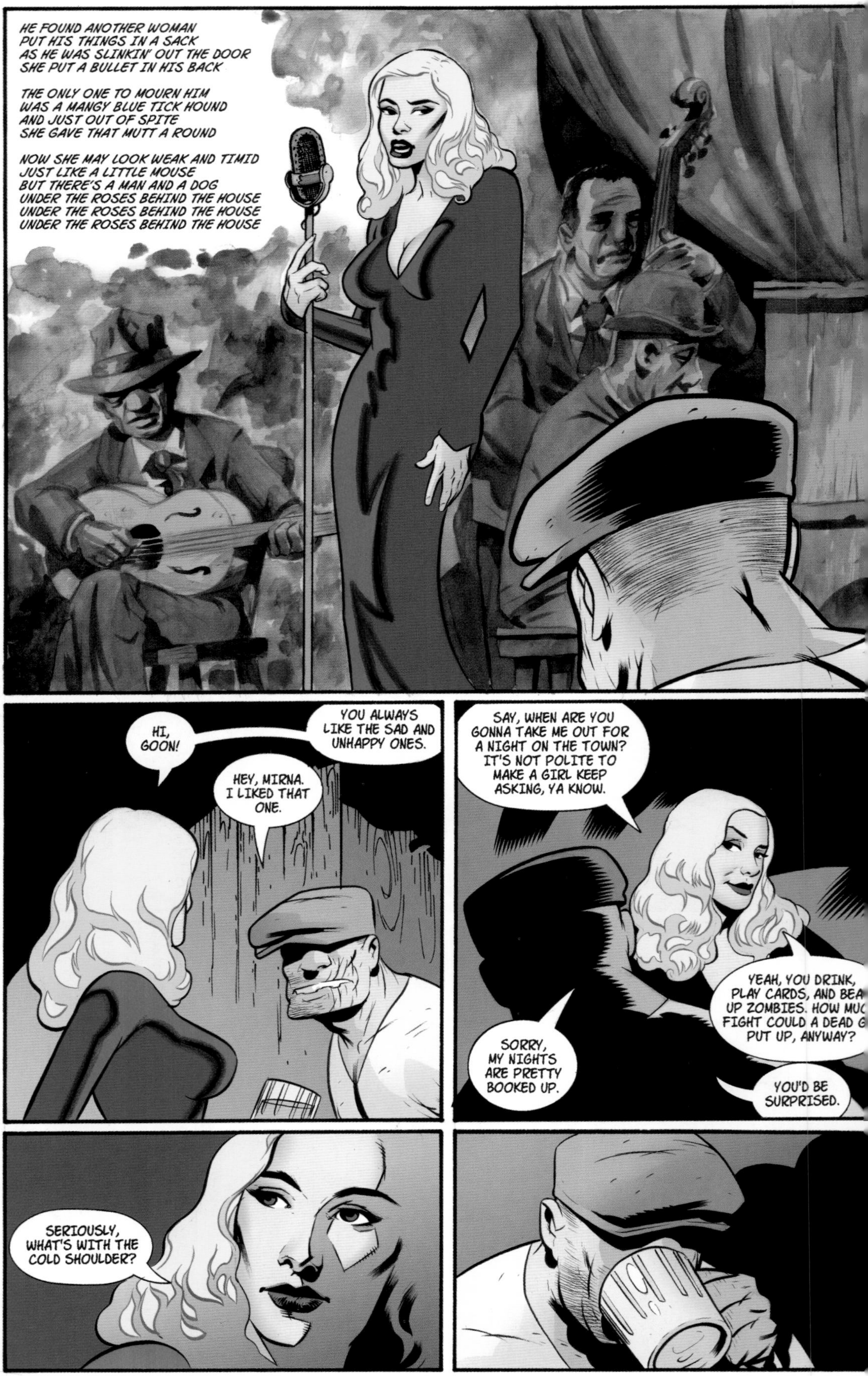
HE FOUND ANOTHER WOMAN
PUT HIS THINGS IN A SACK
AS HE WAS SLINKIN' OUT THE DOOR
SHE PUT A BULLET IN HIS BACK

THE ONLY ONE TO MOURN HIM
WAS A MANGY BLUE TICK HOUND
AND JUST OUT OF SPITE
SHE GAVE THAT MUTT A ROUND

NOW SHE MAY LOOK WEAK AND TIMID
JUST LIKE A LITTLE MOUSE
BUT THERE'S A MAN AND A DOG
UNDER THE ROSES BEHIND THE HOUSE
UNDER THE ROSES BEHIND THE HOUSE
UNDER THE ROSES BEHIND THE HOUSE
HI, GOON!
HEY, MIRNA. I LIKED THAT ONE.
YOU ALWAYS LIKE THE SAD AND UNHAPPY ONES.
SAY, WHEN ARE YOU GONNA TAKE ME OUT FOR A NIGHT ON THE TOWN? IT'S NOT POLITE TO MAKE A GIRL KEEP ASKING, YA KNOW.
SORRY, MY NIGHTS ARE PRETTY BOOKED UP.
YEAH, YOU DRINK, PLAY CARDS, AND BEA UP ZOMBIES. HOW MUC FIGHT COULD A DEAD G PUT UP, ANYWAY?
YOU'D BE SURPRISED.
SERIOUSLY, WHAT'S WITH THE COLD SHOULDER?

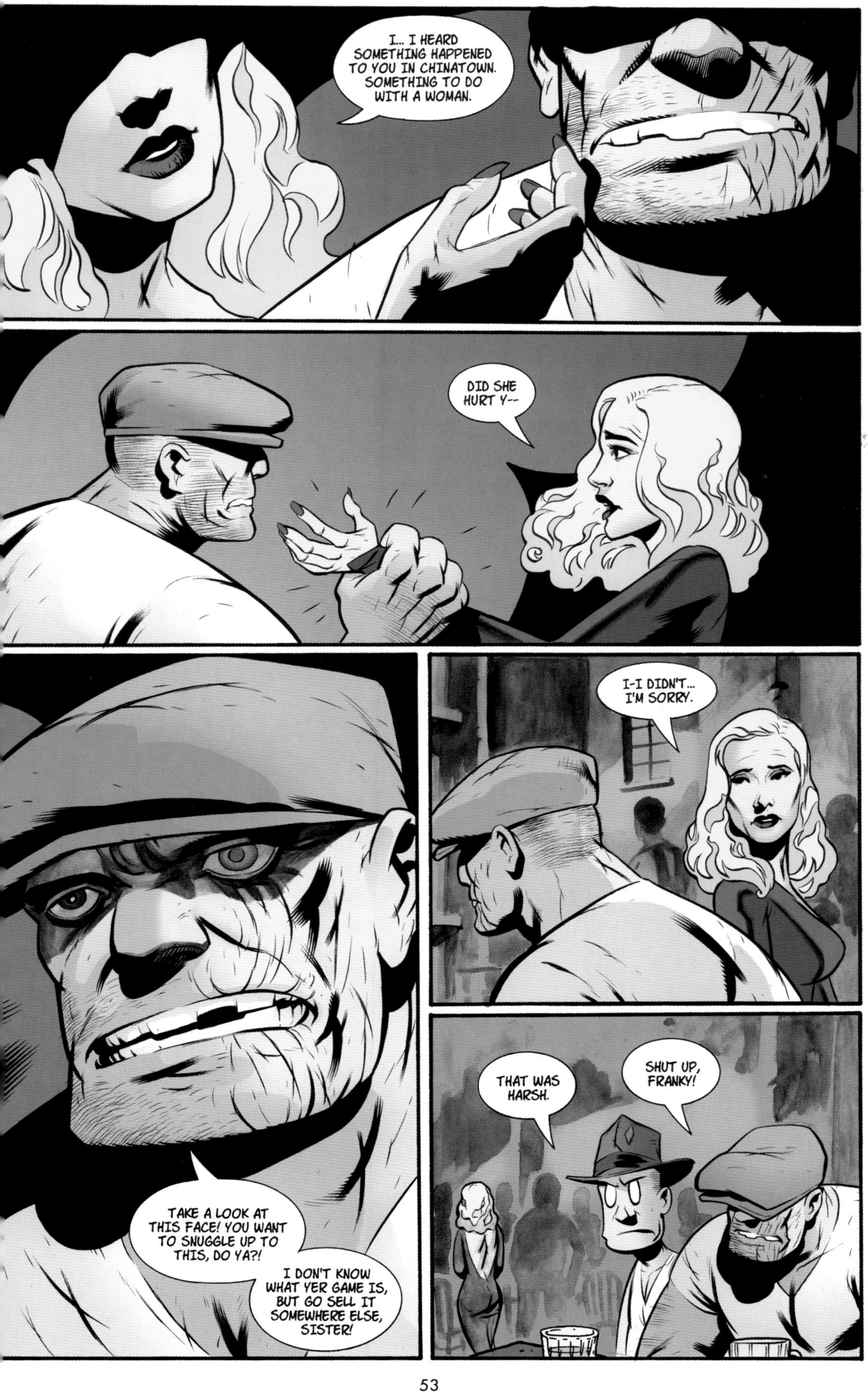
I... I HEARD SOMETHING HAPPENED TO YOU IN CHINATOWN. SOMETHING TO DO WITH A WOMAN.
DID SHE HURT Y--
TAKE A LOOK AT THIS FACE! YOU WANT TO SNUGGLE UP TO THIS, DO YA?!
I DON'T KNOW WHAT YER GAME IS, BUT GO SELL IT SOMEWHERE ELSE, SISTER!
I-I DIDN'T... I'M SORRY.
THAT WAS HARSH.
SHUT UP, FRANKY!

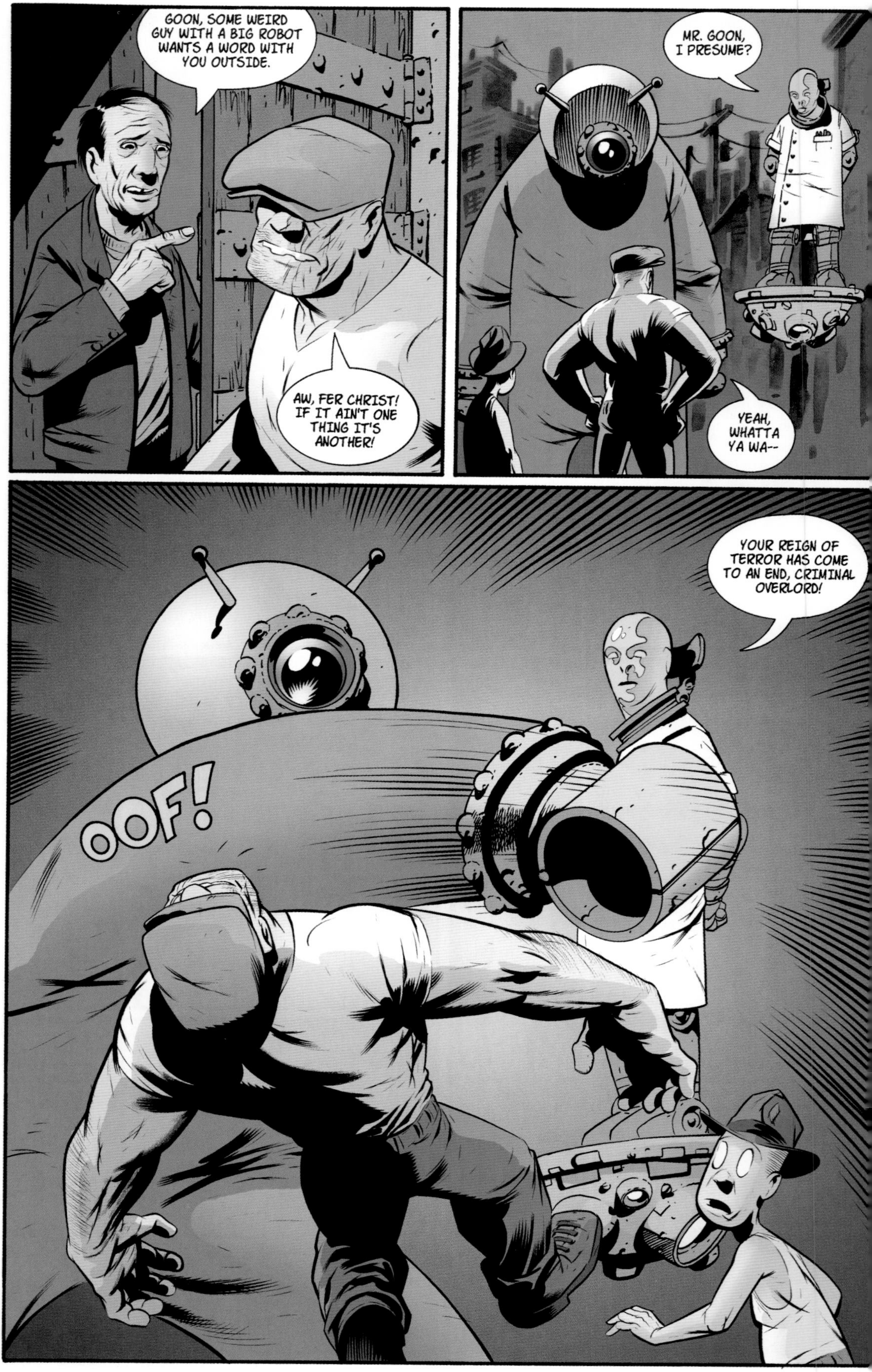
GOON, SOME WEIRD GUY WITH A BIG ROBOT WANTS A WORD WITH YOU OUTSIDE.
AW, FER CHRIST! IF IT AIN'T ONE THING IT'S ANOTHER!
MR. GOON, I PRESUME?
YEAH, WHATTA YA WA--
YOUR REIGN OF TERROR HAS COME TO AN END, CRIMINAL OVERLORD!
OOF!

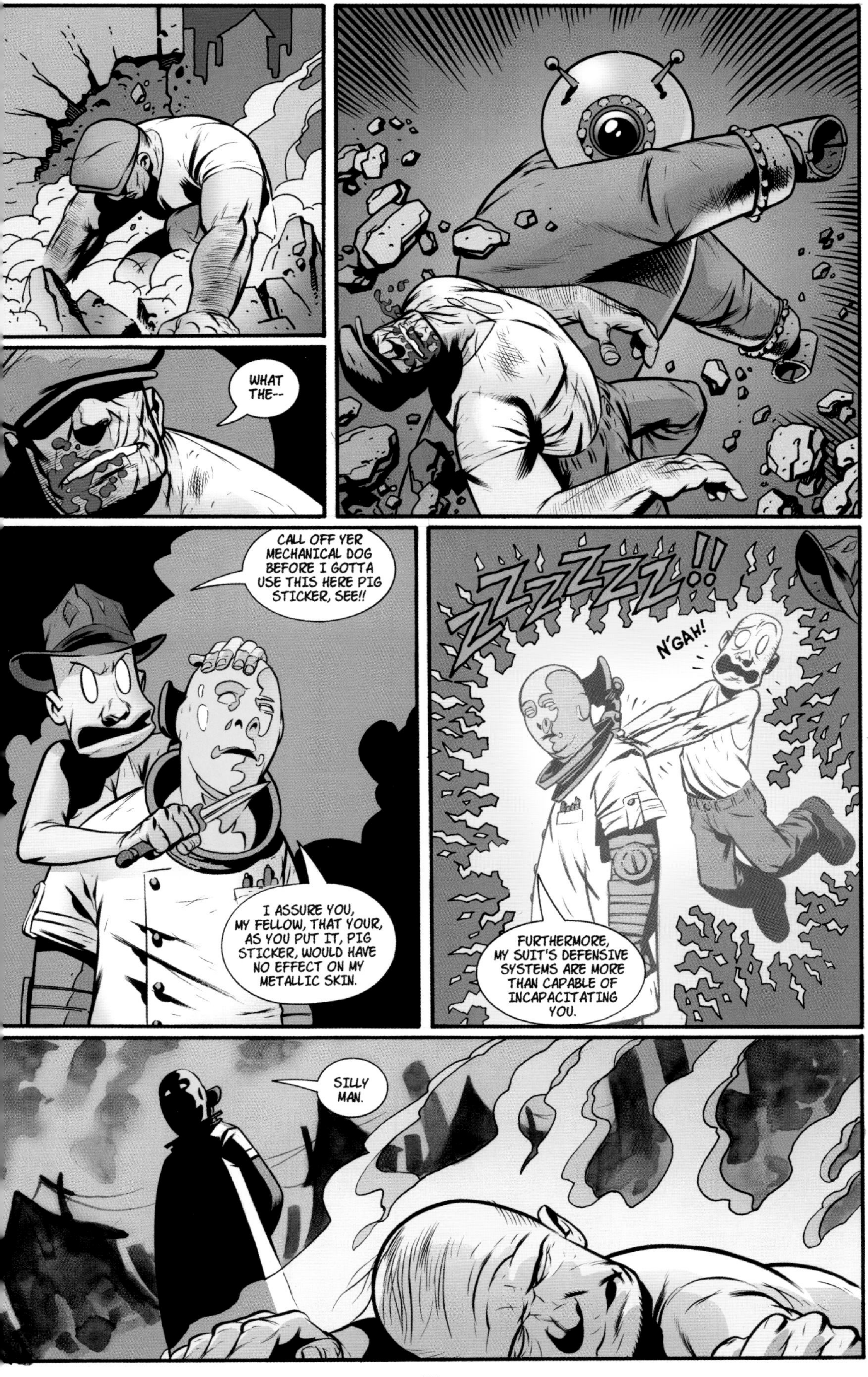
WHAT THE--
CALL OFF YER MECHANICAL DOG BEFORE I GOTTA USE THIS HERE PIG STICKER, SEE!!
I ASSURE YOU, MY FELLOW, THAT YOUR, AS YOU PUT IT, PIG STICKER, WOULD HAVE NO EFFECT ON MY METALLIC SKIN.
ZZZZZZ!!
N'GAH!
FURTHERMORE, MY SUIT'S DEFENSIVE SYSTEMS ARE MORE THAN CAPABLE OF INCAPACITATING YOU.
SILLY MAN.

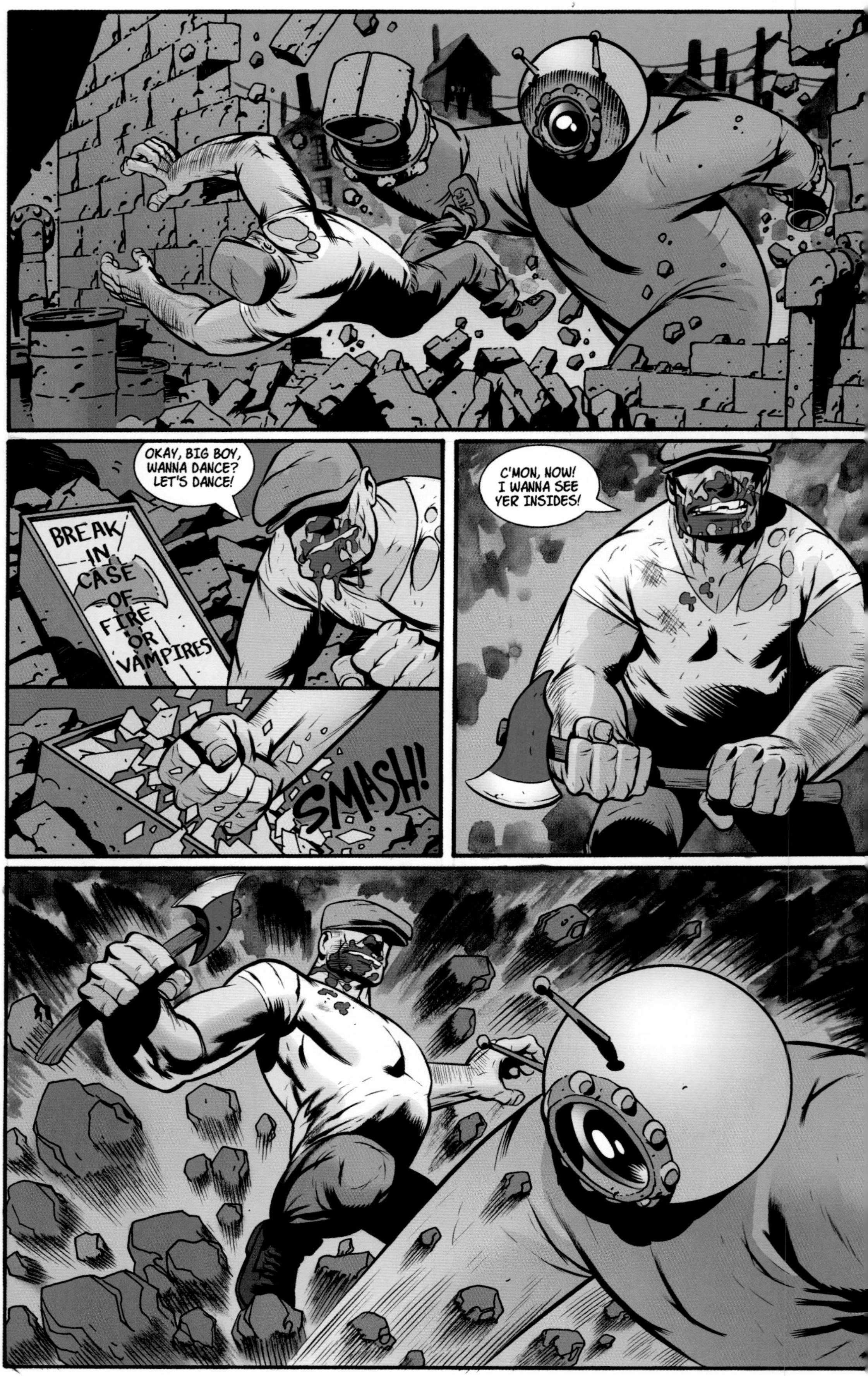
OKAY, BIG BOY, WANNA DANCE? LET'S DANCE!
BREAK IN CASE OF FIRE OR VAMPIRES
SMASH!
C'MON, NOW! I WANNA SEE YER INSIDES!

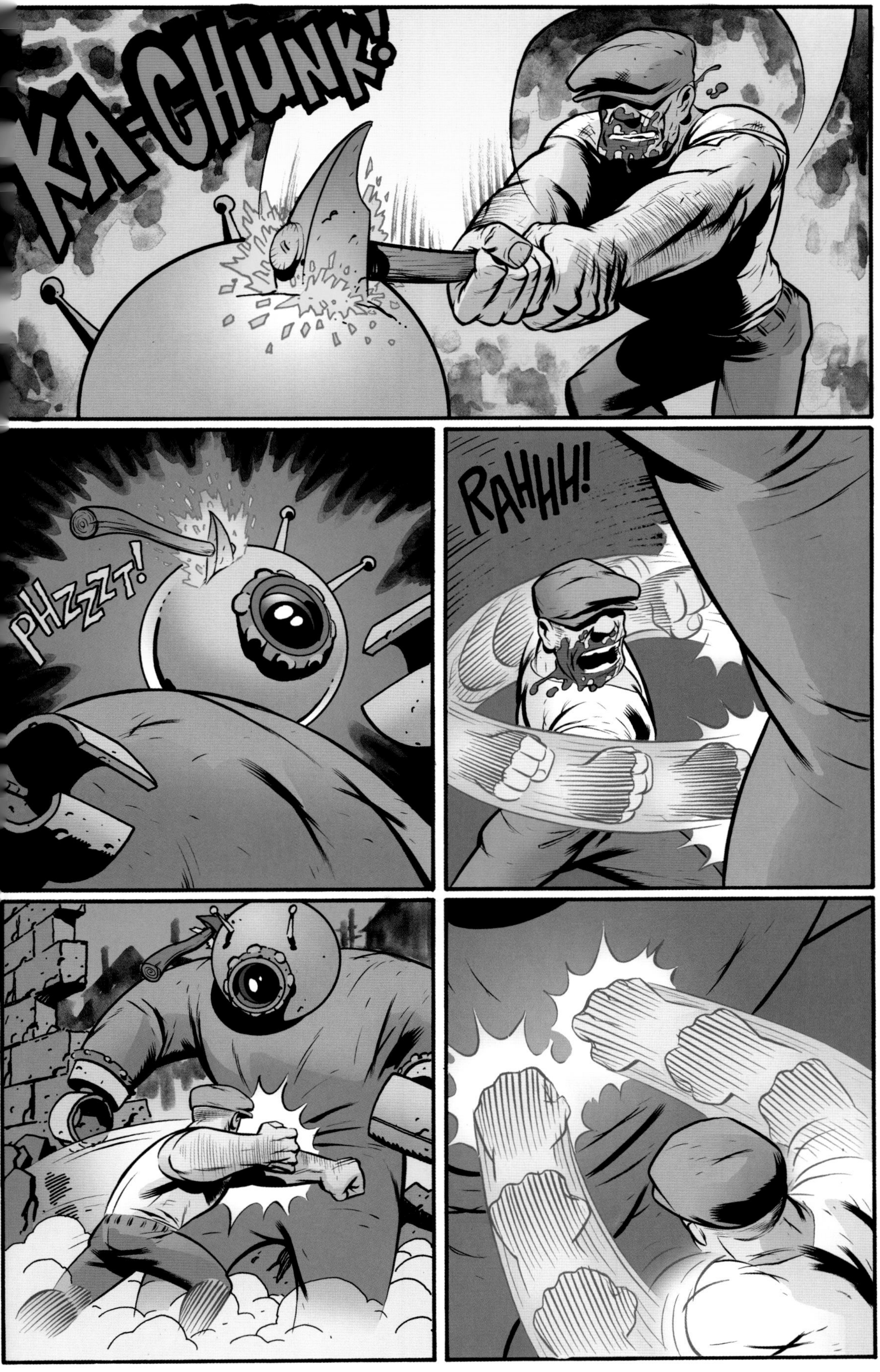
KA-CHUNK!
PHZZZT!
RAHHH!

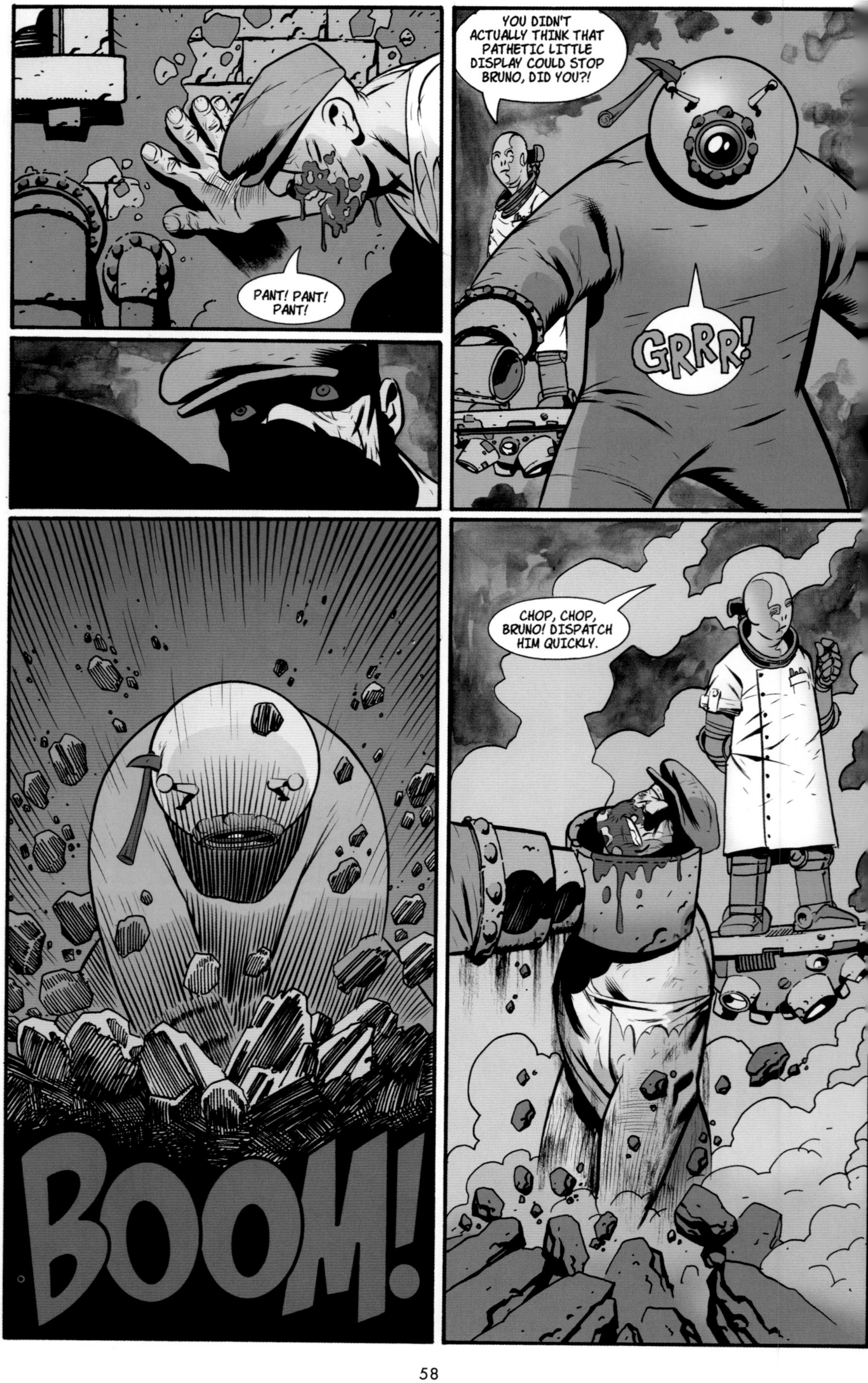
PANT! PANT! PANT!
YOU DIDN'T ACTUALLY THINK THAT PATHETIC LITTLE DISPLAY COULD STOP BRUNO, DID YOU?!
GRRR!
BOOM!
CHOP, CHOP, BRUNO! DISPATCH HIM QUICKLY.

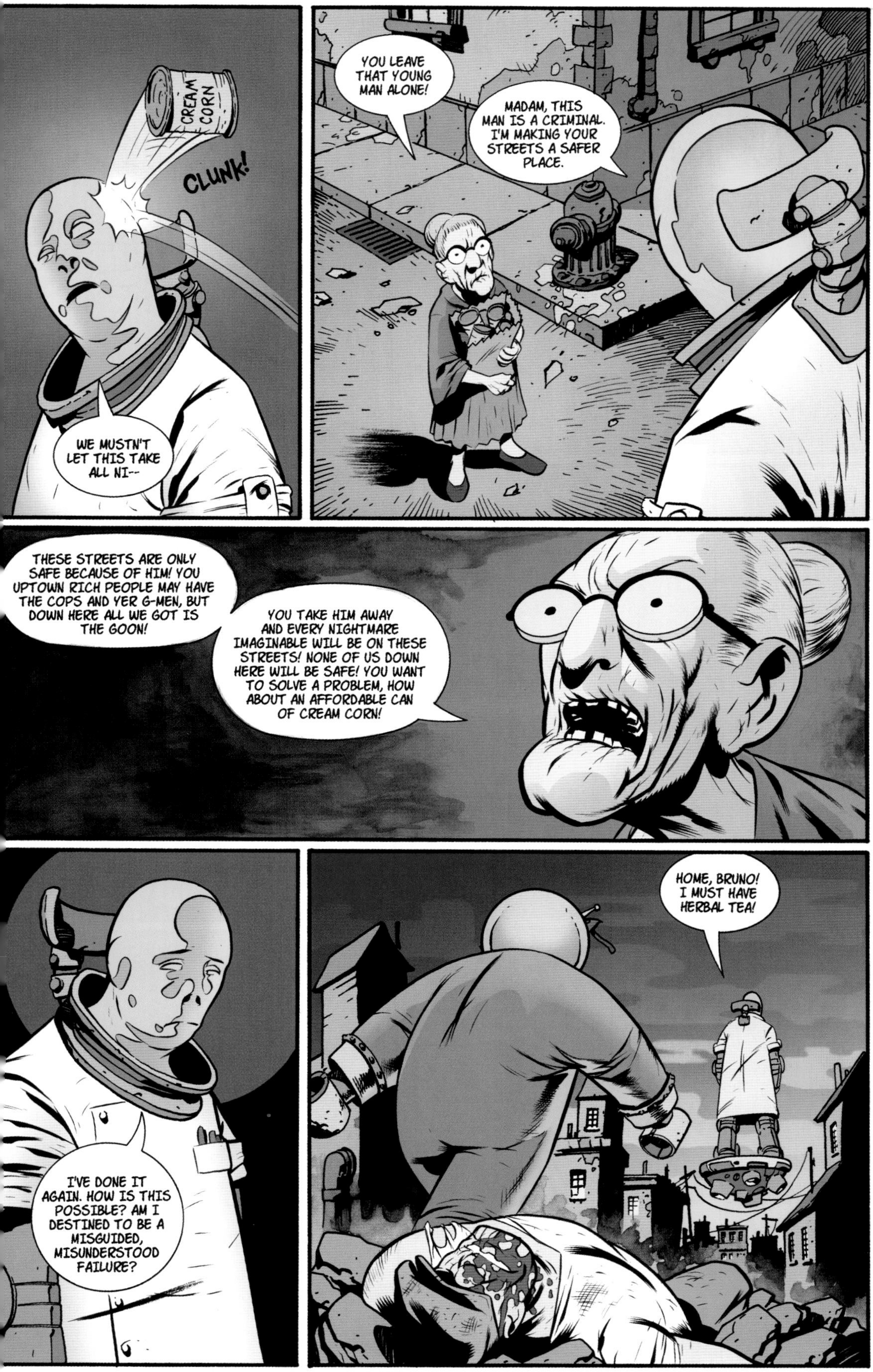
CREAM CORN
CLUNK!
WE MUSTN'T LET THIS TAKE ALL NI--
YOU LEAVE THAT YOUNG MAN ALONE!
MADAM, THIS MAN IS A CRIMINAL. I'M MAKING YOUR STREETS A SAFER PLACE.
THESE STREETS ARE ONLY SAFE BECAUSE OF HIM! YOU UPTOWN RICH PEOPLE MAY HAVE THE COPS AND YER G-MEN, BUT DOWN HERE ALL WE GOT IS THE GOON!
YOU TAKE HIM AWAY AND EVERY NIGHTMARE IMAGINABLE WILL BE ON THESE STREETS! NONE OF US DOWN HERE WILL BE SAFE! YOU WANT TO SOLVE A PROBLEM, HOW ABOUT AN AFFORDABLE CAN OF CREAM CORN!
I'VE DONE IT AGAIN. HOW IS THIS POSSIBLE? AM I DESTINED TO BE A MISGUIDED, MISUNDERSTOOD FAILURE?
HOME, BRUNO! I MUST HAVE HERBAL TEA!

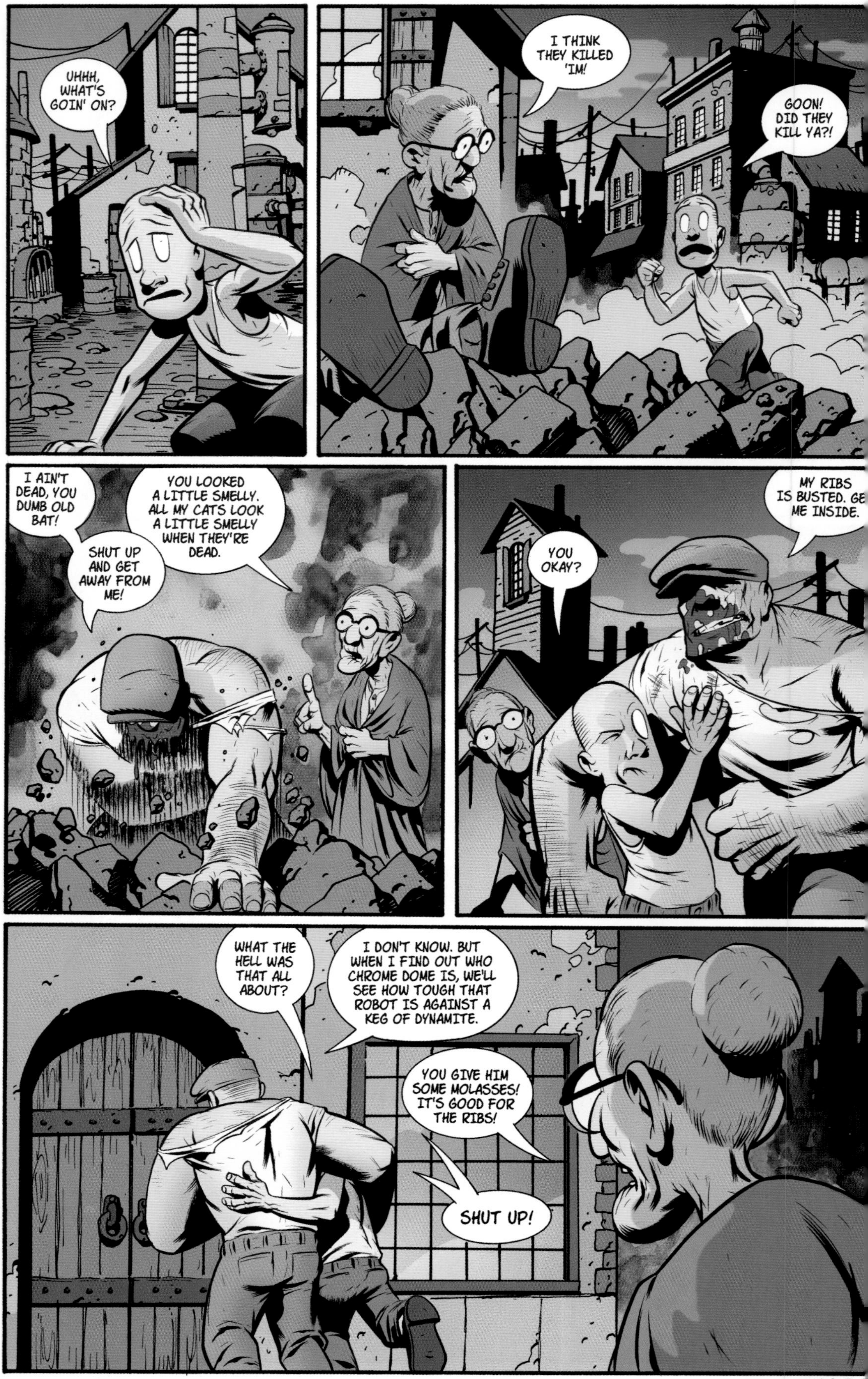
UHHH, WHAT'S GOIN' ON?
I THINK THEY KILLED 'IM!
GOON! DID THEY KILL YA?!
I AIN'T DEAD, YOU DUMB OLD BAT!
YOU LOOKED A LITTLE SMELLY. ALL MY CATS LOOK A LITTLE SMELLY WHEN THEY'RE DEAD.
SHUT UP AND GET AWAY FROM ME!
YOU OKAY?
MY RIBS IS BUSTED. GE
ME INSIDE.
WHAT THE HELL WAS THAT ALL ABOUT?
I DON'T KNOW. BUT WHEN I FIND OUT WHO CHROME DOME IS, WE'LL SEE HOW TOUGH THAT ROBOT IS AGAINST A KEG OF DYNAMITE.
YOU GIVE HIM SOME MOLASSES! IT'S GOOD FOR THE RIBS!
SHUT UP!

END!

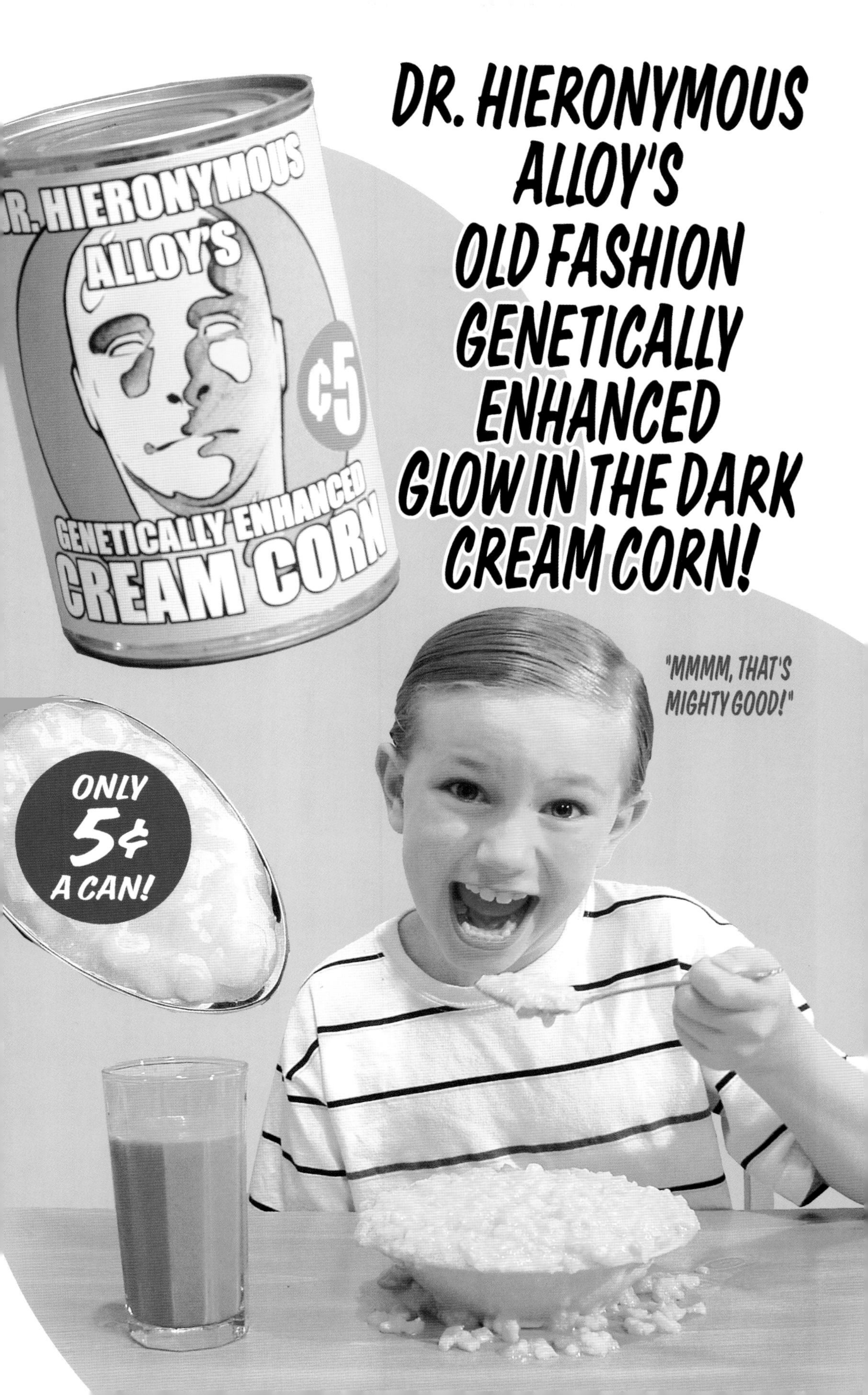
DR. HIERONYMOUS ALLOY'S
GENETICALLY ENHANCED CREAM CORN
¢5
DR. HIERONYMOUS ALLOY'S OLD FASHION GENETICALLY ENHANCED GLOW IN THE DARK CREAM CORN!
"MMMM, THAT'S MIGHTY GOOD!"
ONLY 5¢ A CAN!

CHAPTER 3

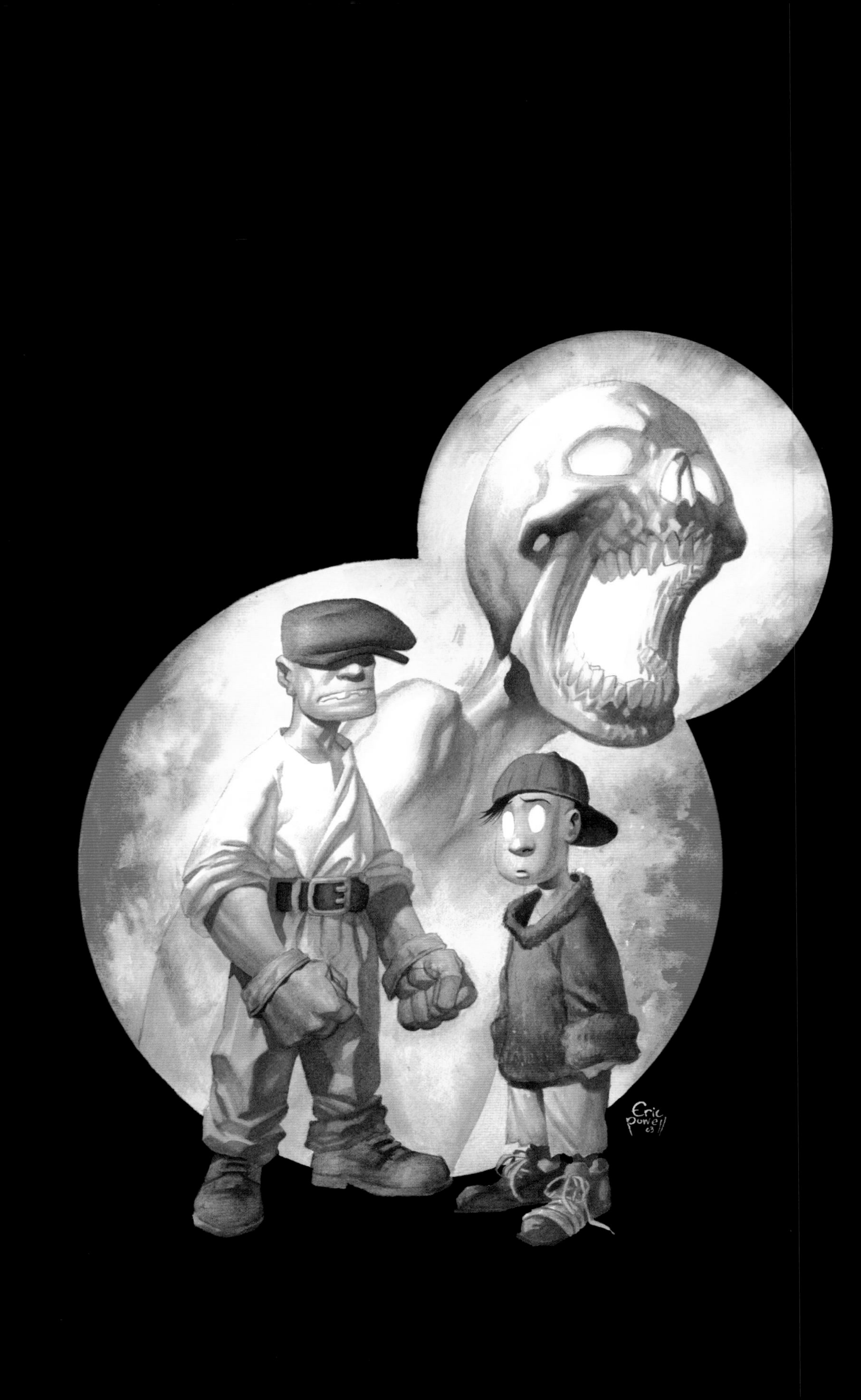
Eric powell
03

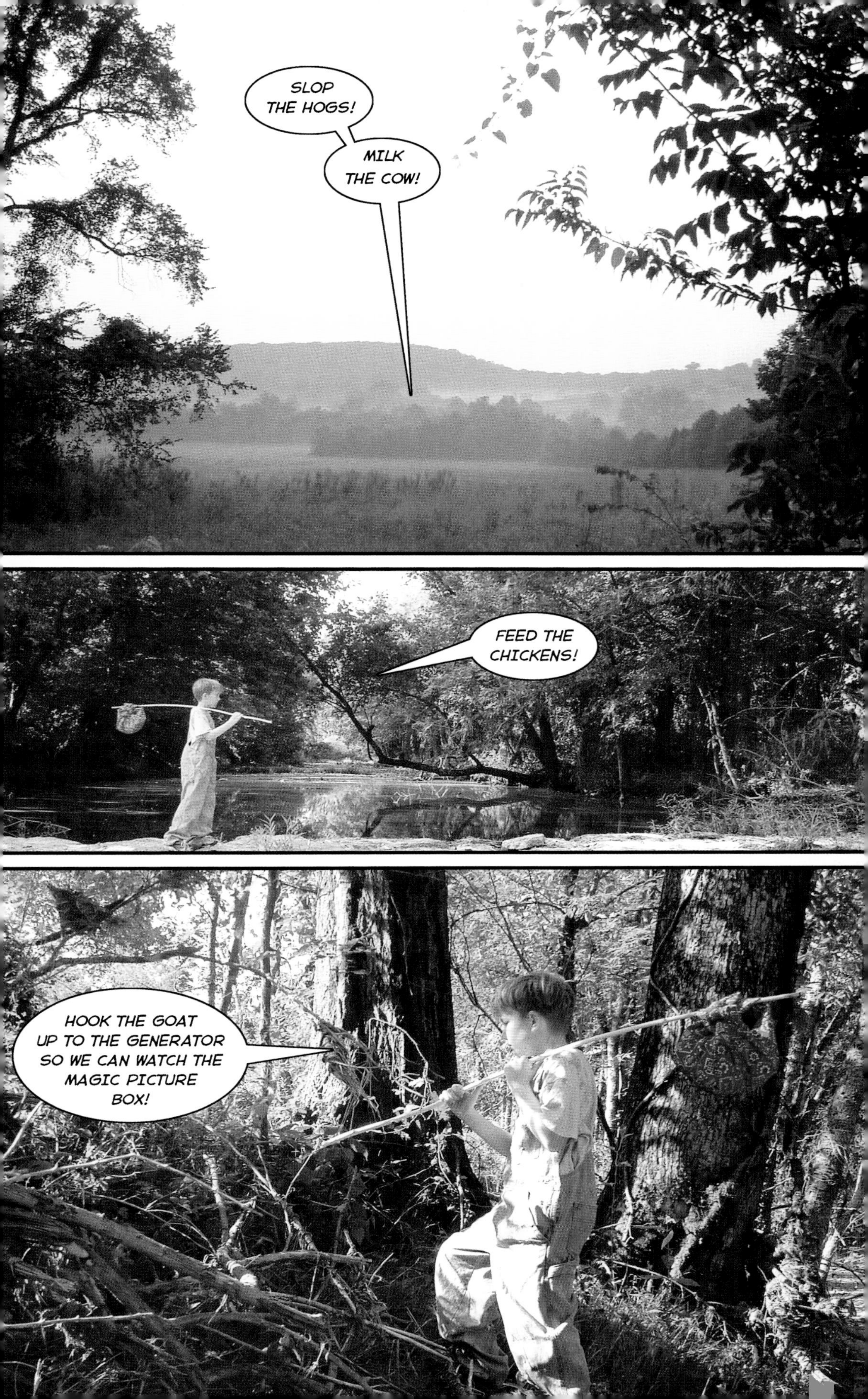
SLOP THE HOGS!
MILK THE COW!
FEED THE CHICKENS!
HOOK THE GOAT UP TO THE GENERATOR SO WE CAN WATCH THE MAGIC PICTURE BOX!

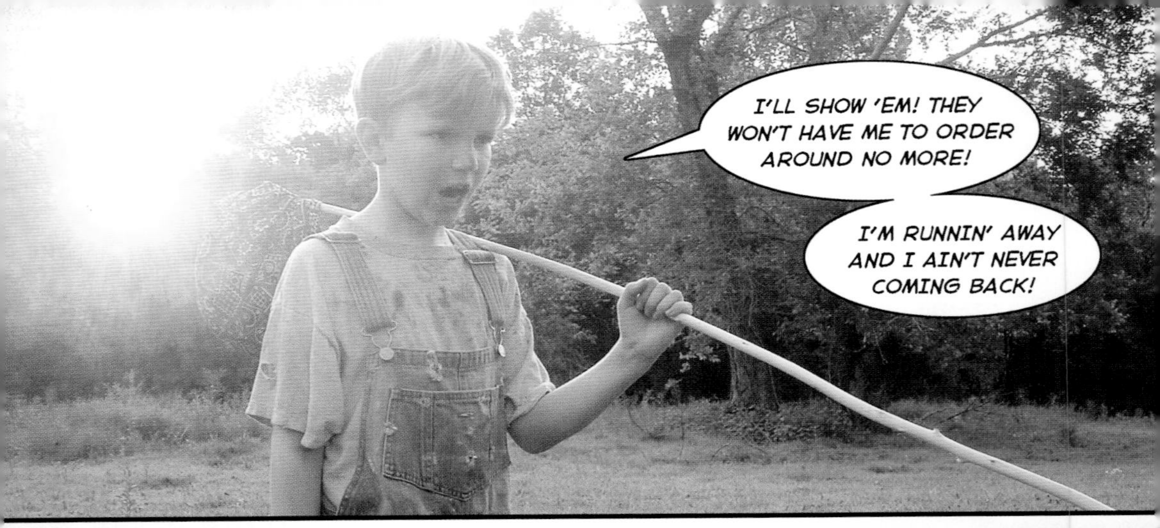
I'LL SHOW 'EM! THEY WON'T HAVE ME TO ORDER AROUND NO MORE!
I'M RUNNIN' AWAY AND I AIN'T NEVER COMING BACK!

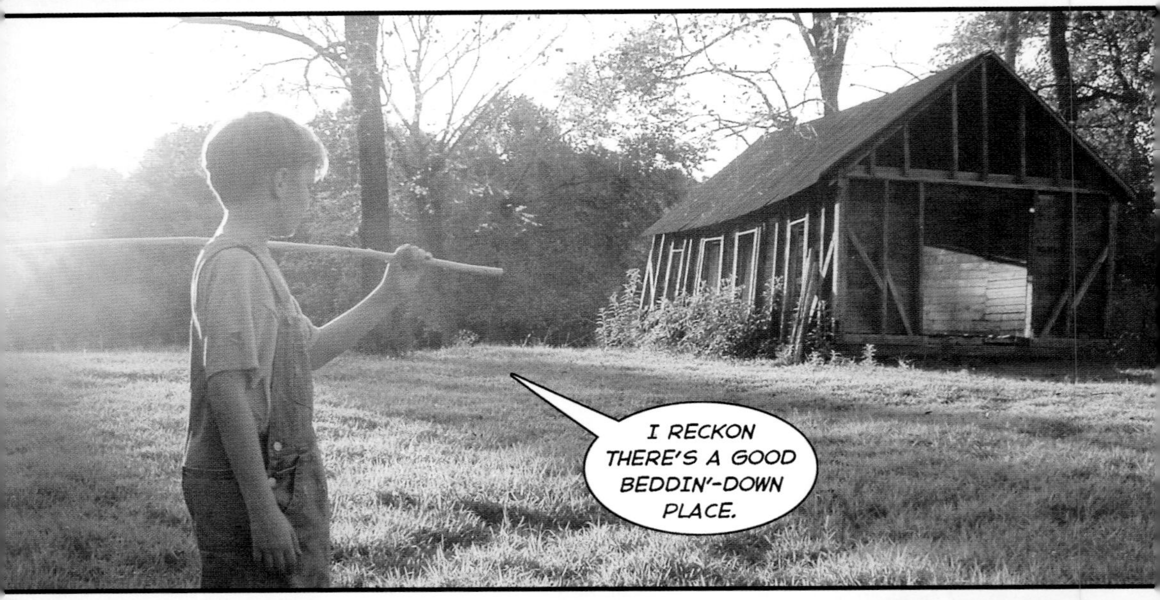
I RECKON THERE'S A GOOD BEDDIN'-DOWN PLACE.

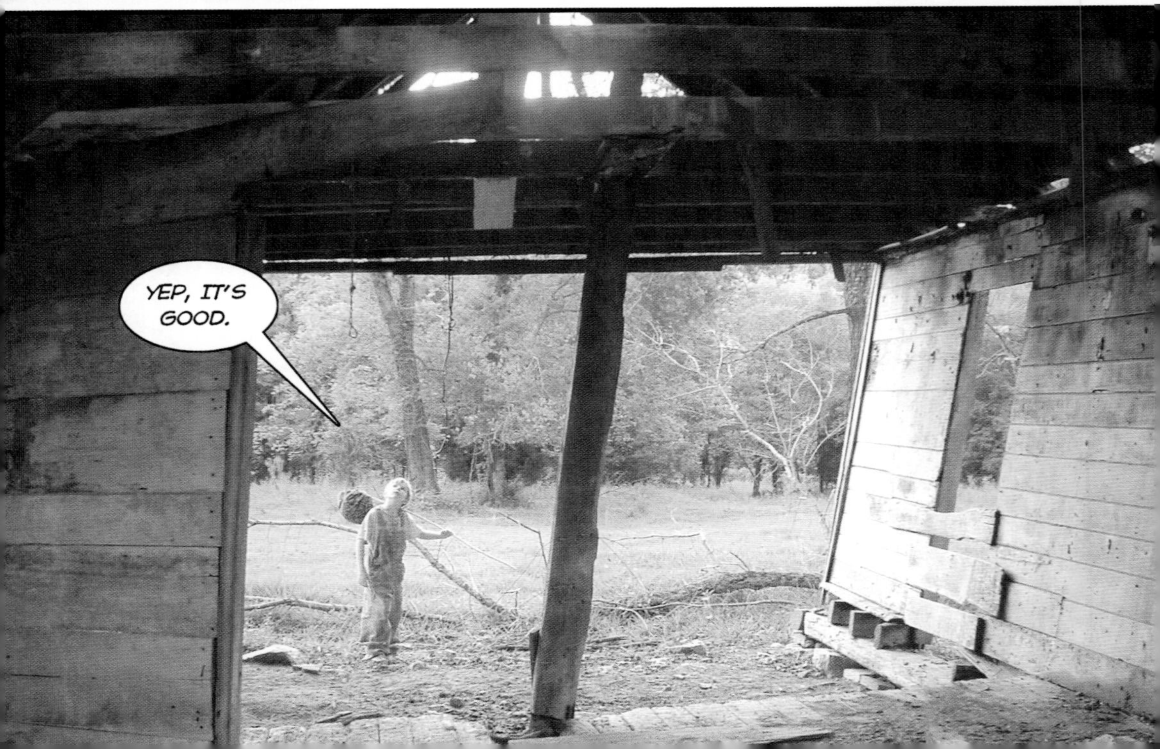
YEP, IT'S GOOD.

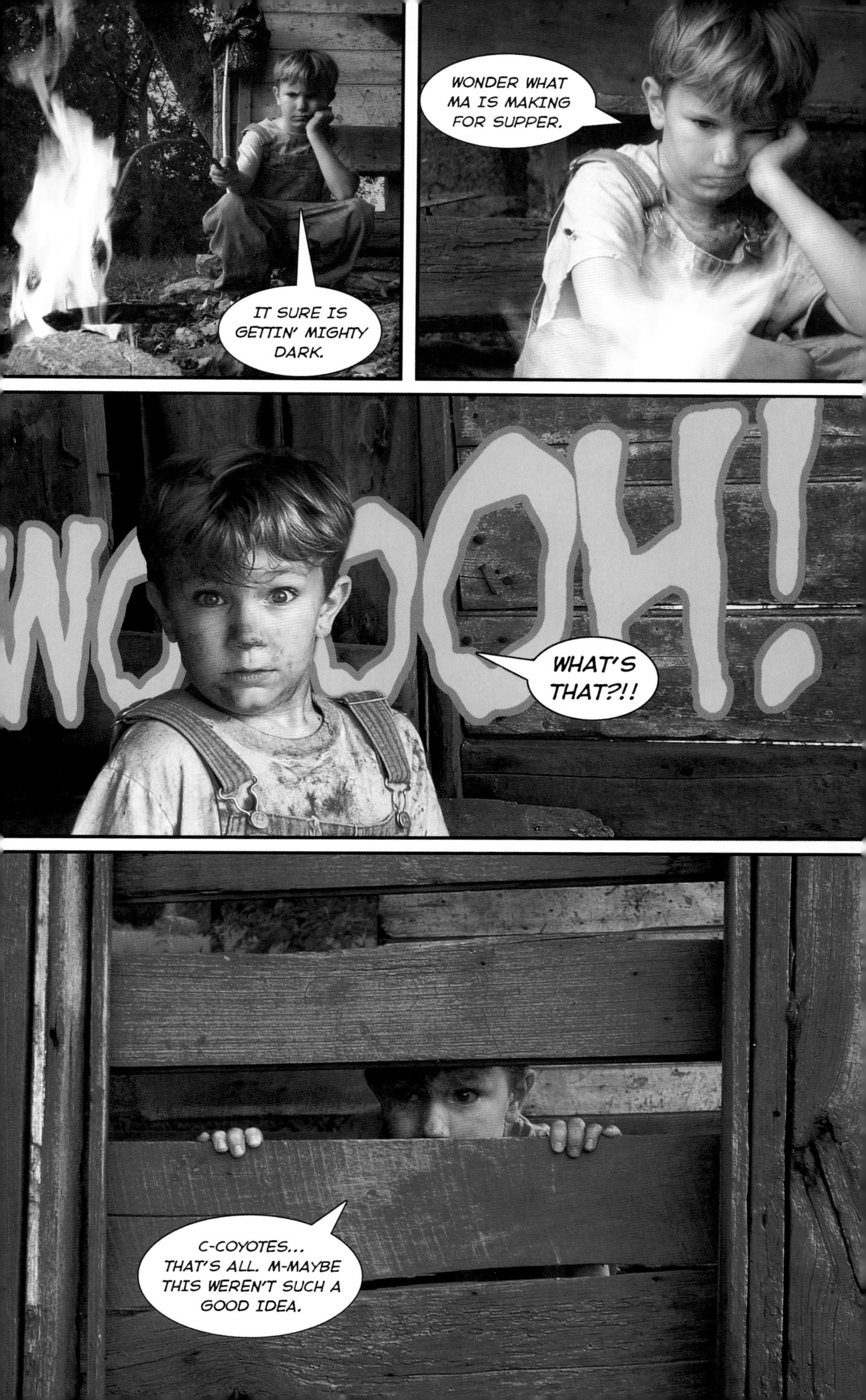
IT SURE IS GETTIN' MIGHTY DARK.
WONDER WHAT MA IS MAKING FOR SUPPER.
WHAT'S THAT?!!
C-COYOTES... THAT'S ALL. M-MAYBE THIS WEREN'T SUCH A GOOD IDEA.

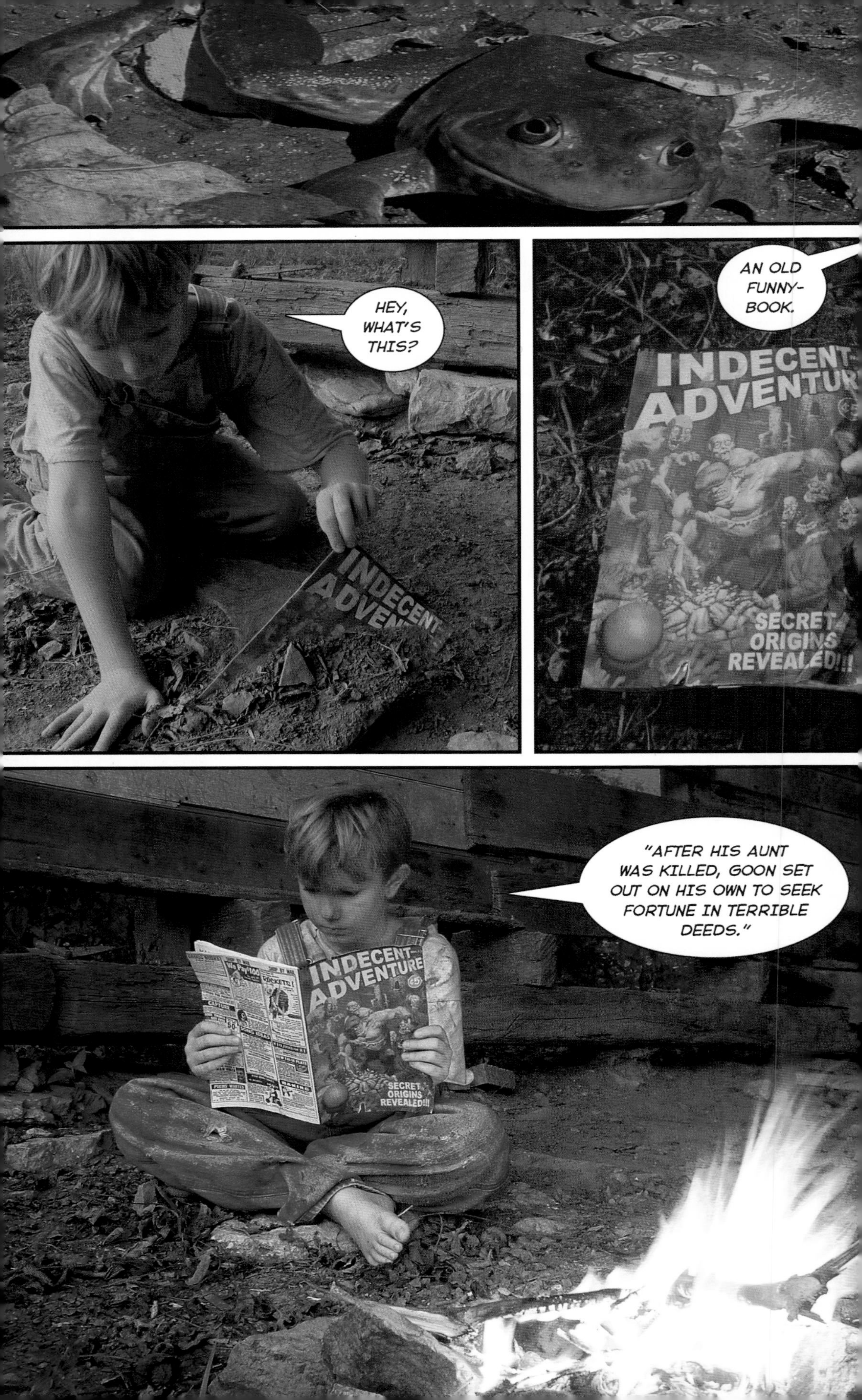
HEY, WHAT'S THIS?
INDECENT- ADVENTURE
AN OLD FUNNY-BOOK.
INDECENT- ADVENTURE
SECRET ORIGINS REVEALED!!!
"AFTER HIS AUNT WAS KILLED, GOON SET OUT ON HIS OWN TO SEEK FORTUNE IN TERRIBLE DEEDS."
INDECENT- ADVENTURE
SECRET ORIGINS REVEALED!!!

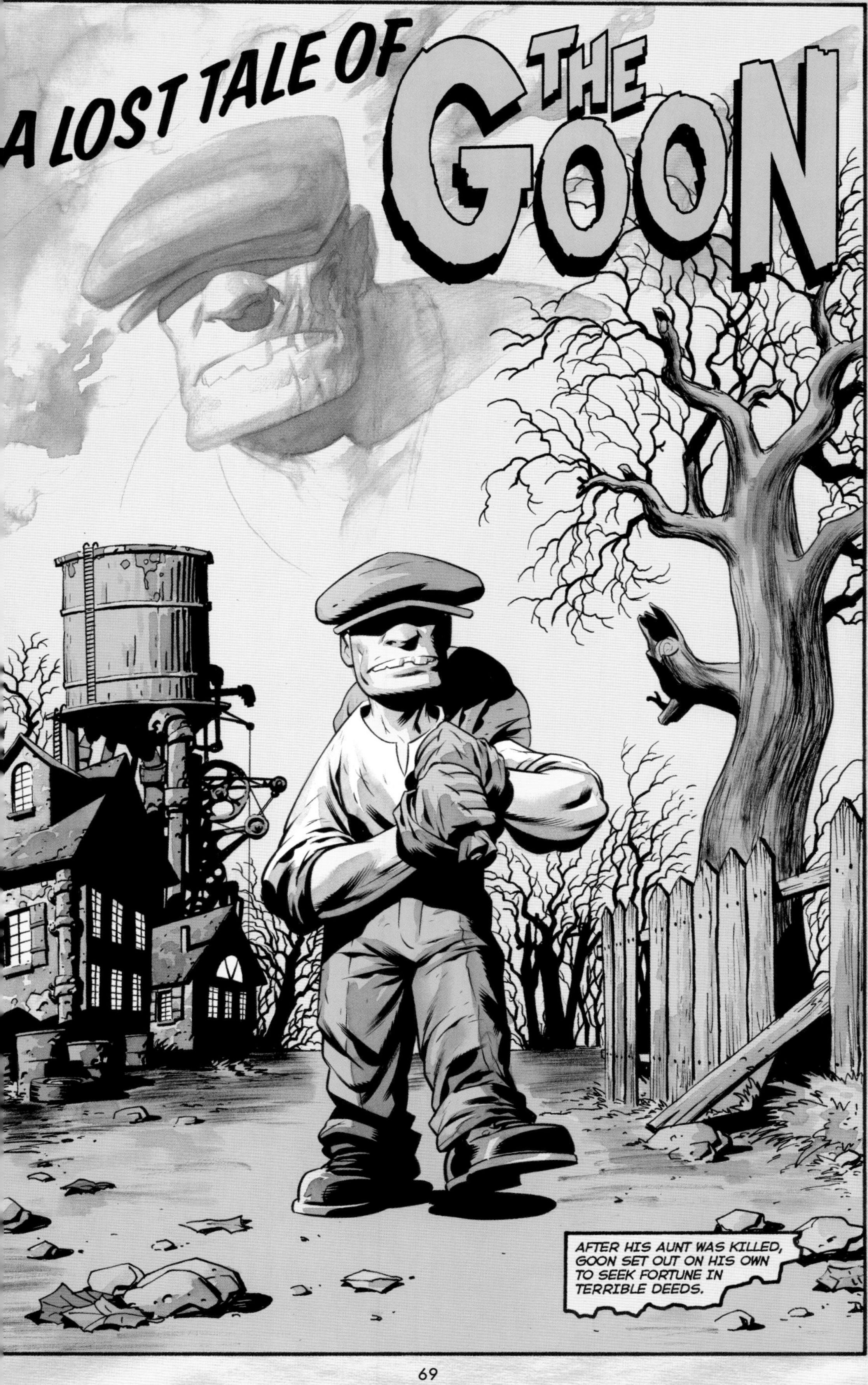

A LOST TALE OF THE GOON
AFTER HIS AUNT WAS KILLED, GOON SET OUT ON HIS OWN TO SEEK FORTUNE IN TERRIBLE DEEDS.

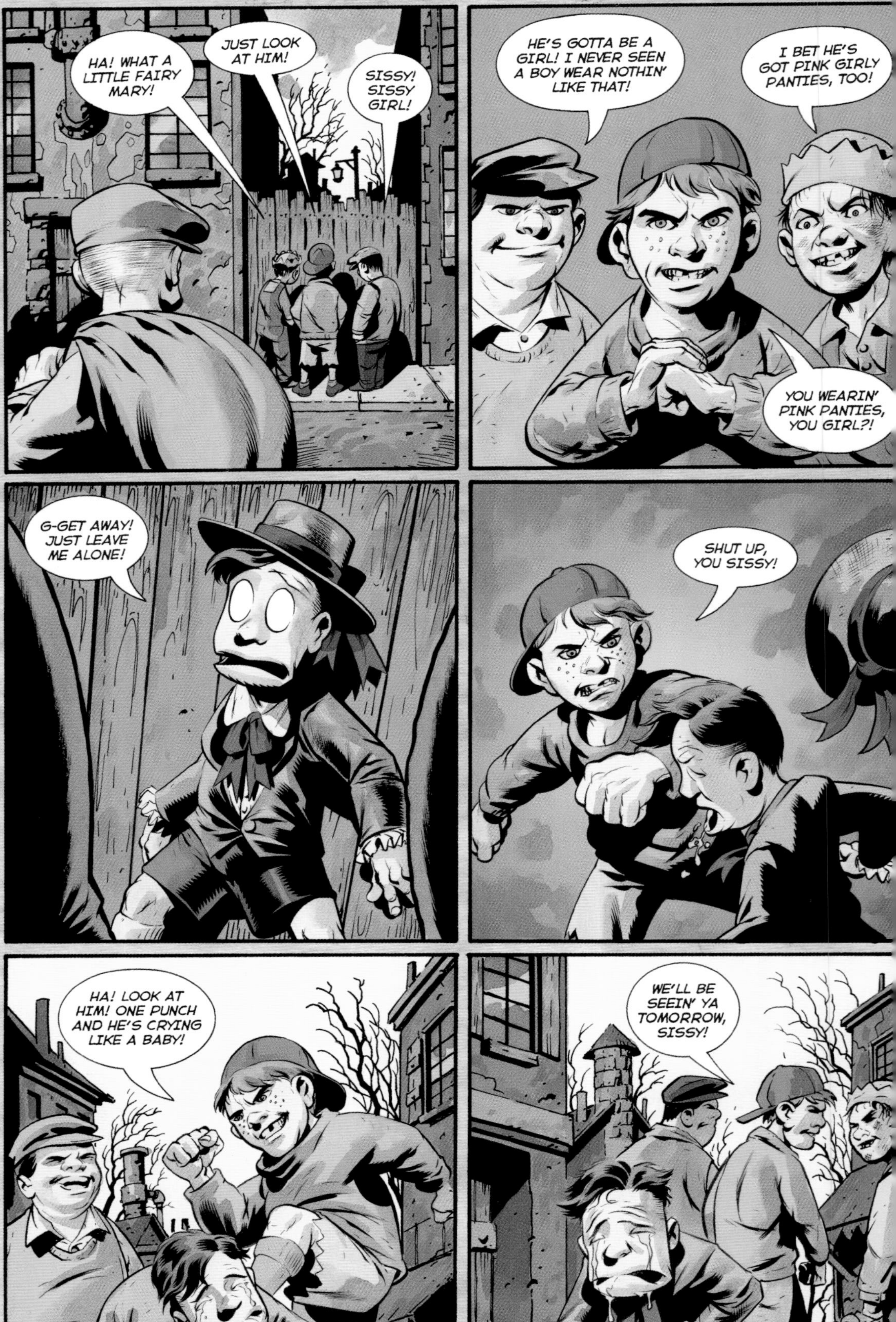
HA! WHAT A LITTLE FAIRY MARY!
JUST LOOK AT HIM!
SISSY! SISSY GIRL!
HE'S GOTTA BE A GIRL! I NEVER SEEN A BOY WEAR NOTHIN' LIKE THAT!
I BET HE'S GOT PINK GIRLY PANTIES, TOO!
YOU WEARIN' PINK PANTIES, YOU GIRL?!
G-GET AWAY! JUST LEAVE ME ALONE!
SHUT UP, YOU SISSY!
HA! LOOK AT HIM! ONE PUNCH AND HE'S CRYING LIKE A BABY!
WE'LL BE SEEIN' YA TOMORROW, SISSY!

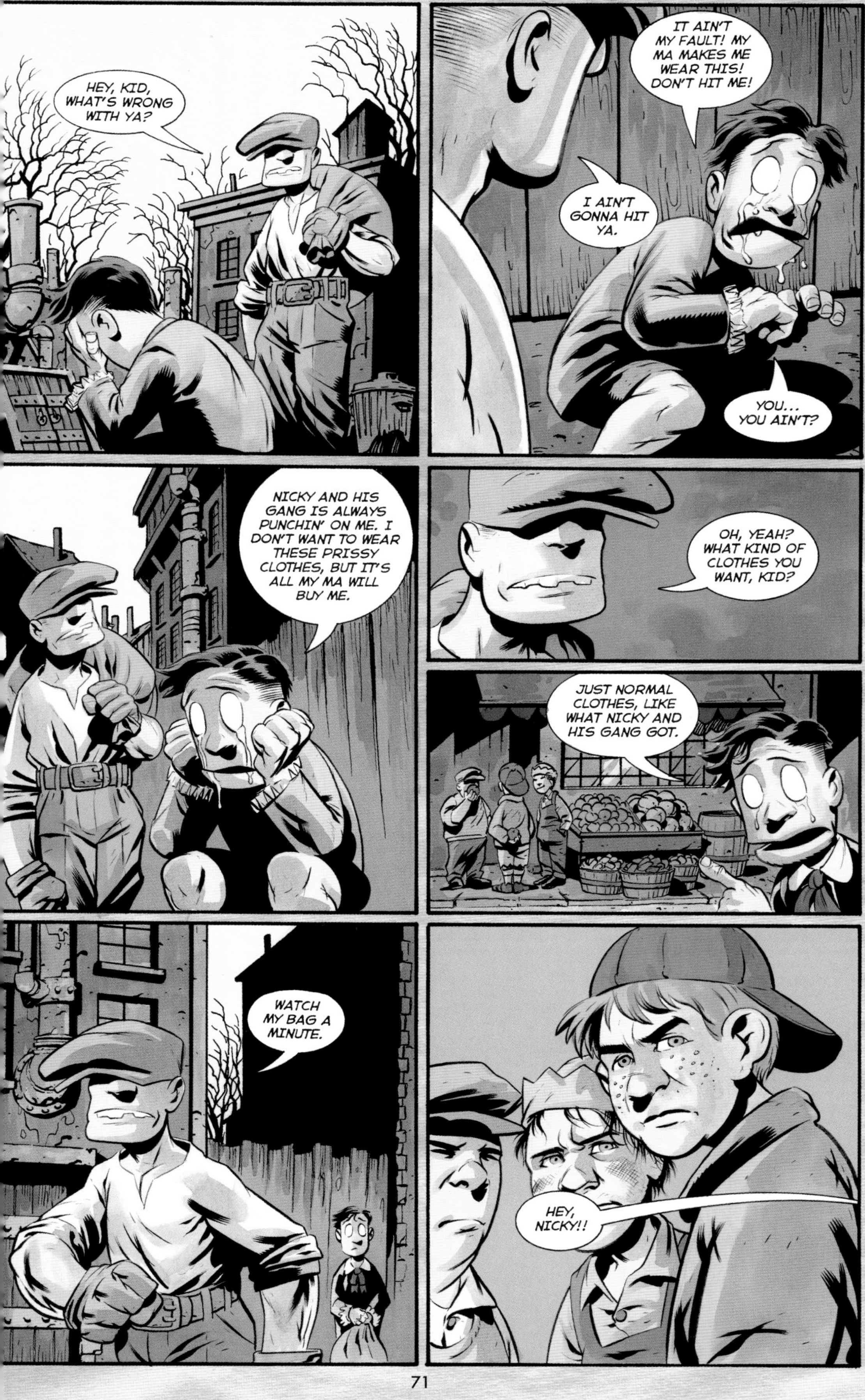
HEY, KID, WHAT'S WRONG WITH YA?
IT AIN'T MY FAULT! MY MA MAKES ME WEAR THIS! DON'T HIT ME!
I AIN'T GONNA HIT YA.
YOU... YOU AIN'T?
NICKY AND HIS GANG IS ALWAYS PUNCHIN' ON ME. I DON'T WANT TO WEAR THESE PRISSY CLOTHES, BUT IT'S ALL MY MA WILL BUY ME.
OH, YEAH? WHAT KIND OF CLOTHES YOU WANT, KID?
JUST NORMAL CLOTHES, LIKE WHAT NICKY AND HIS GANG GOT.
WATCH MY BAG A MINUTE.
HEY, NICKY!!

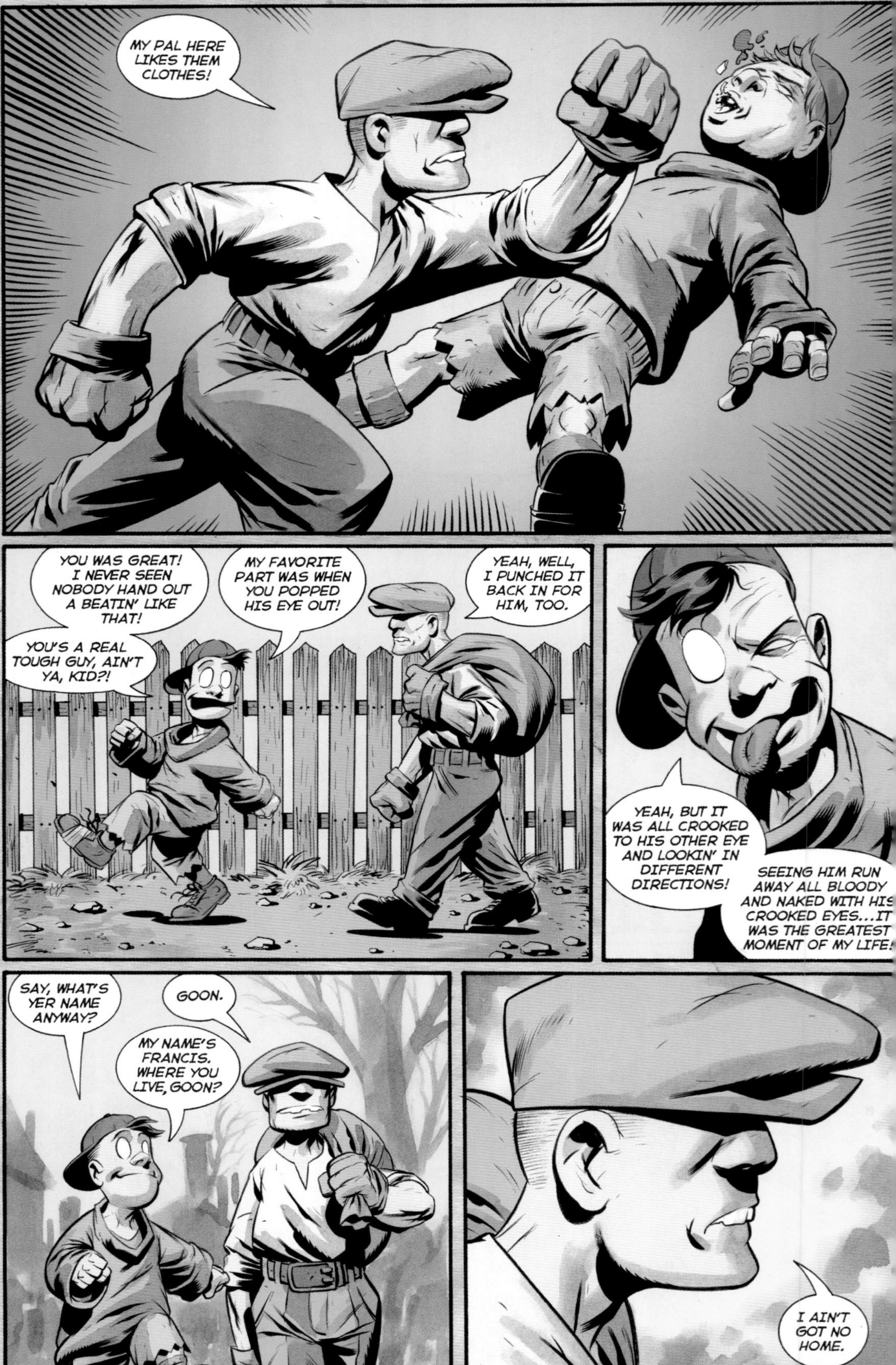
MY PAL HERE LIKES THEM CLOTHES!
YOU WAS GREAT! I NEVER SEEN NOBODY HAND OUT A BEATIN' LIKE THAT!
YOU'S A REAL TOUGH GUY, AIN'T YA, KID?!
MY FAVORITE PART WAS WHEN YOU POPPED HIS EYE OUT!
YEAH, WELL, I PUNCHED IT BACK IN FOR HIM, TOO.
YEAH, BUT IT WAS ALL CROOKED TO HIS OTHER EYE AND LOOKIN' IN DIFFERENT DIRECTIONS!
SEEING HIM RUN AWAY ALL BLOODY AND NAKED WITH HIS CROOKED EYES...IT WAS THE GREATEST MOMENT OF MY LIFE!
SAY, WHAT'S YER NAME ANYWAY?
GOON.
MY NAME'S FRANCIS. WHERE YOU LIVE, GOON?
I AIN'T GOT NO HOME.

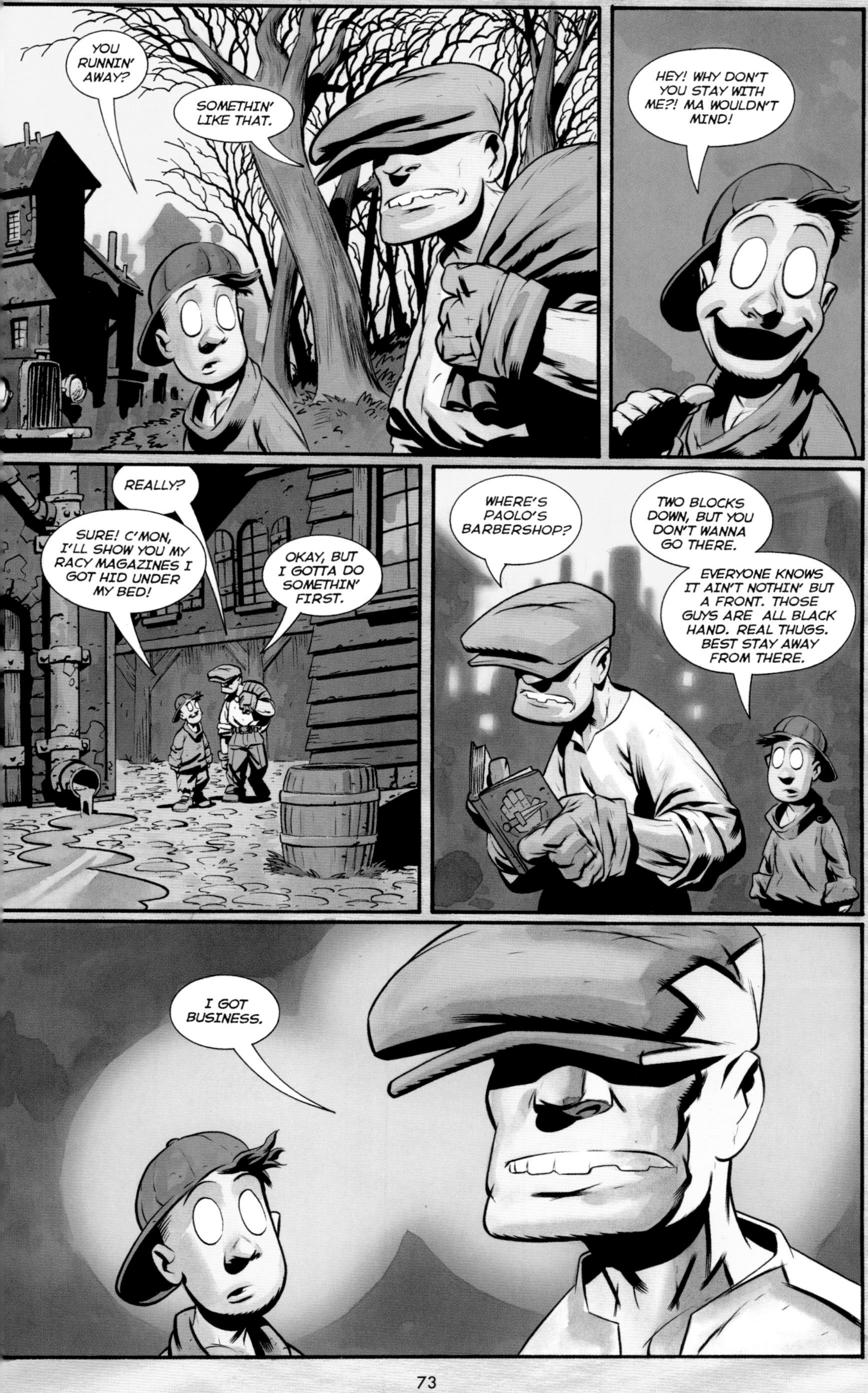
YOU RUNNIN' AWAY?
SOMETHIN' LIKE THAT.
HEY! WHY DON'T YOU STAY WITH ME?! MA WOULDN'T MIND!
REALLY?
SURE! C'MON, I'LL SHOW YOU MY RACY MAGAZINES I GOT HID UNDER MY BED!
OKAY, BUT I GOTTA DO SOMETHIN' FIRST.
WHERE'S PAOLO'S BARBERSHOP?
TWO BLOCKS DOWN, BUT YOU DON'T WANNA GO THERE.
EVERYONE KNOWS IT AIN'T NOTHIN' BUT A FRONT. THOSE GUYS ARE ALL BLACK HAND. REAL THUGS. BEST STAY AWAY FROM THERE.
I GOT BUSINESS.

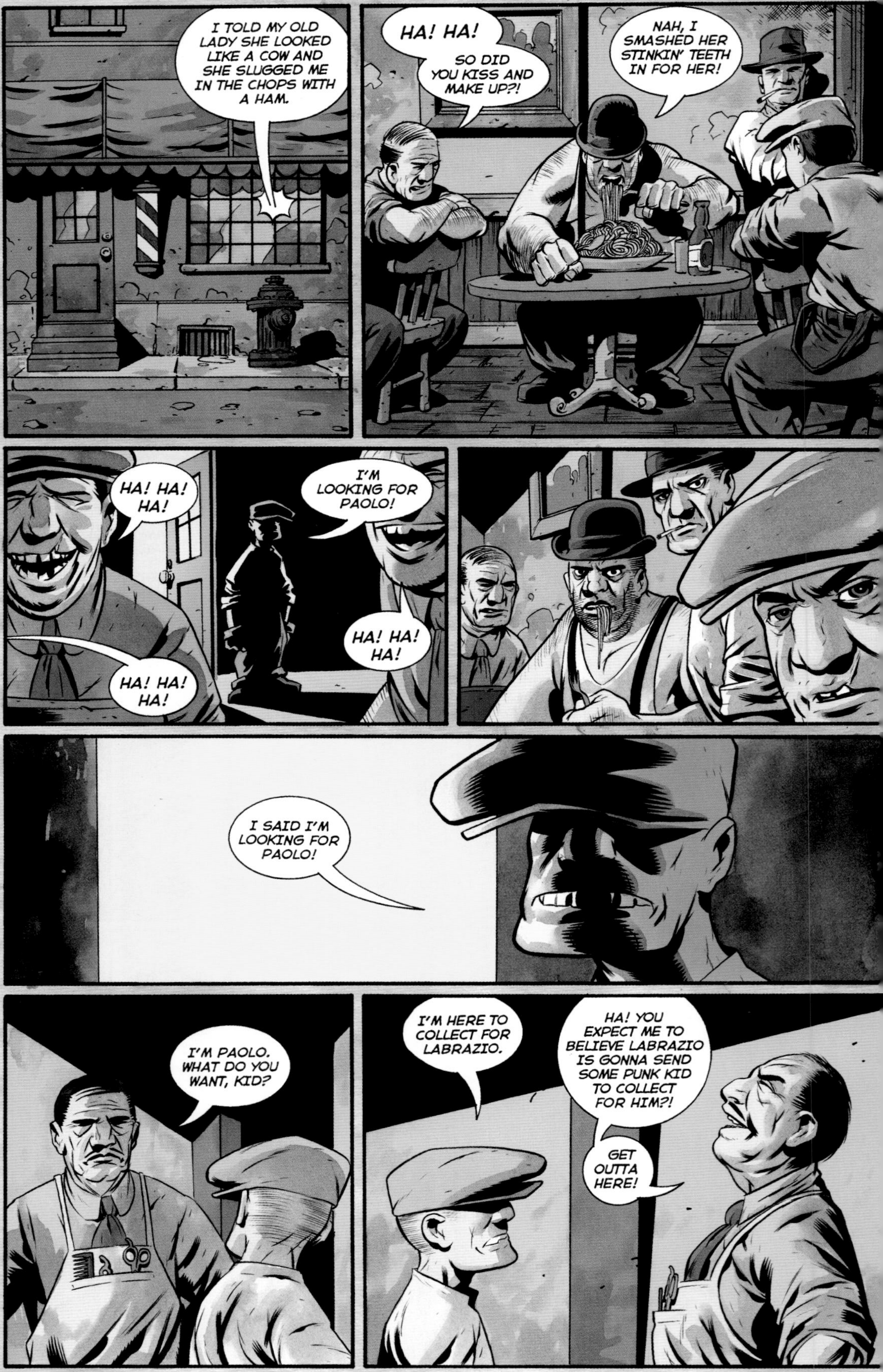
I TOLD MY OLD LADY SHE LOOKED LIKE A COW AND SHE SLUGGED ME IN THE CHOPS WITH A HAM.
HA! HA!
SO DID YOU KISS AND MAKE UP?!
NAH, I SMASHED HER STINKIN' TEETH IN FOR HER!
HA! HA! HA!
HA! HA! HA!
I'M LOOKING FOR PAOLO!
HA! HA! HA!
I SAID I'M LOOKING FOR PAOLO!
I'M PAOLO. WHAT DO YOU WANT, KID?
I'M HERE TO COLLECT FOR LABRAZIO.
HA! YOU EXPECT ME TO BELIEVE LABRAZIO IS GONNA SEND SOME PUNK KID TO COLLECT FOR HIM?!
GET OUTTA HERE!

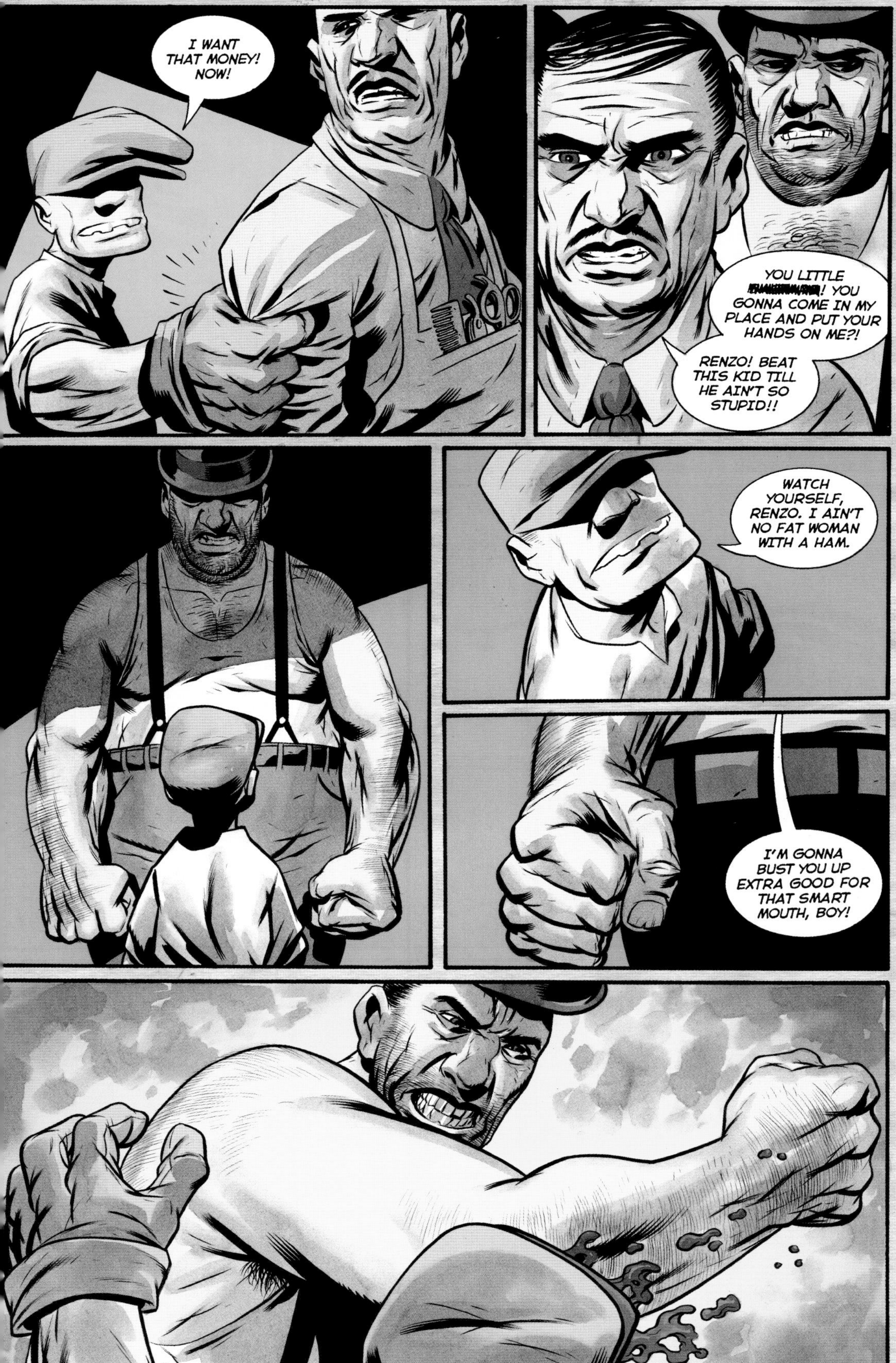
I WANT THAT MONEY! NOW!
YOU LITTLE [redacted]! YOU GONNA COME IN MY PLACE AND PUT YOUR HANDS ON ME?!
RENZO! BEAT THIS KID TILL HE AIN'T SO STUPID!!
WATCH YOURSELF, RENZO. I AIN'T NO FAT WOMAN WITH A HAM.
I'M GONNA BUST YOU UP EXTRA GOOD FOR THAT SMART MOUTH, BOY!

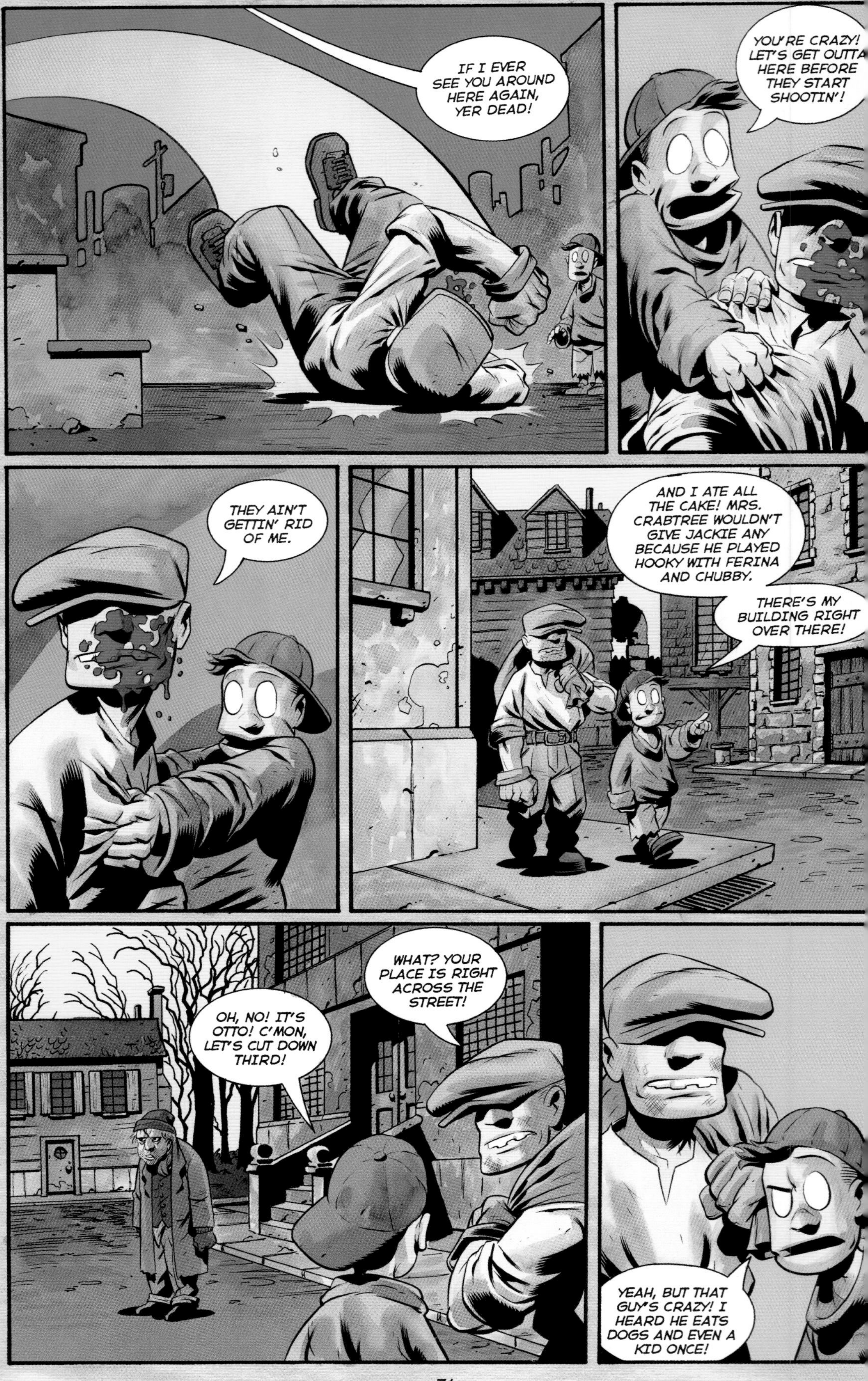
IF I EVER SEE YOU AROUND HERE AGAIN, YER DEAD!
YOU'RE CRAZY! LET'S GET OUTTA HERE BEFORE THEY START SHOOTIN'!
THEY AIN'T GETTIN' RID OF ME.
AND I ATE ALL THE CAKE! MRS. CRABTREE WOULDN'T GIVE JACKIE ANY BECAUSE HE PLAYED HOOKY WITH FERINA AND CHUBBY.
THERE'S MY BUILDING RIGHT OVER THERE!
WHAT? YOUR PLACE IS RIGHT ACROSS THE STREET!
OH, NO! IT'S OTTO! C'MON, LET'S CUT DOWN THIRD!
YEAH, BUT THAT GUY'S CRAZY! I HEARD HE EATS DOGS AND EVEN A KID ONCE!

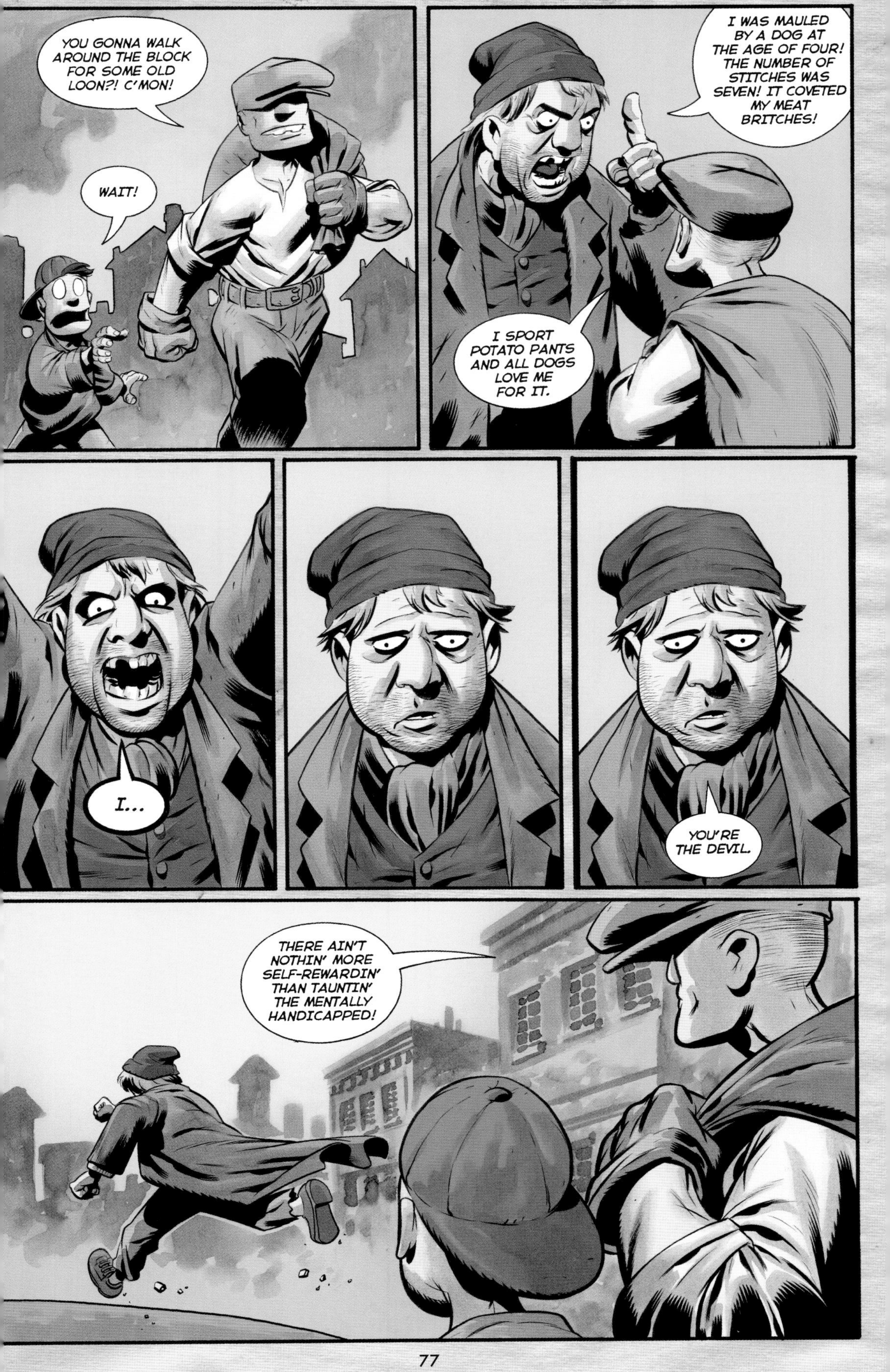
YOU GONNA WALK AROUND THE BLOCK FOR SOME OLD LOON?! C'MON!
WAIT!
I WAS MAULED BY A DOG AT THE AGE OF FOUR! THE NUMBER OF STITCHES WAS SEVEN! IT COVETED MY MEAT BRITCHES!
I SPORT POTATO PANTS AND ALL DOGS LOVE ME FOR IT.
I...
YOU'RE THE DEVIL.
THERE AIN'T NOTHIN' MORE SELF-REWARDIN' THAN TAUNTIN' THE MENTALLY HANDICAPPED!

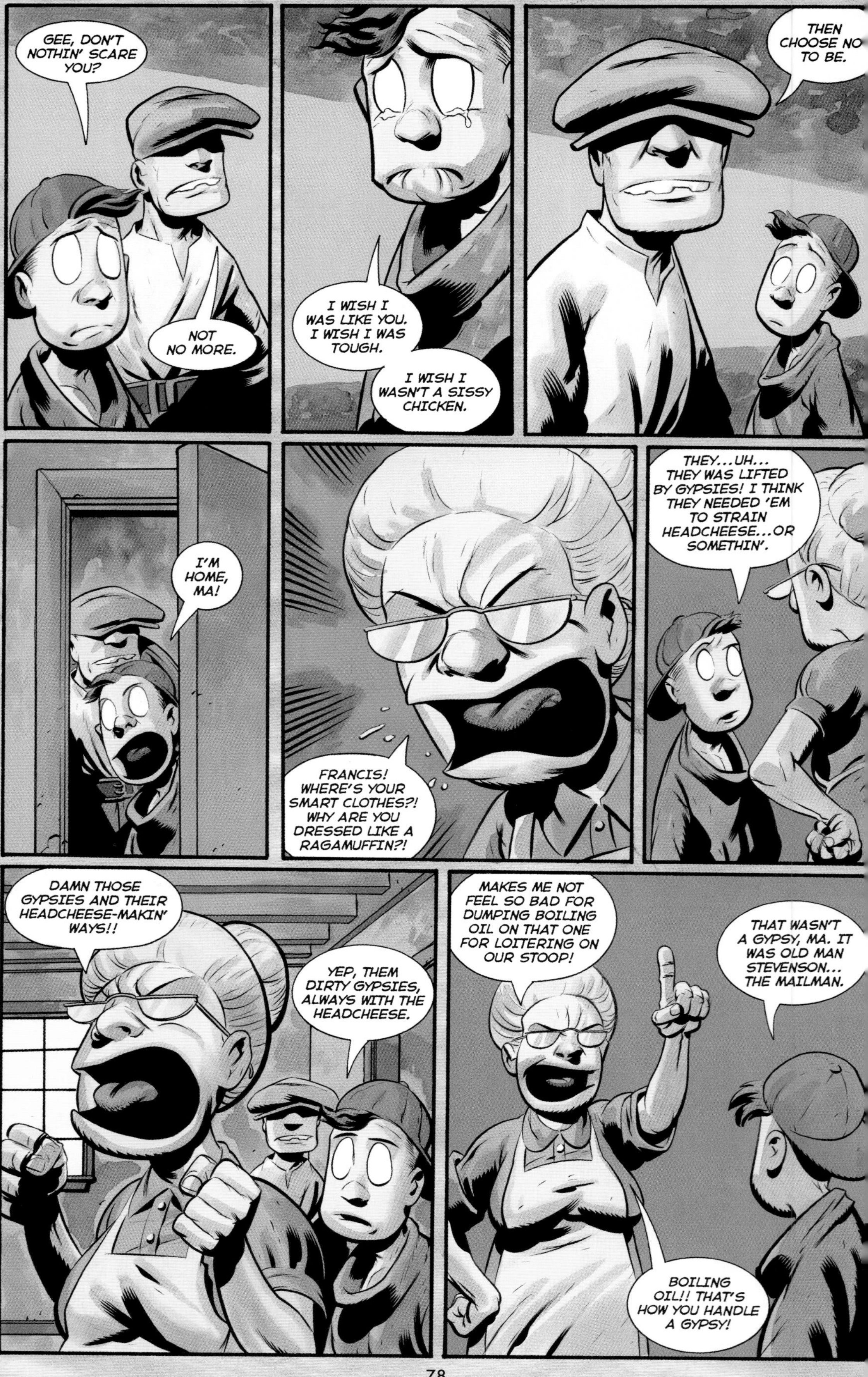
GEE, DON'T NOTHIN' SCARE YOU?
NOT NO MORE.
I WISH I WAS LIKE YOU. I WISH I WAS TOUGH.
I WISH I WASN'T A SISSY CHICKEN.
THEN CHOOSE NO TO BE.
I'M HOME, MA!
FRANCIS! WHERE'S YOUR SMART CLOTHES?! WHY ARE YOU DRESSED LIKE A RAGAMUFFIN?!
THEY...UH... THEY WAS LIFTED BY GYPSIES! I THINK THEY NEEDED 'EM TO STRAIN HEADCHEESE...OR SOMETHIN'.
DAMN THOSE GYPSIES AND THEIR HEADCHEESE-MAKIN' WAYS!!
YEP, THEM DIRTY GYPSIES, ALWAYS WITH THE HEADCHEESE.
MAKES ME NOT FEEL SO BAD FOR DUMPING BOILING OIL ON THAT ONE FOR LOITERING ON OUR STOOP!
THAT WASN'T A GYPSY, MA. IT WAS OLD MAN STEVENSON... THE MAILMAN.
BOILING OIL!! THAT'S HOW YOU HANDLE A GYPSY!

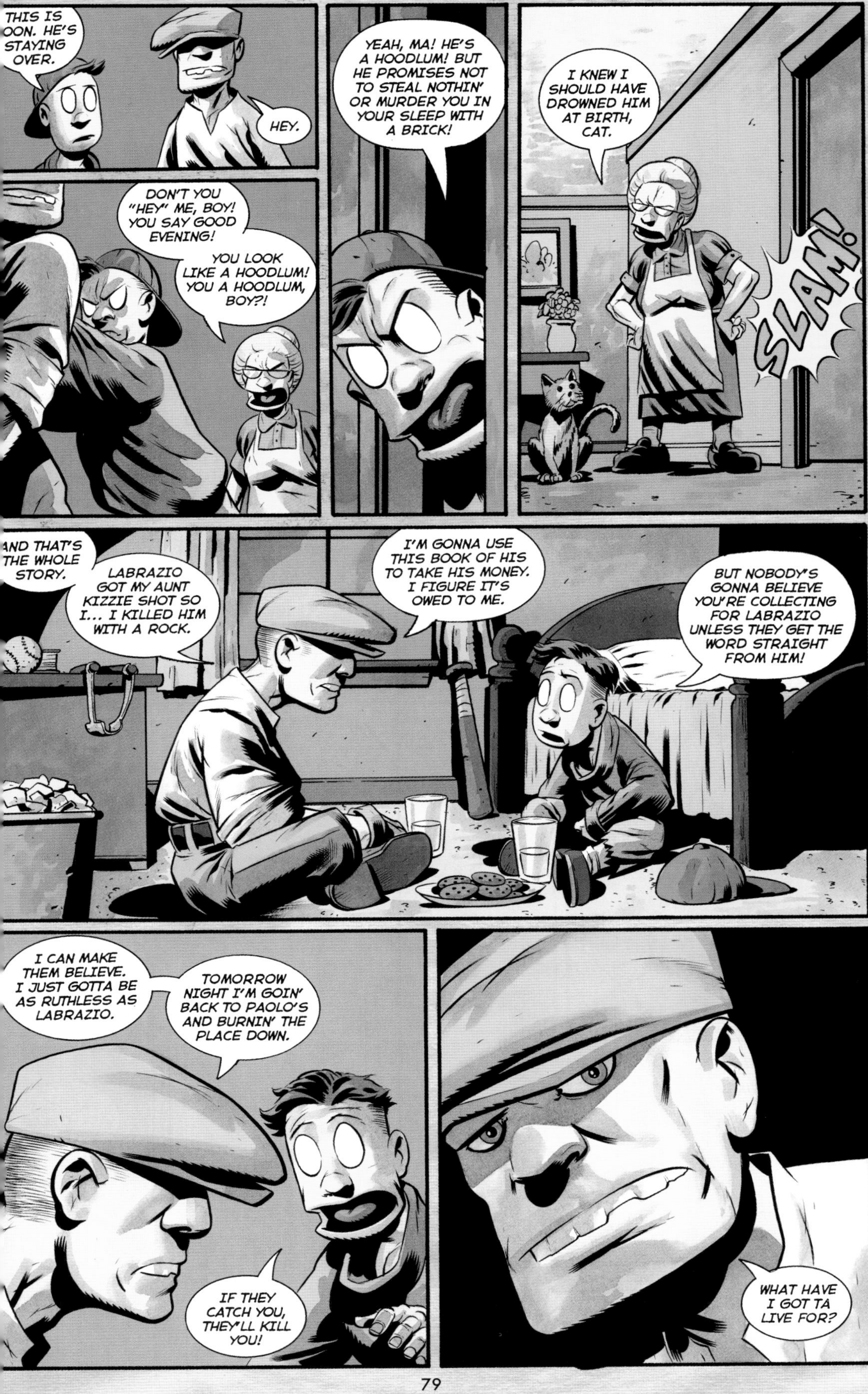
THIS IS
OON. HE'S STAYING OVER.
HEY.
DON'T YOU "HEY" ME, BOY! YOU SAY GOOD EVENING!
YOU LOOK LIKE A HOODLUM! YOU A HOODLUM, BOY?!
YEAH, MA! HE'S A HOODLUM! BUT HE PROMISES NOT TO STEAL NOTHIN' OR MURDER YOU IN YOUR SLEEP WITH A BRICK!
I KNEW I SHOULD HAVE DROWNED HIM AT BIRTH, CAT.
SLAM!
AND THAT'S THE WHOLE STORY.
LABRAZIO GOT MY AUNT KIZZIE SHOT SO I... I KILLED HIM WITH A ROCK.
I'M GONNA USE THIS BOOK OF HIS TO TAKE HIS MONEY. I FIGURE IT'S OWED TO ME.
BUT NOBODY'S GONNA BELIEVE YOU'RE COLLECTING FOR LABRAZIO UNLESS THEY GET THE WORD STRAIGHT FROM HIM!
I CAN MAKE THEM BELIEVE. I JUST GOTTA BE AS RUTHLESS AS LABRAZIO.
TOMORROW NIGHT I'M GOIN' BACK TO PAOLO'S AND BURNIN' THE PLACE DOWN.
IF THEY CATCH YOU, THEY'LL KILL YOU!
WHAT HAVE I GOT TA LIVE FOR?

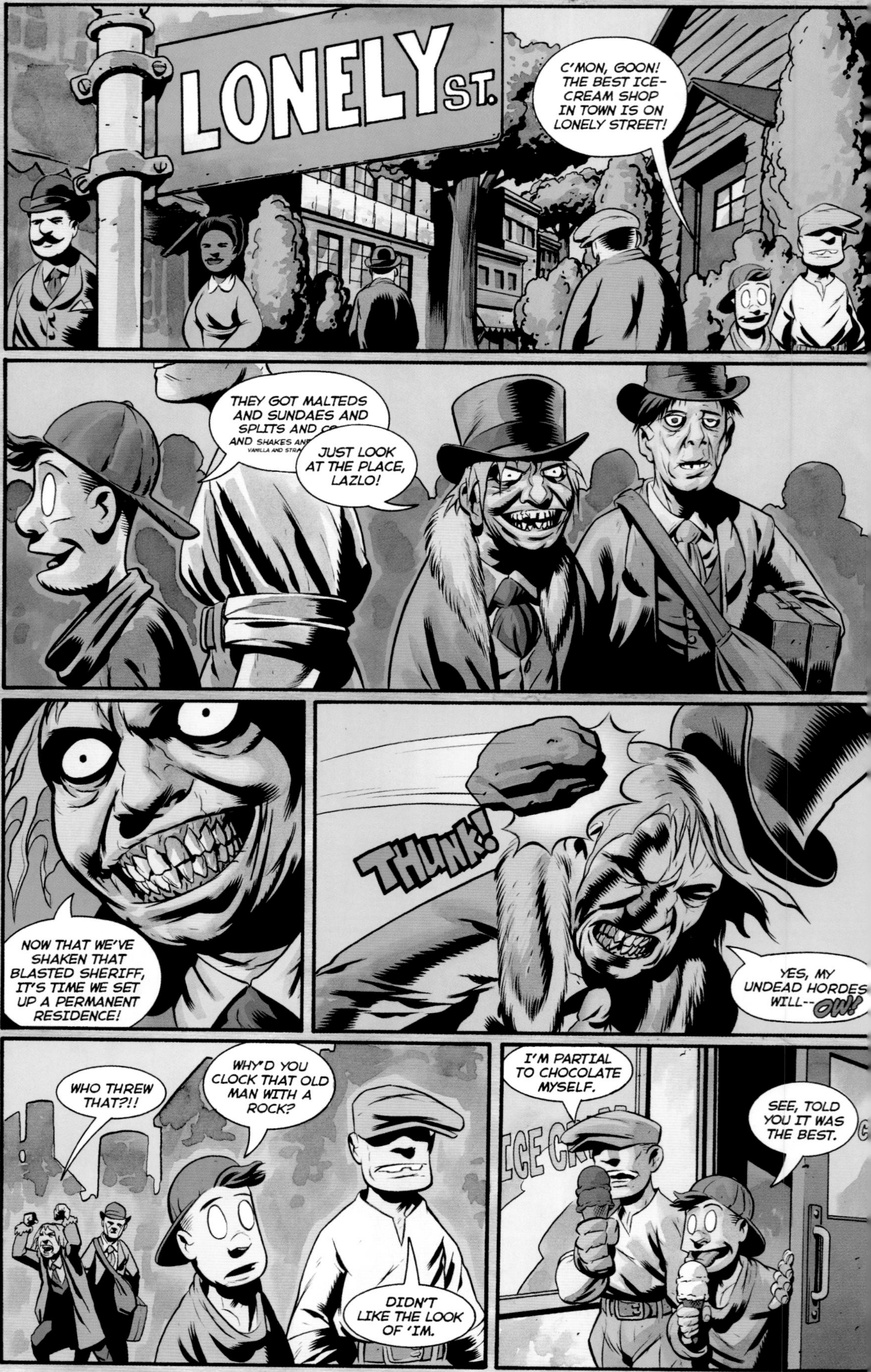

LONELY ST.
C'MON, GOON! THE BEST ICE-CREAM SHOP IN TOWN IS ON LONELY STREET!
THEY GOT MALTEDS AND SUNDAES AND SPLITS AND
AND SHAKES
JUST LOOK AT THE PLACE, LAZLO!
NOW THAT WE'VE SHAKEN THAT BLASTED SHERIFF, IT'S TIME WE SET UP A PERMANENT RESIDENCE!
THUNK!
YES, MY UNDEAD HORDES WILL--OW!
WHO THREW THAT?!!
WHY'D YOU CLOCK THAT OLD MAN WITH A ROCK?
DIDN'T LIKE THE LOOK OF 'IM.
I'M PARTIAL TO CHOCOLATE MYSELF.
SEE, TOLD YOU IT WAS THE BEST.

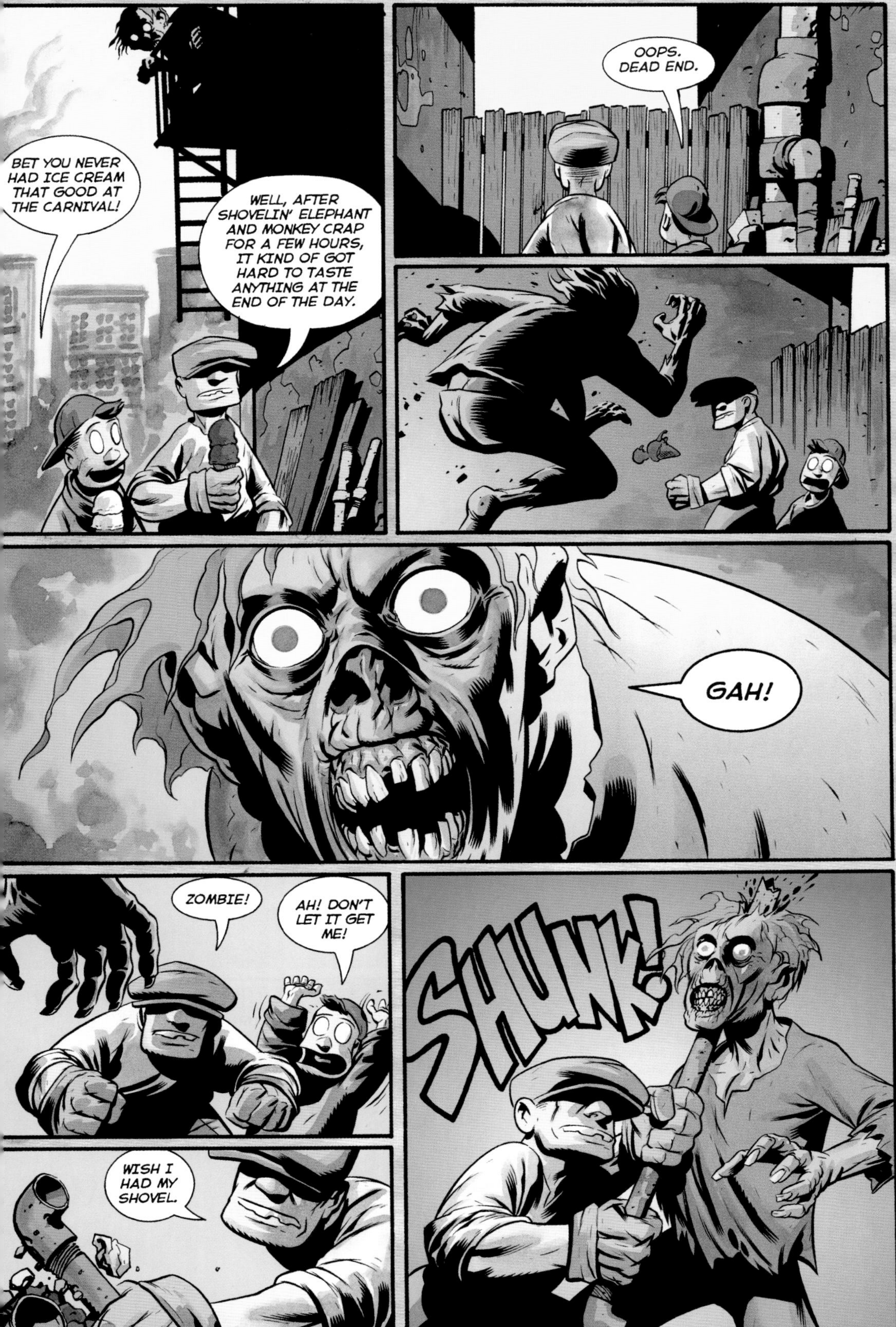
BET YOU NEVER HAD ICE CREAM THAT GOOD AT THE CARNIVAL!
WELL, AFTER SHOVELIN' ELEPHANT AND MONKEY CRAP FOR A FEW HOURS, IT KIND OF GOT HARD TO TASTE ANYTHING AT THE END OF THE DAY.
OOPS. DEAD END.
GAH!
ZOMBIE!
AH! DON'T LET IT GET ME!
WISH I HAD MY SHOVEL.
SHUNK!

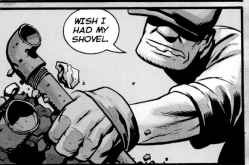

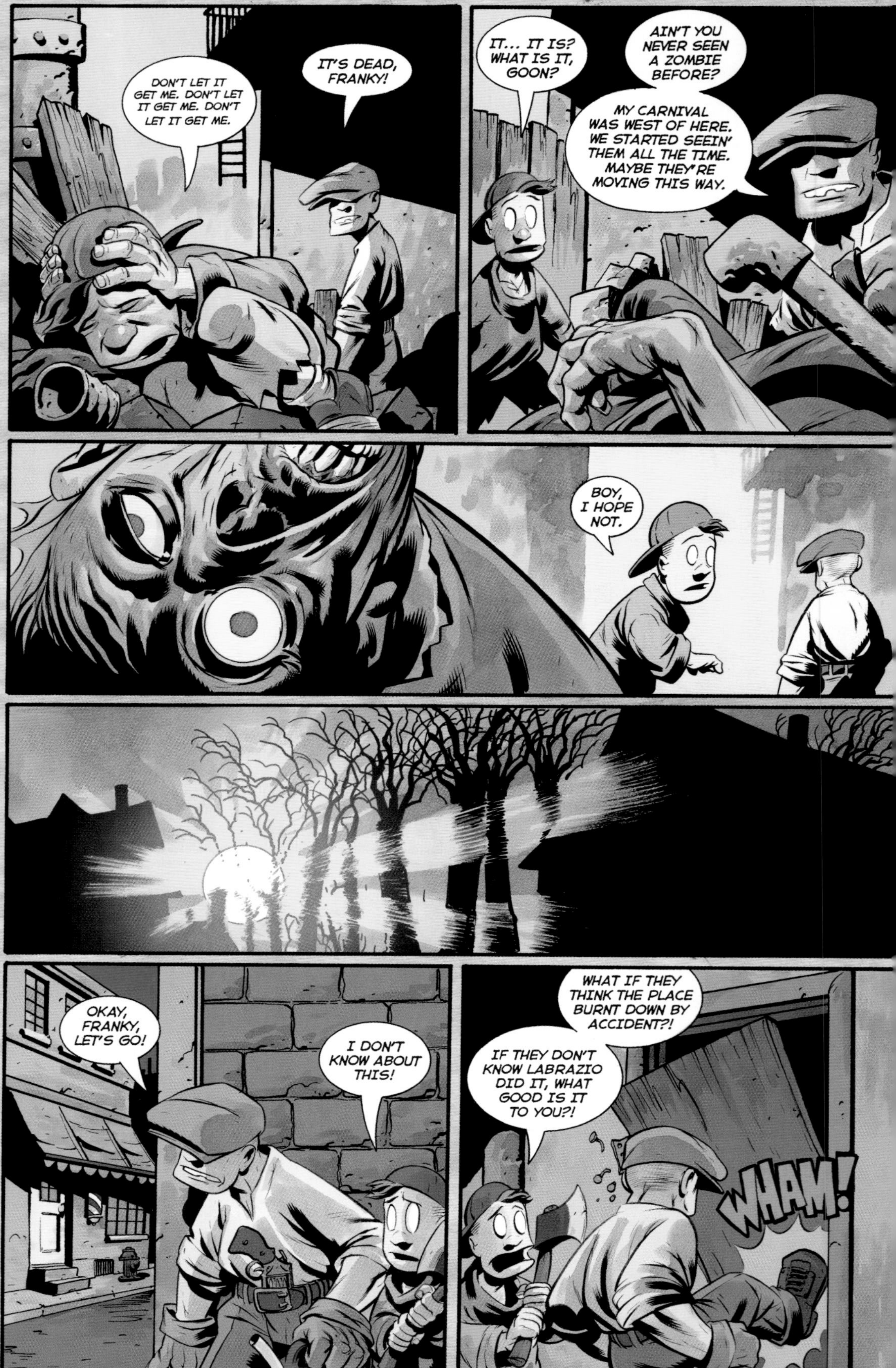
DON'T LET IT GET ME. DON'T LET IT GET ME. DON'T LET IT GET ME.
IT'S DEAD, FRANKY!
IT... IT IS? WHAT IS IT, GOON?
AIN'T YOU NEVER SEEN A ZOMBIE BEFORE?
MY CARNIVAL WAS WEST OF HERE. WE STARTED SEEIN' THEM ALL THE TIME. MAYBE THEY'RE MOVING THIS WAY.
BOY, I HOPE NOT.
OKAY, FRANKY, LET'S GO!
I DON'T KNOW ABOUT THIS!
GAS
WHAT IF THEY THINK THE PLACE BURNT DOWN BY ACCIDENT?!
IF THEY DON'T KNOW LABRAZIO DID IT, WHAT GOOD IS IT TO YOU?!
WHAM!

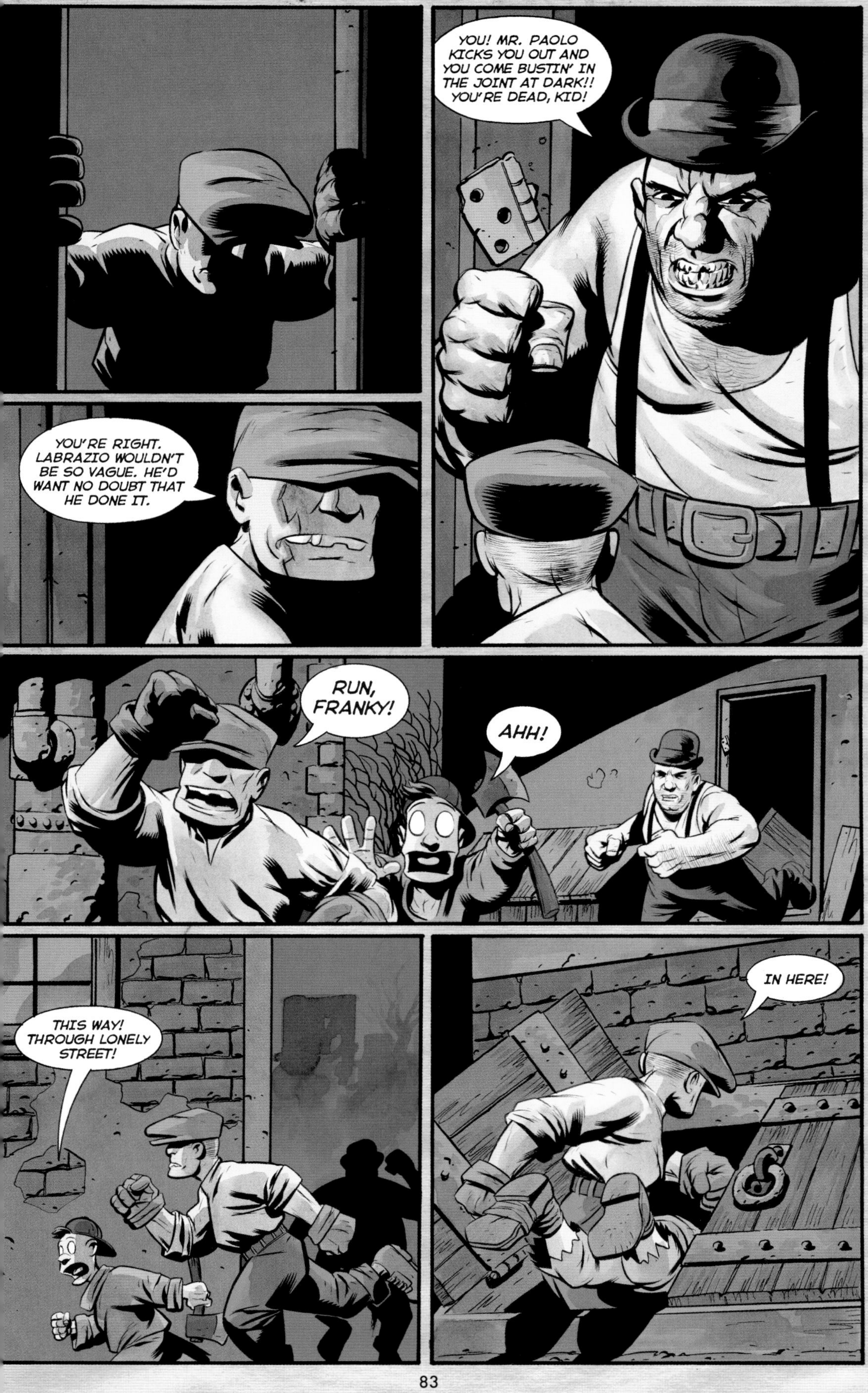
YOU! MR. PAOLO KICKS YOU OUT AND YOU COME BUSTIN' IN THE JOINT AT DARK!! YOU'RE DEAD, KID!
YOU'RE RIGHT. LABRAZIO WOULDN'T BE SO VAGUE. HE'D WANT NO DOUBT THAT HE DONE IT.
RUN, FRANKY!
AHH!
THIS WAY! THROUGH LONELY STREET!
IN HERE!

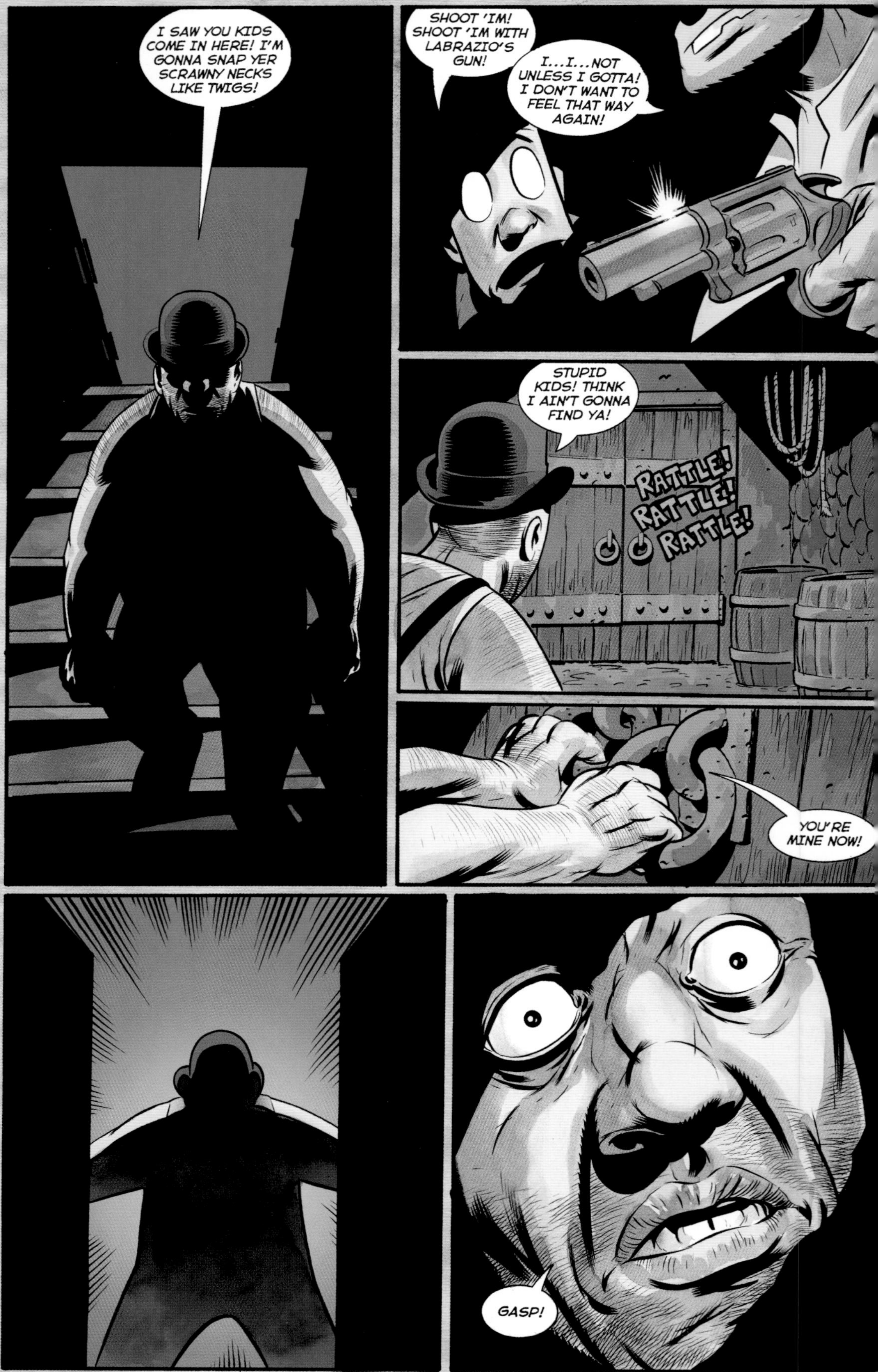

I SAW YOU KIDS COME IN HERE! I'M GONNA SNAP YER SCRAWNY NECKS LIKE TWIGS!
SHOOT 'IM! SHOOT 'IM WITH LABRAZIO'S GUN!
I...I...NOT UNLESS I GOTTA! I DON'T WANT TO FEEL THAT WAY AGAIN!
STUPID KIDS! THINK I AIN'T GONNA FIND YA!
RATTLE! RATTLE! RATTLE!
YOU'RE MINE NOW!
GASP!

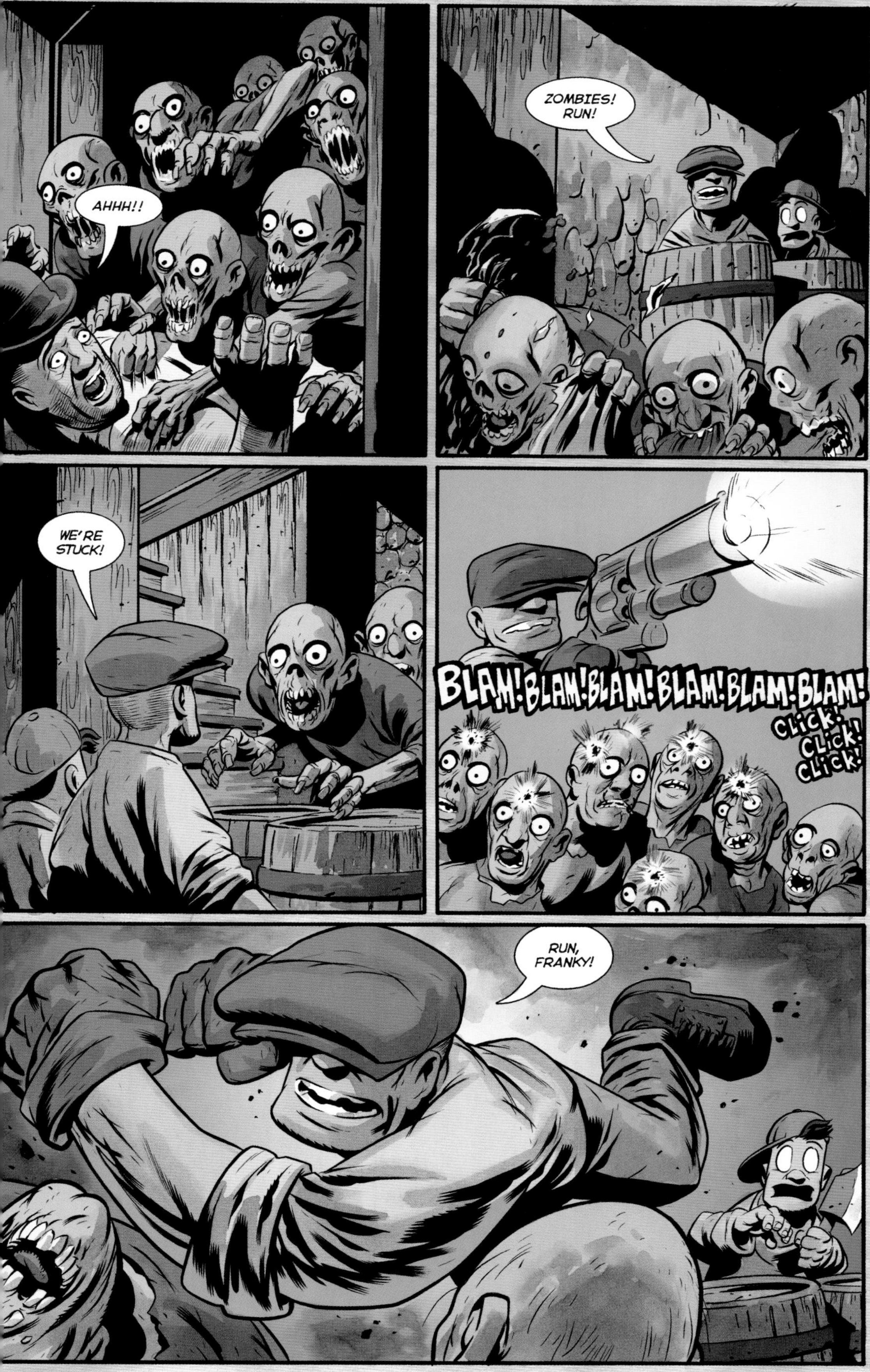
AHHH!!
ZOMBIES! RUN!
WE'RE STUCK!
BLAM! BLAM! BLAM! BLAM! BLAM! BLAM!
CLICK! CLICK! CLICK!
RUN, FRANKY!

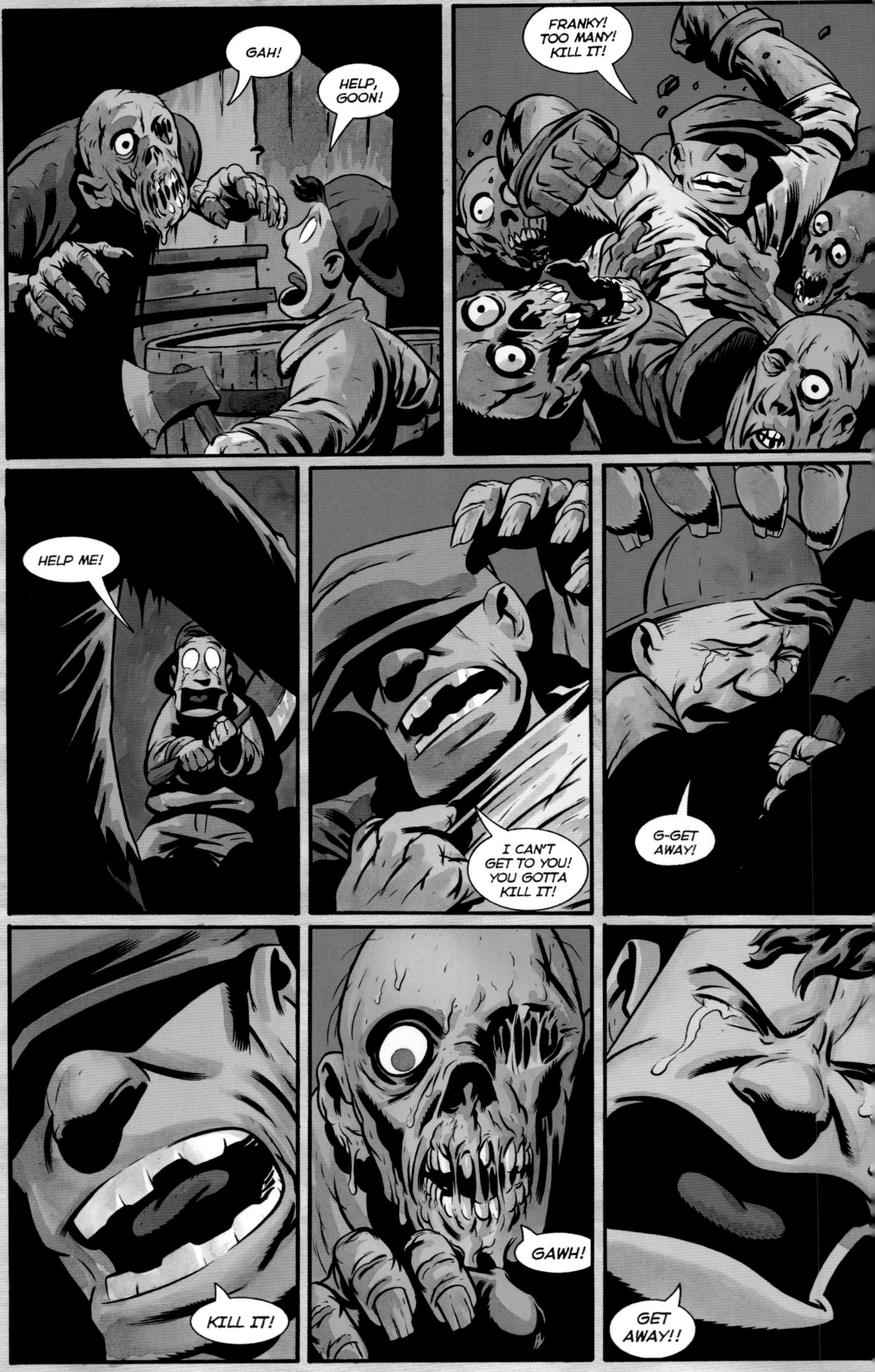
GAH!
HELP, GOON!
FRANKY! TOO MANY! KILL IT!
HELP ME!
I CAN'T GET TO YOU! YOU GOTTA KILL IT!
G-GET AWAY!
KILL IT!
GAWH!
GET AWAY!!

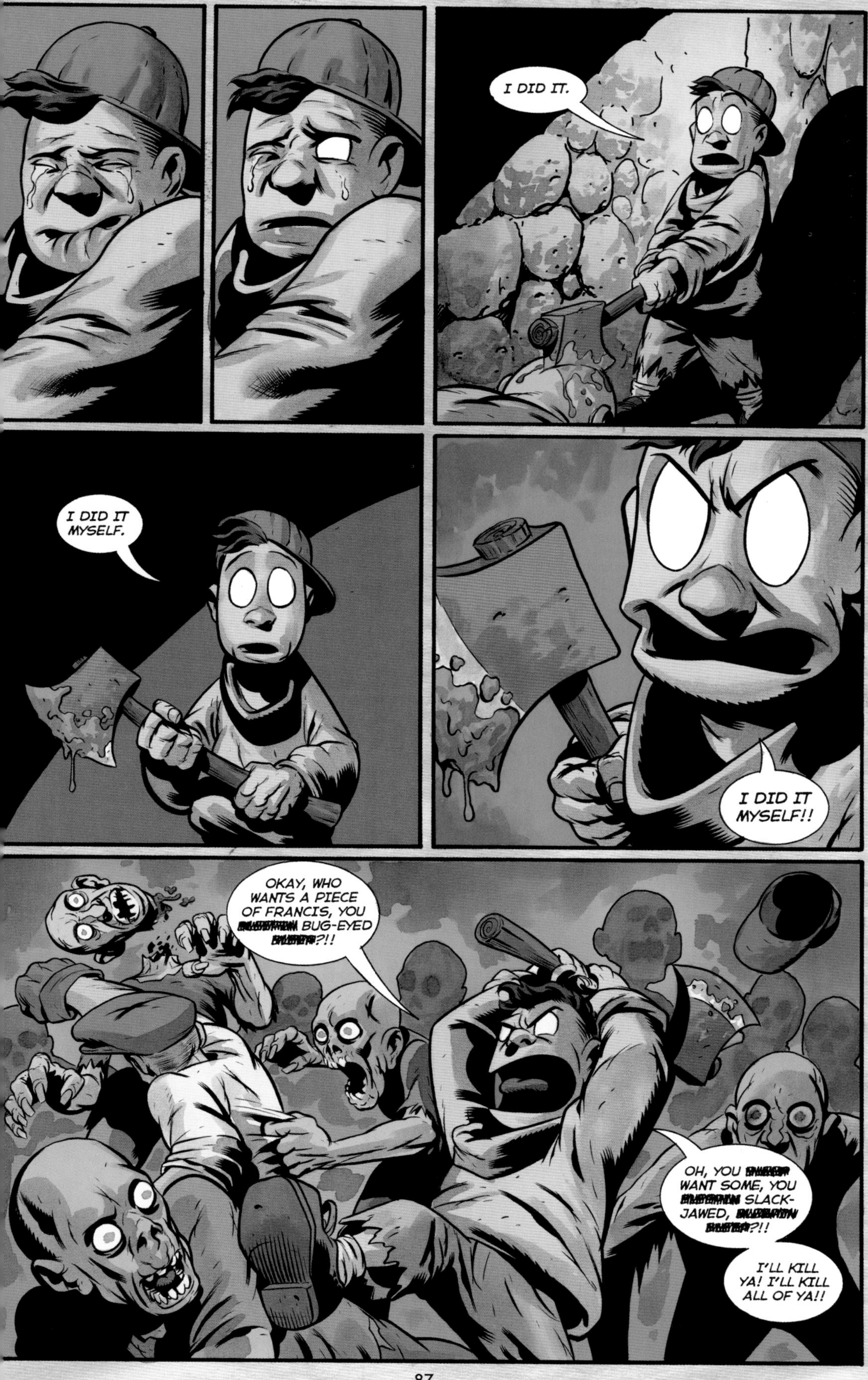
I DID IT.
I DID IT MYSELF.
I DID IT MYSELF!!
OKAY, WHO WANTS A PIECE OF FRANCIS, YOU [redacted] BUG-EYED [redacted]?!!
OH, YOU [redacted] WANT SOME, YOU [redacted] SLACK-JAWED, [redacted]?!!
I'LL KILL YA! I'LL KILL ALL OF YA!!

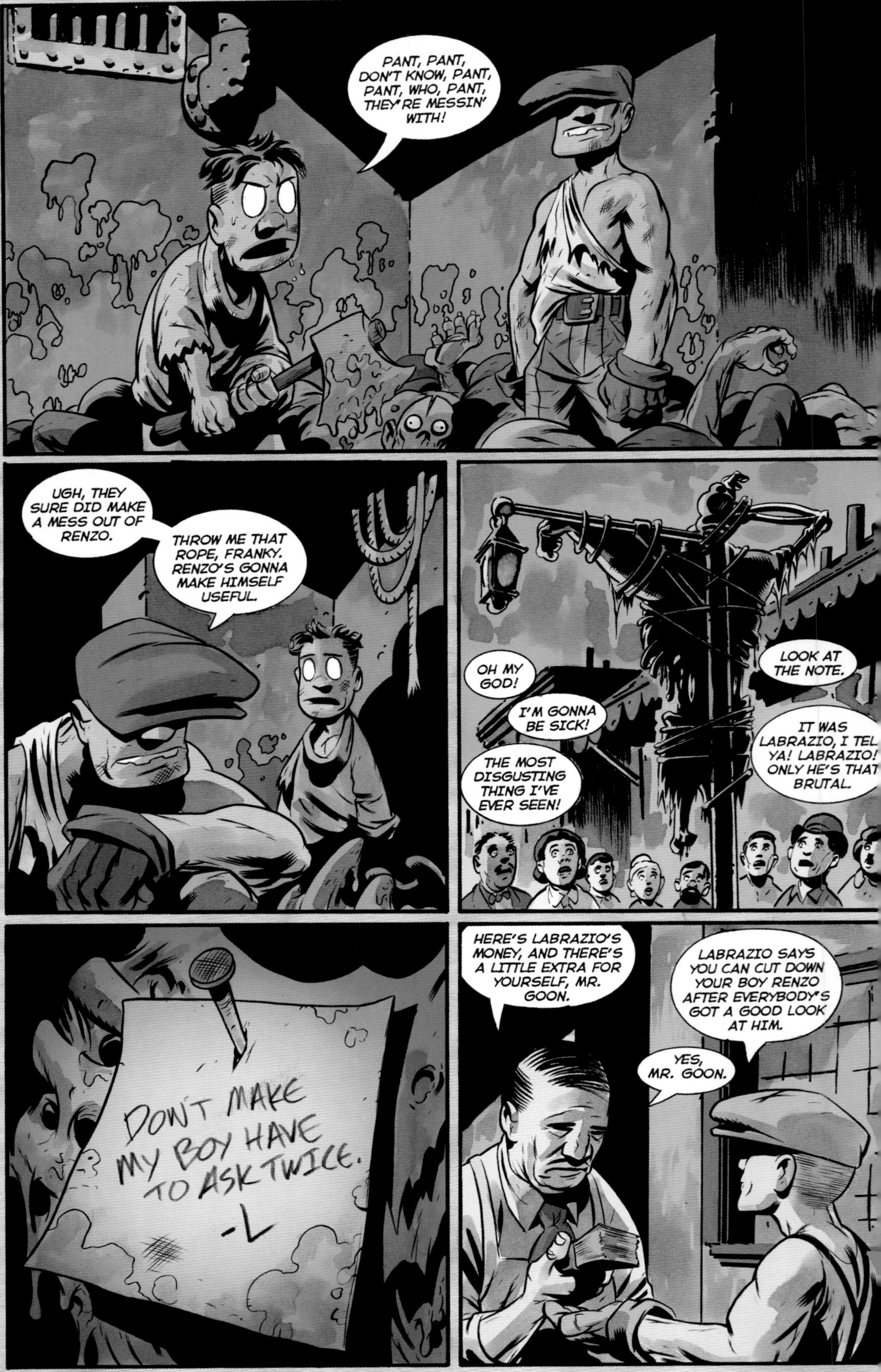
PANT, PANT, DON'T KNOW, PANT, PANT, WHO, PANT, THEY'RE MESSIN' WITH!
UGH, THEY SURE DID MAKE A MESS OUT OF RENZO.
THROW ME THAT ROPE, FRANKY. RENZO'S GONNA MAKE HIMSELF USEFUL.
OH MY GOD!
I'M GONNA BE SICK!
THE MOST DISGUSTING THING I'VE EVER SEEN!
LOOK AT THE NOTE.
IT WAS LABRAZIO, I TEL YA! LABRAZIO! ONLY HE'S THAT BRUTAL.
DON'T MAKE MY BOY HAVE TO ASK TWICE. -L
HERE'S LABRAZIO'S MONEY, AND THERE'S A LITTLE EXTRA FOR YOURSELF, MR. GOON.
LABRAZIO SAYS YOU CAN CUT DOWN YOUR BOY RENZO AFTER EVERYBODY'S GOT A GOOD LOOK AT HIM.
YES, MR. GOON.

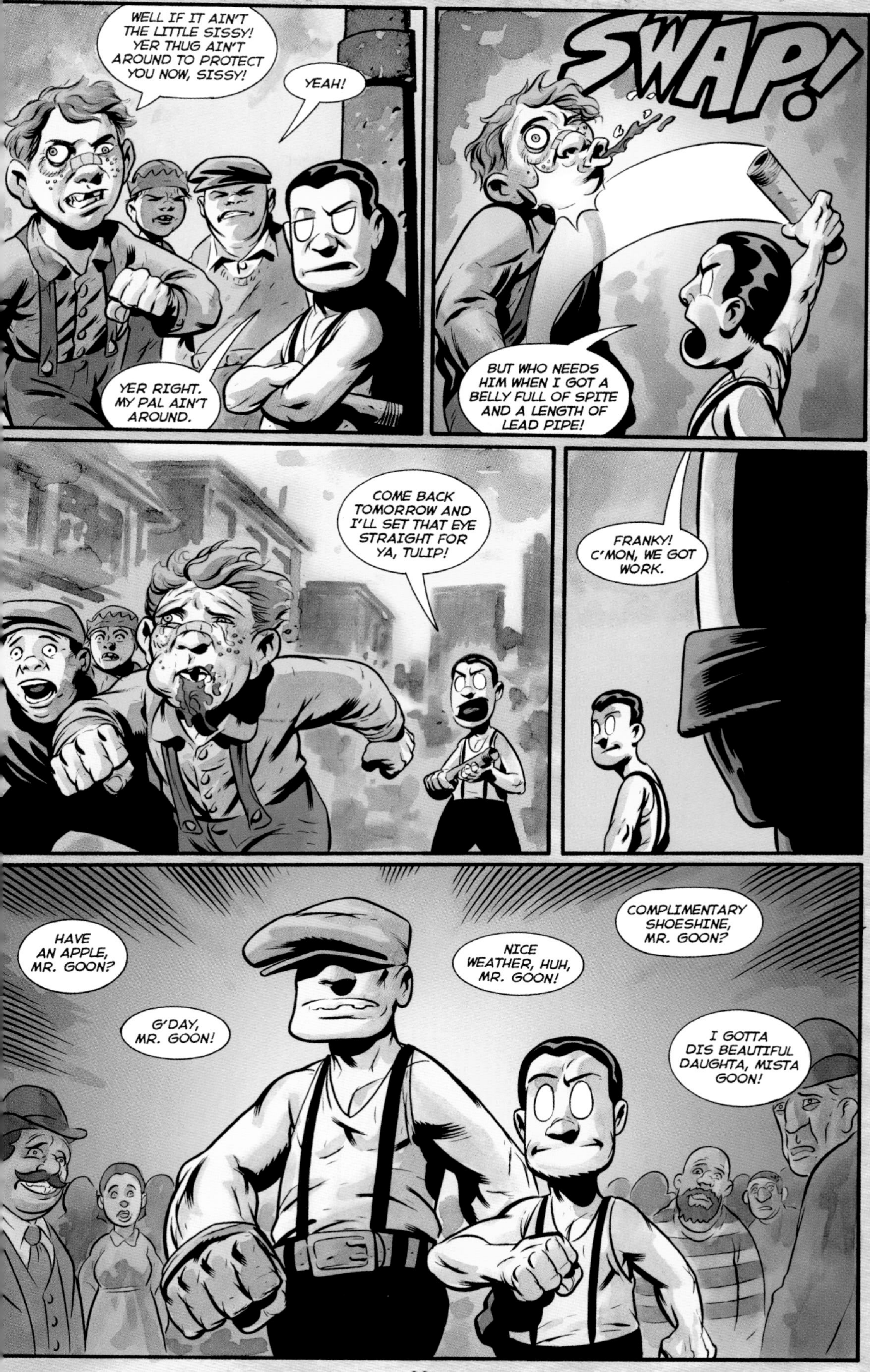
WELL IF IT AIN'T THE LITTLE SISSY! YER THUG AIN'T AROUND TO PROTECT YOU NOW, SISSY!
YEAH!
YER RIGHT. MY PAL AIN'T AROUND.
SWAP!
BUT WHO NEEDS HIM WHEN I GOT A BELLY FULL OF SPITE AND A LENGTH OF LEAD PIPE!
COME BACK TOMORROW AND I'LL SET THAT EYE STRAIGHT FOR YA, TULIP!
FRANKY! C'MON, WE GOT WORK.
HAVE AN APPLE, MR. GOON?
G'DAY, MR. GOON!
NICE WEATHER, HUH, MR. GOON!
COMPLIMENTARY SHOESHINE, MR. GOON?
I GOTTA DIS BEAUTIFUL DAUGHTA, MISTA GOON!

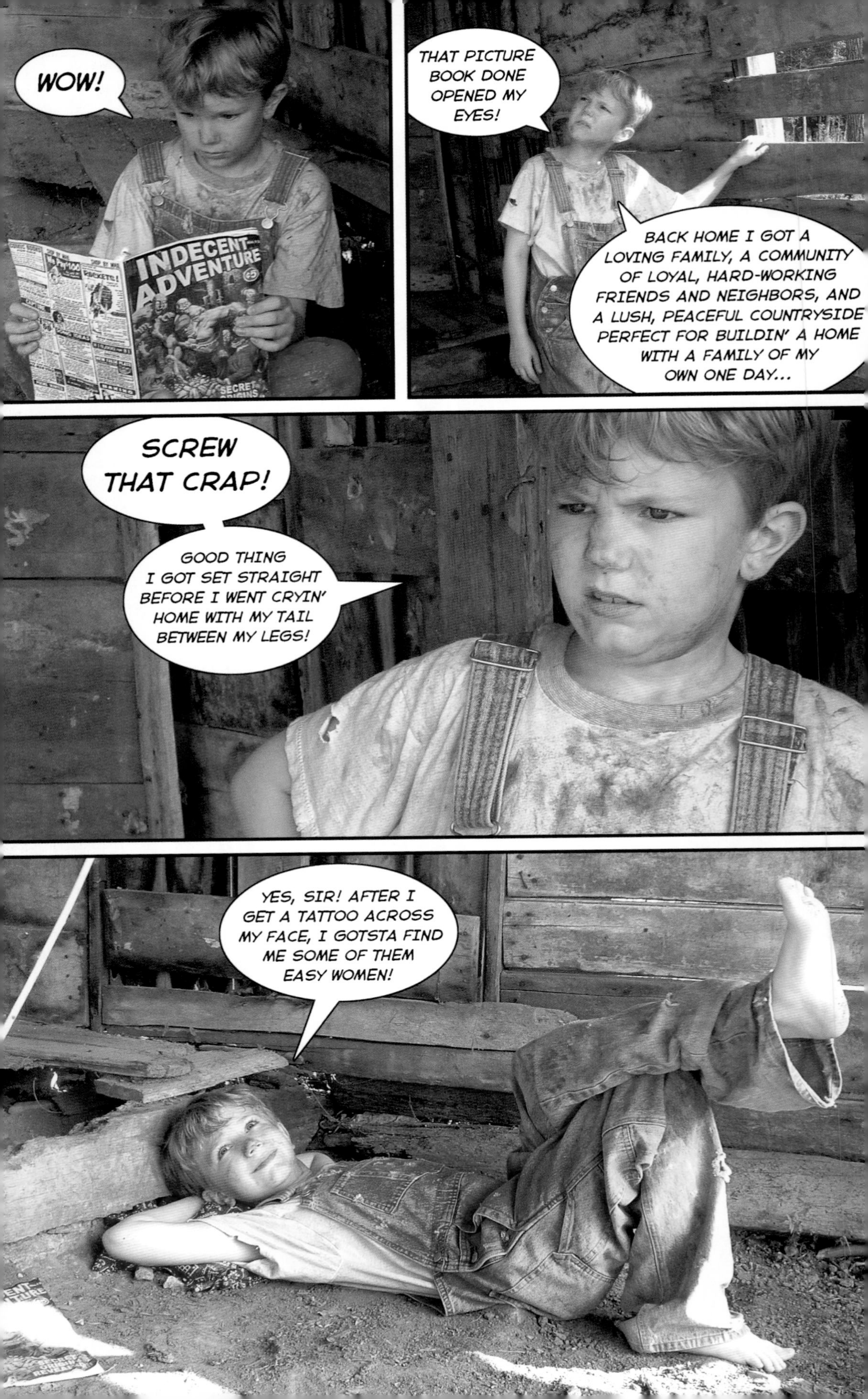
WOW!
INDECENT ADVENTURE
THAT PICTURE BOOK DONE OPENED MY EYES!
BACK HOME I GOT A LOVING FAMILY, A COMMUNITY OF LOYAL, HARD-WORKING FRIENDS AND NEIGHBORS, AND A LUSH, PEACEFUL COUNTRYSIDE PERFECT FOR BUILDIN' A HOME WITH A FAMILY OF MY OWN ONE DAY...
SCREW THAT CRAP!
GOOD THING I GOT SET STRAIGHT BEFORE I WENT CRYIN' HOME WITH MY TAIL BETWEEN MY LEGS!
YES, SIR! AFTER I GET A TATTOO ACROSS MY FACE, I GOTSTA FIND ME SOME OF THEM EASY WOMEN!

CHAPTER 4

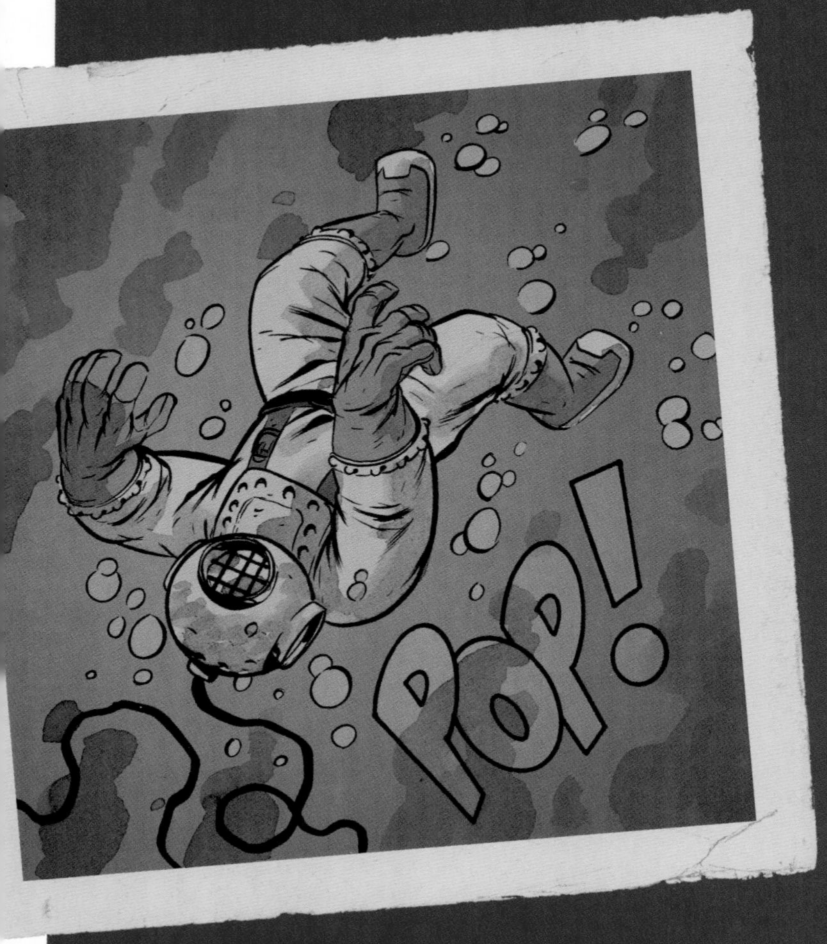
POP!

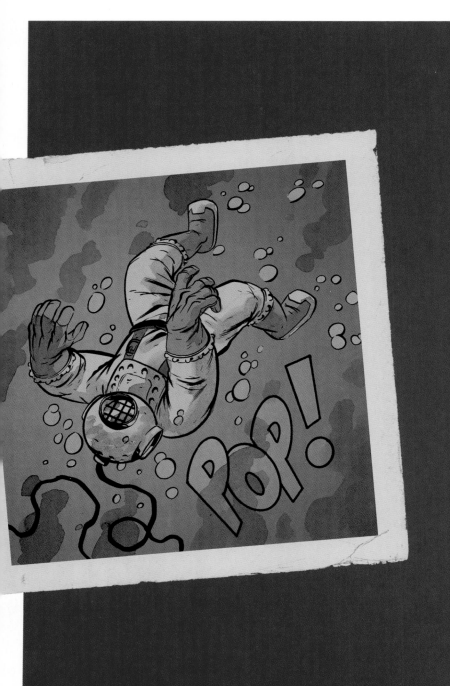

THE GOON™

3 EPIC THRILLERS!!

BY ERIC POWELL AND KYLE HOTZ

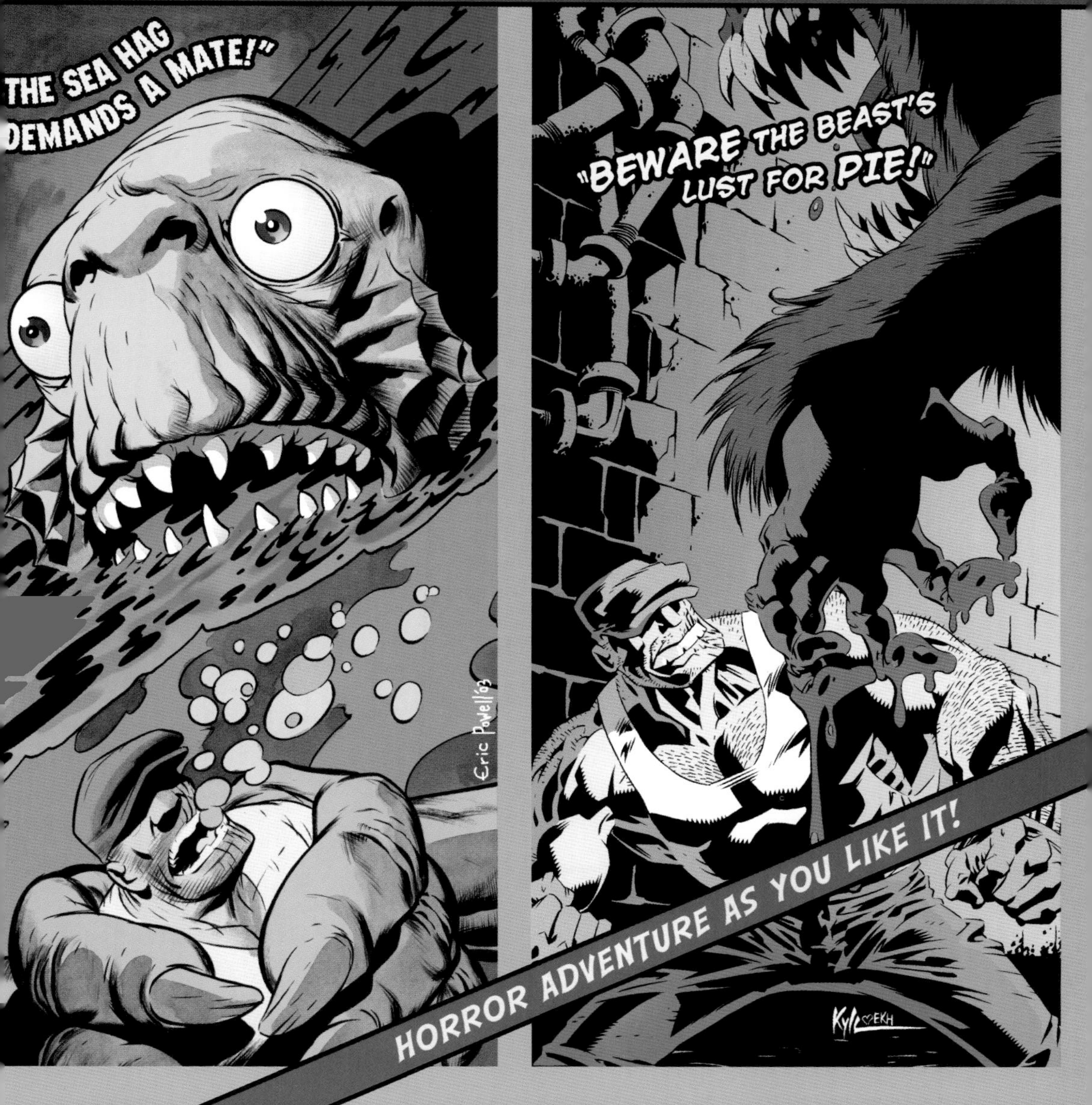

"THE SEA HAG DEMANDS A MATE!"
Eric Powell '03
"BEWARE THE BEAST'S LUST FOR PIE!"
HORROR ADVENTURE AS YOU LIKE IT!

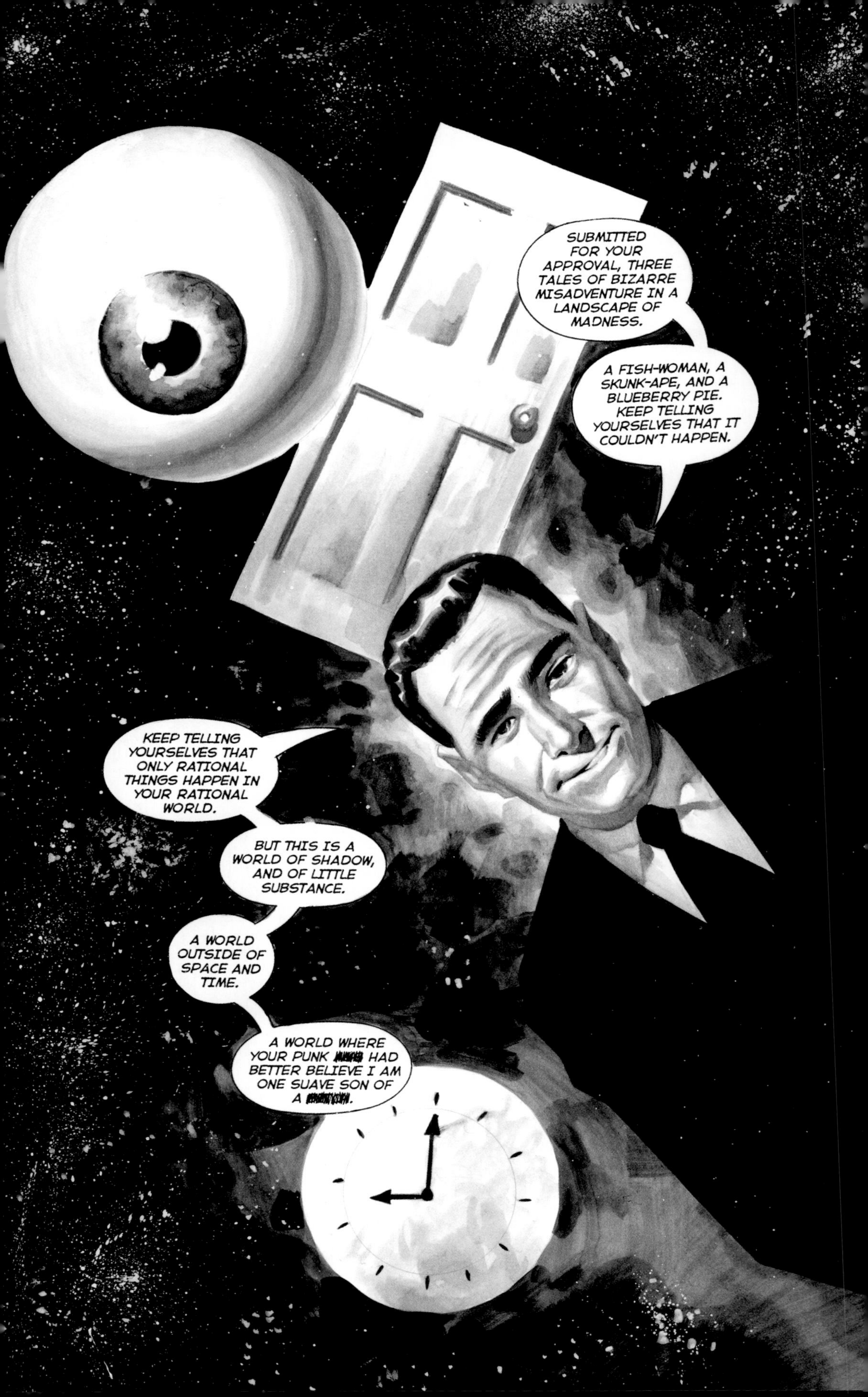
SUBMITTED FOR YOUR APPROVAL, THREE TALES OF BIZARRE MISADVENTURE IN A LANDSCAPE OF MADNESS.
A FISH-WOMAN, A SKUNK-APE, AND A BLUEBERRY PIE. KEEP TELLING YOURSELVES THAT IT COULDN'T HAPPEN.
KEEP TELLING YOURSELVES THAT ONLY RATIONAL THINGS HAPPEN IN YOUR RATIONAL WORLD.
BUT THIS IS A WORLD OF SHADOW, AND OF LITTLE SUBSTANCE.
A WORLD OUTSIDE OF SPACE AND TIME.
A WORLD WHERE YOUR PUNK HAD BETTER BELIEVE I AM ONE SUAVE SON OF A.

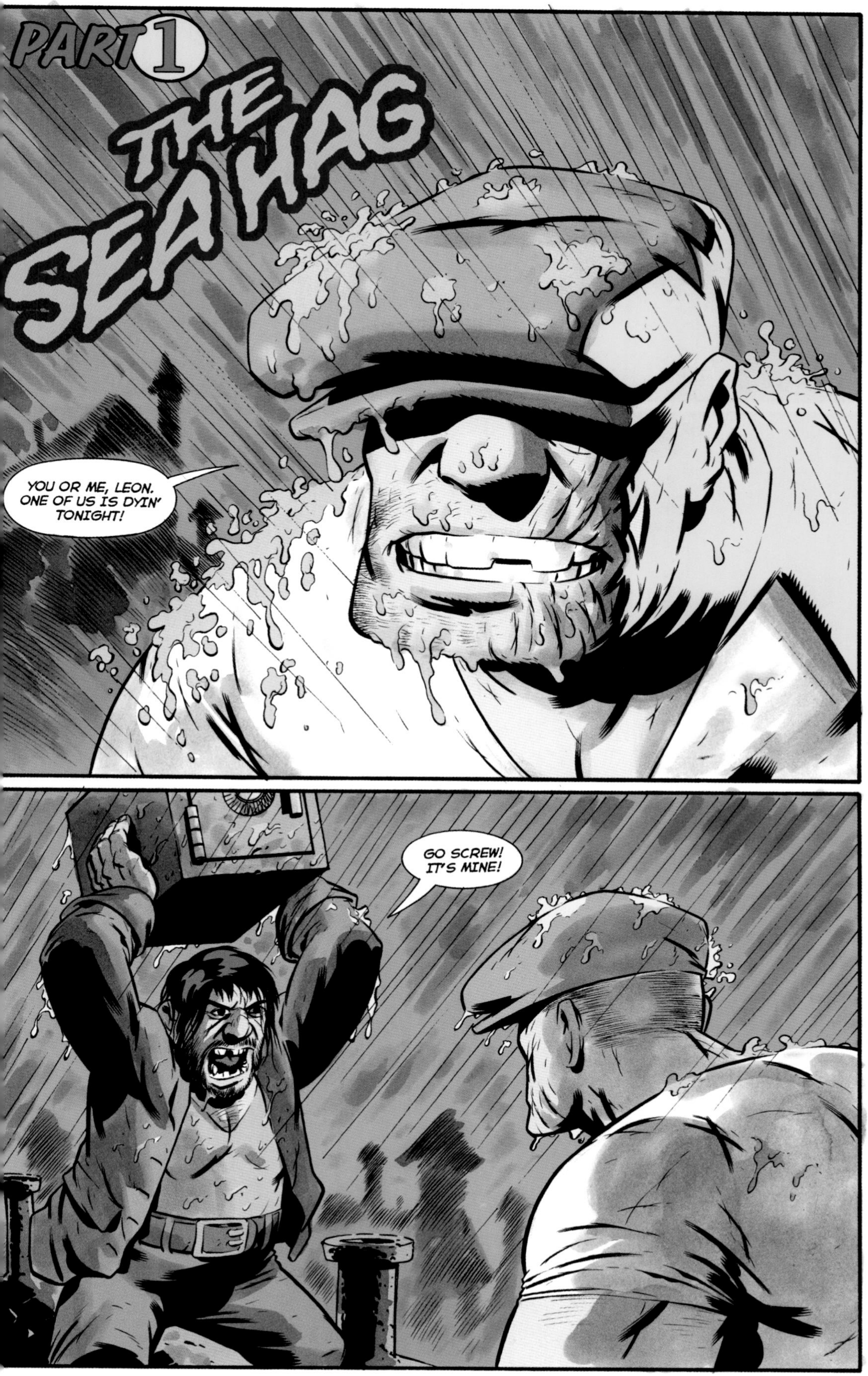
PART 1
THE SEA HAG
YOU OR ME, LEON. ONE OF US IS DYIN' TONIGHT!
GO SCREW! IT'S MINE!

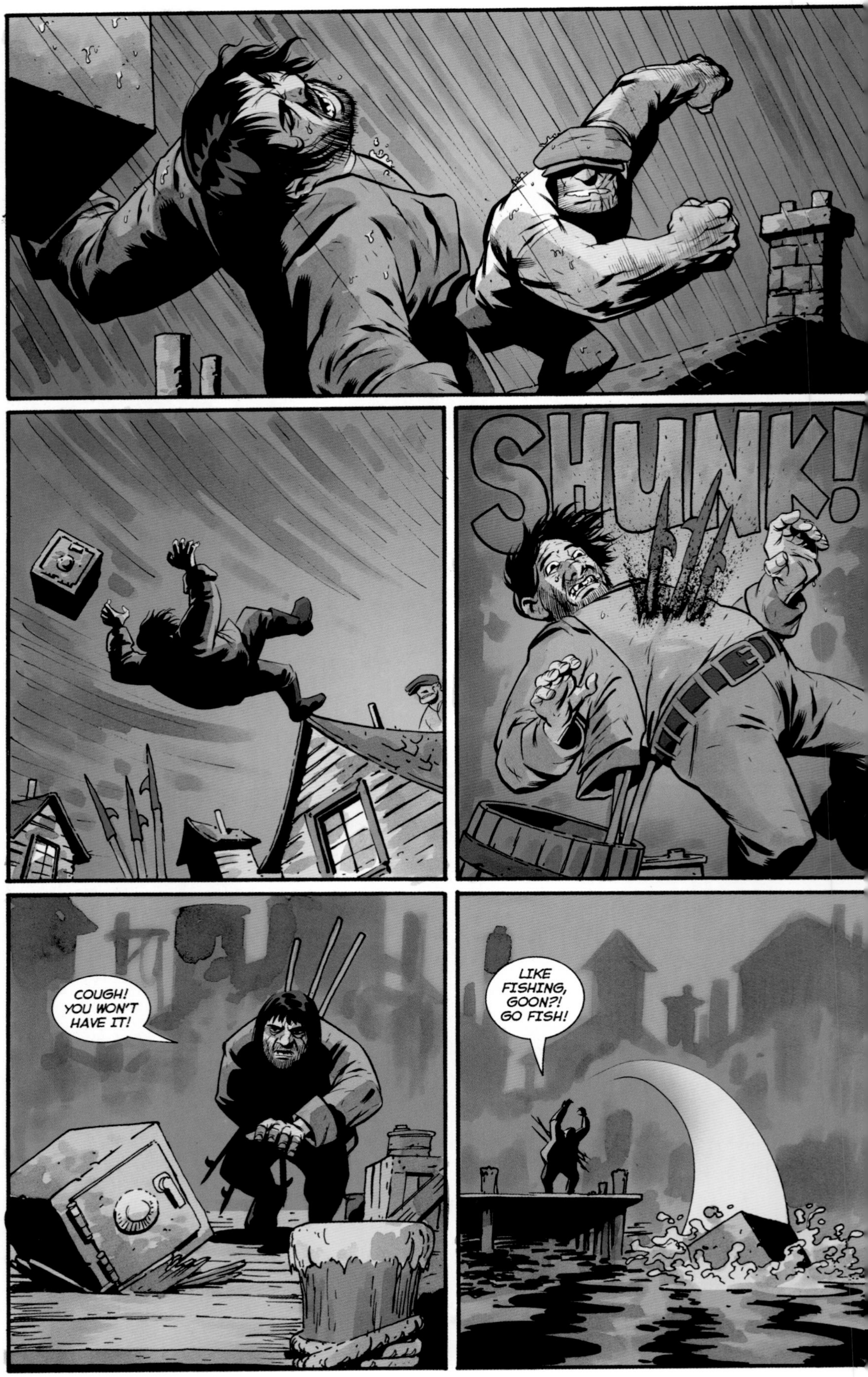
SHUNK!
COUGH! YOU WON'T HAVE IT!
LIKE FISHING, GOON?! GO FISH!

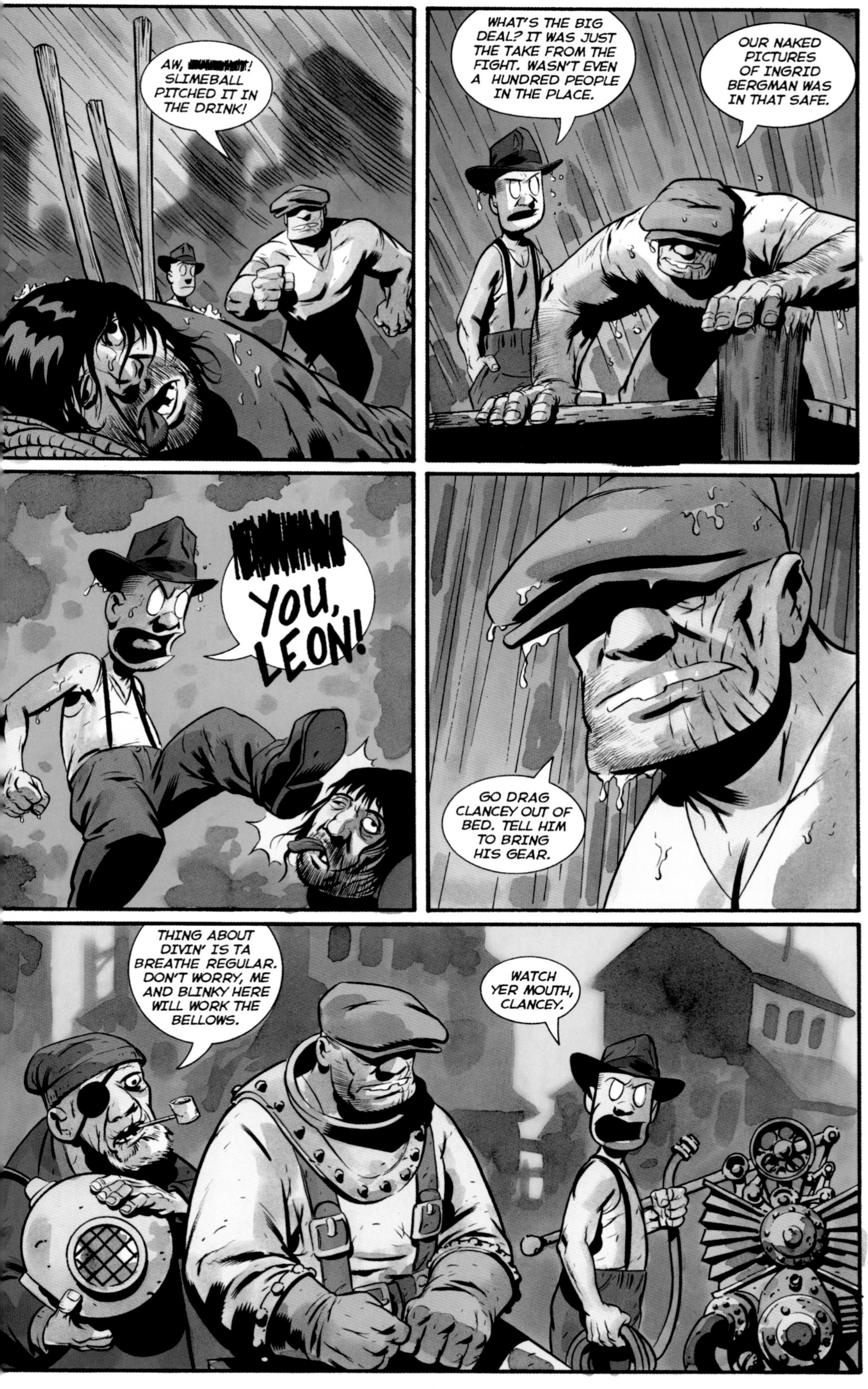
AW, [redacted]! SLIMEBALL PITCHED IT IN THE DRINK!
WHAT'S THE BIG DEAL? IT WAS JUST THE TAKE FROM THE FIGHT. WASN'T EVEN A HUNDRED PEOPLE IN THE PLACE.
OUR NAKED PICTURES OF INGRID BERGMAN WAS IN THAT SAFE.
[redacted] YOU, LEON!
GO DRAG CLANCEY OUT OF BED. TELL HIM TO BRING HIS GEAR.
THING ABOUT DIVIN' IS TA BREATHE REGULAR. DON'T WORRY, ME AND BLINKY HERE WILL WORK THE BELLOWS.
WATCH YER MOUTH, CLANCEY.

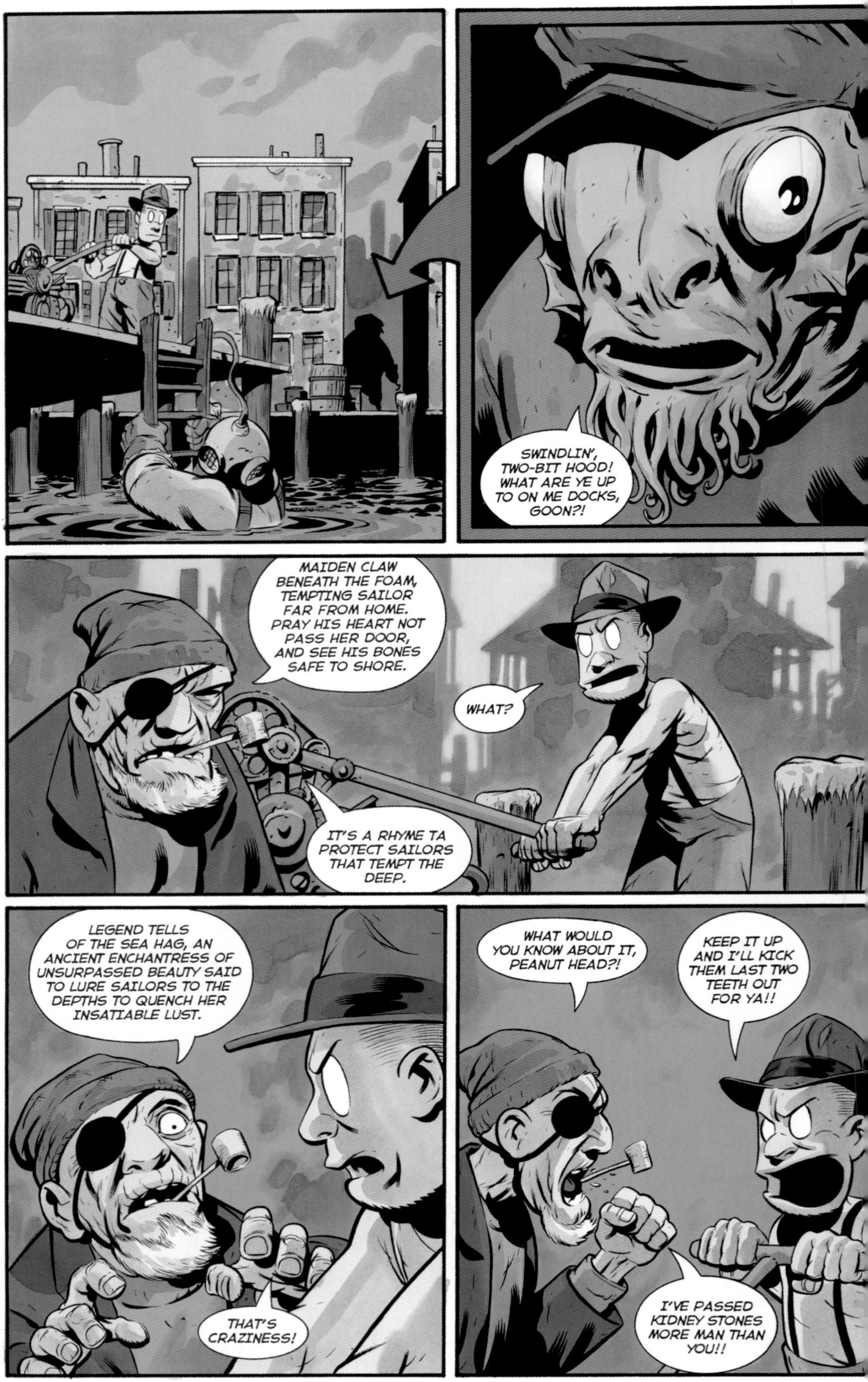
SWINDLIN', TWO-BIT HOOD! WHAT ARE YE UP TO ON ME DOCKS, GOON?!
MAIDEN CLAW BENEATH THE FOAM, TEMPTING SAILOR FAR FROM HOME. PRAY HIS HEART NOT PASS HER DOOR, AND SEE HIS BONES SAFE TO SHORE.
WHAT?
IT'S A RHYME TA PROTECT SAILORS THAT TEMPT THE DEEP.
LEGEND TELLS OF THE SEA HAG, AN ANCIENT ENCHANTRESS OF UNSURPASSED BEAUTY SAID TO LURE SAILORS TO THE DEPTHS TO QUENCH HER INSATIABLE LUST.
THAT'S CRAZINESS!
WHAT WOULD YOU KNOW ABOUT IT, PEANUT HEAD?!
KEEP IT UP AND I'LL KICK THEM LAST TWO TEETH OUT FOR YA!!
I'VE PASSED KIDNEY STONES MORE MAN THAN YOU!!

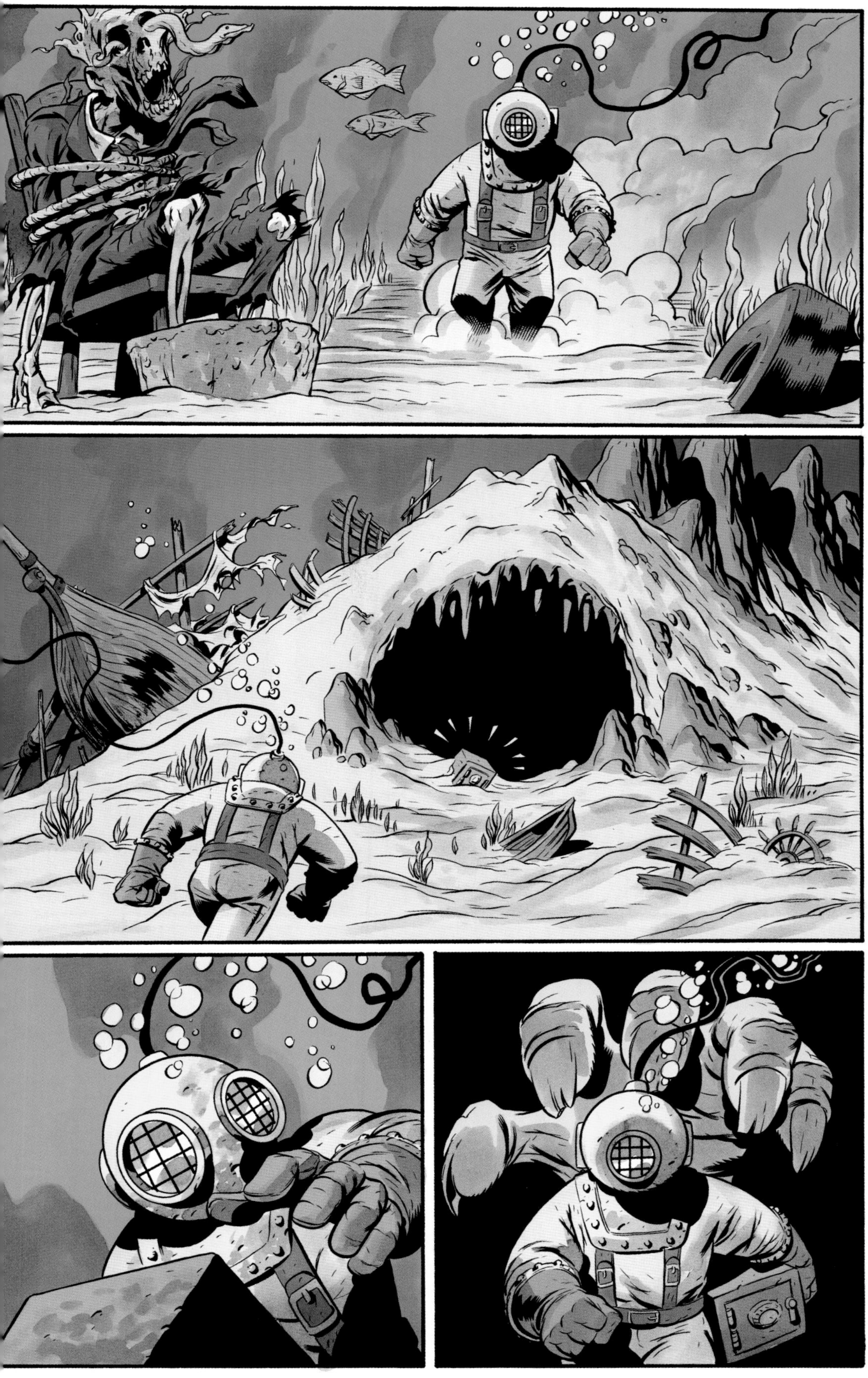

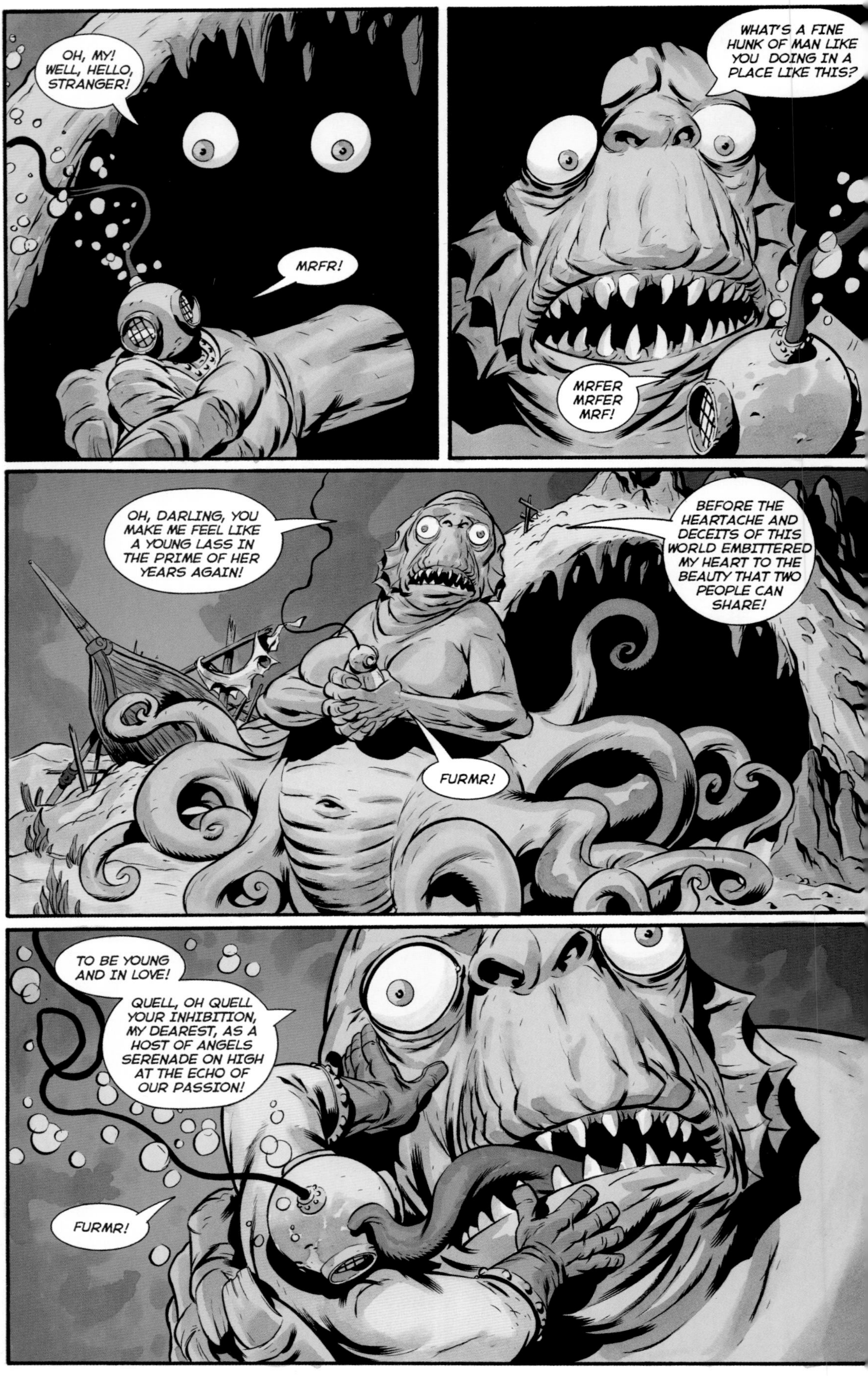
OH, MY! WELL, HELLO, STRANGER!
MRFR!
WHAT'S A FINE HUNK OF MAN LIKE YOU DOING IN A PLACE LIKE THIS?
MRFER MRFER MRF!
OH, DARLING, YOU MAKE ME FEEL LIKE A YOUNG LASS IN THE PRIME OF HER YEARS AGAIN!
BEFORE THE HEARTACHE AND DECEITS OF THIS WORLD EMBITTERED MY HEART TO THE BEAUTY THAT TWO PEOPLE CAN SHARE!
FURMR!
TO BE YOUNG AND IN LOVE!
QUELL, OH QUELL YOUR INHIBITION, MY DEAREST, AS A HOST OF ANGELS SERENADE ON HIGH AT THE ECHO OF OUR PASSION!
FURMR!

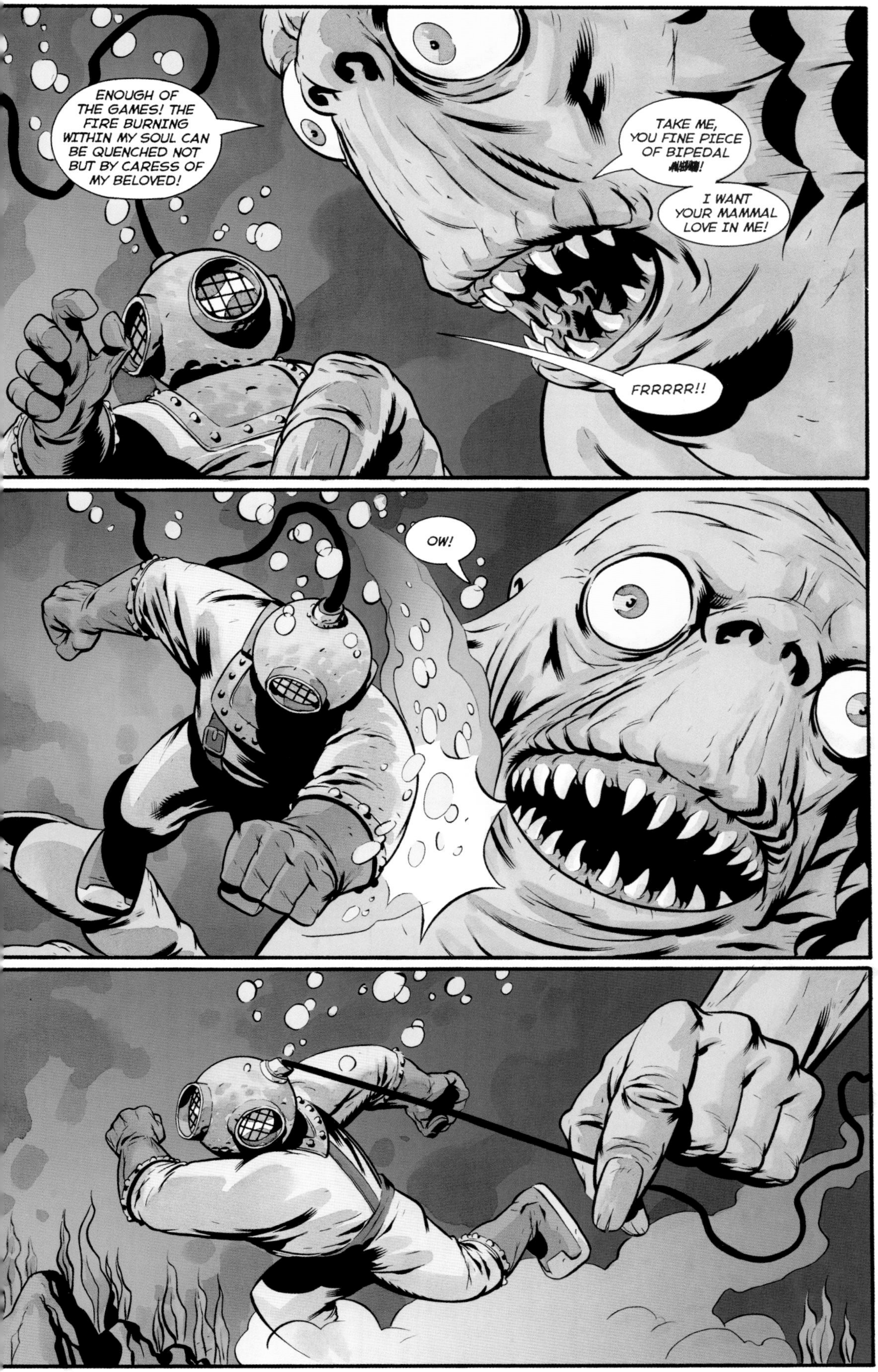
ENOUGH OF THE GAMES! THE FIRE BURNING WITHIN MY SOUL CAN BE QUENCHED NOT BUT BY CARESS OF MY BELOVED!
TAKE ME, YOU FINE PIECE OF BIPEDAL [redacted]!
I WANT YOUR MAMMAL LOVE IN ME!
FRRRRR!!
OW!

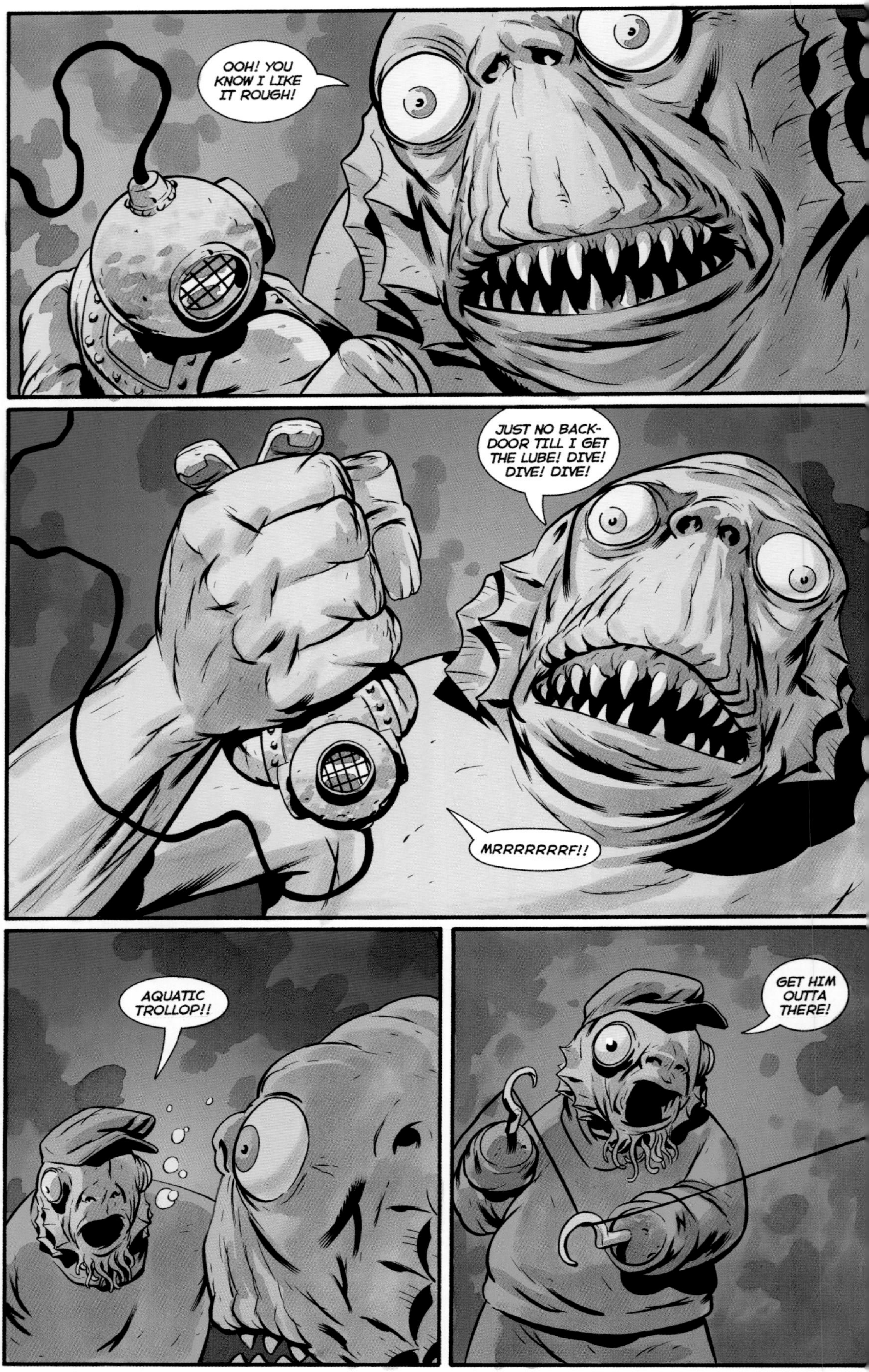
OOH! YOU KNOW I LIKE IT ROUGH!
JUST NO BACK-DOOR TILL I GET THE LUBE! DIVE! DIVE! DIVE!
MRRRRRRRF!!
AQUATIC TROLLOP!!
GET HIM OUTTA THERE!

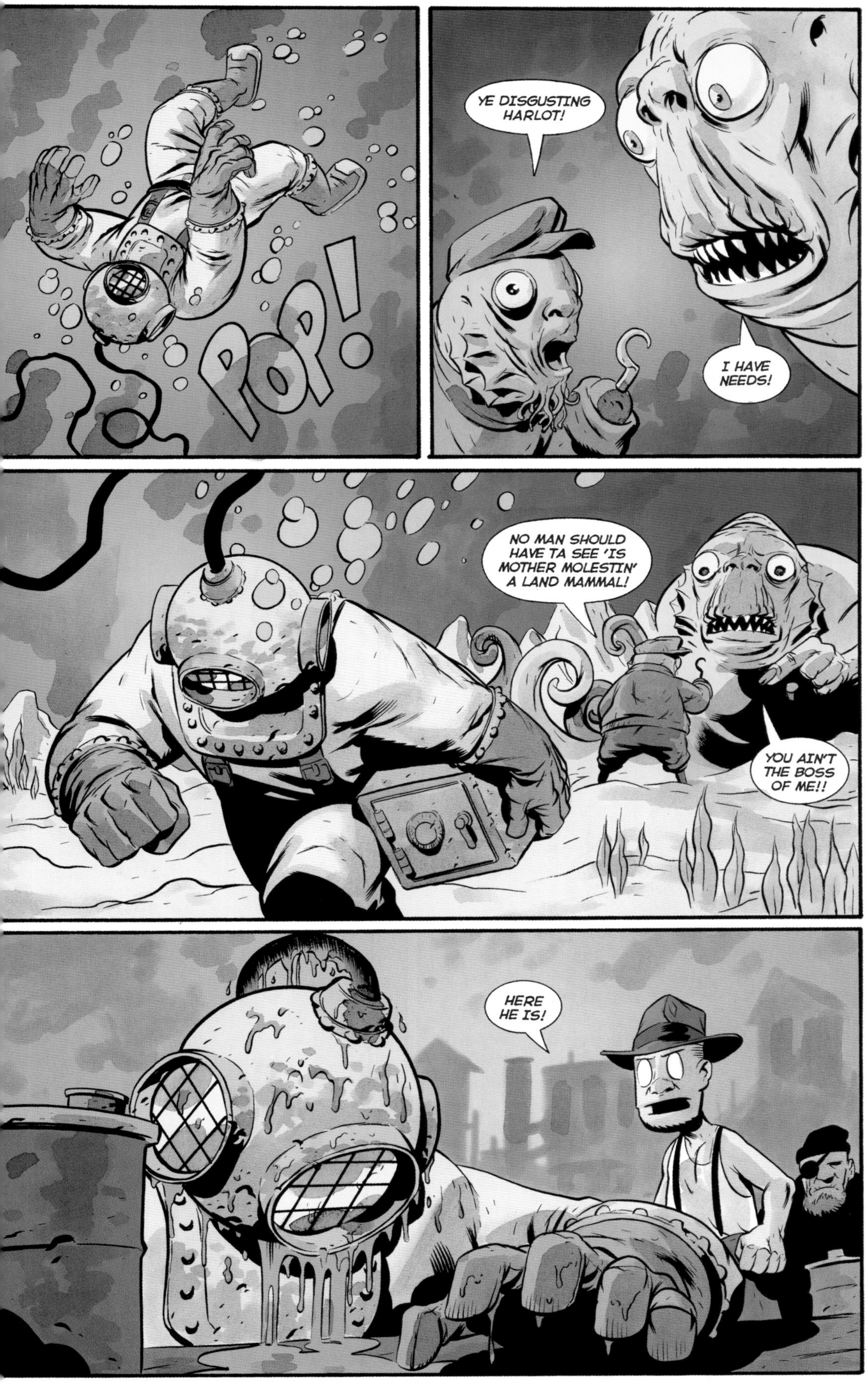
POP!
YE DISGUSTING HARLOT!
I HAVE NEEDS!
NO MAN SHOULD HAVE TA SEE 'IS MOTHER MOLESTIN' A LAND MAMMAL!
YOU AIN'T THE BOSS OF ME!!
HERE HE IS!

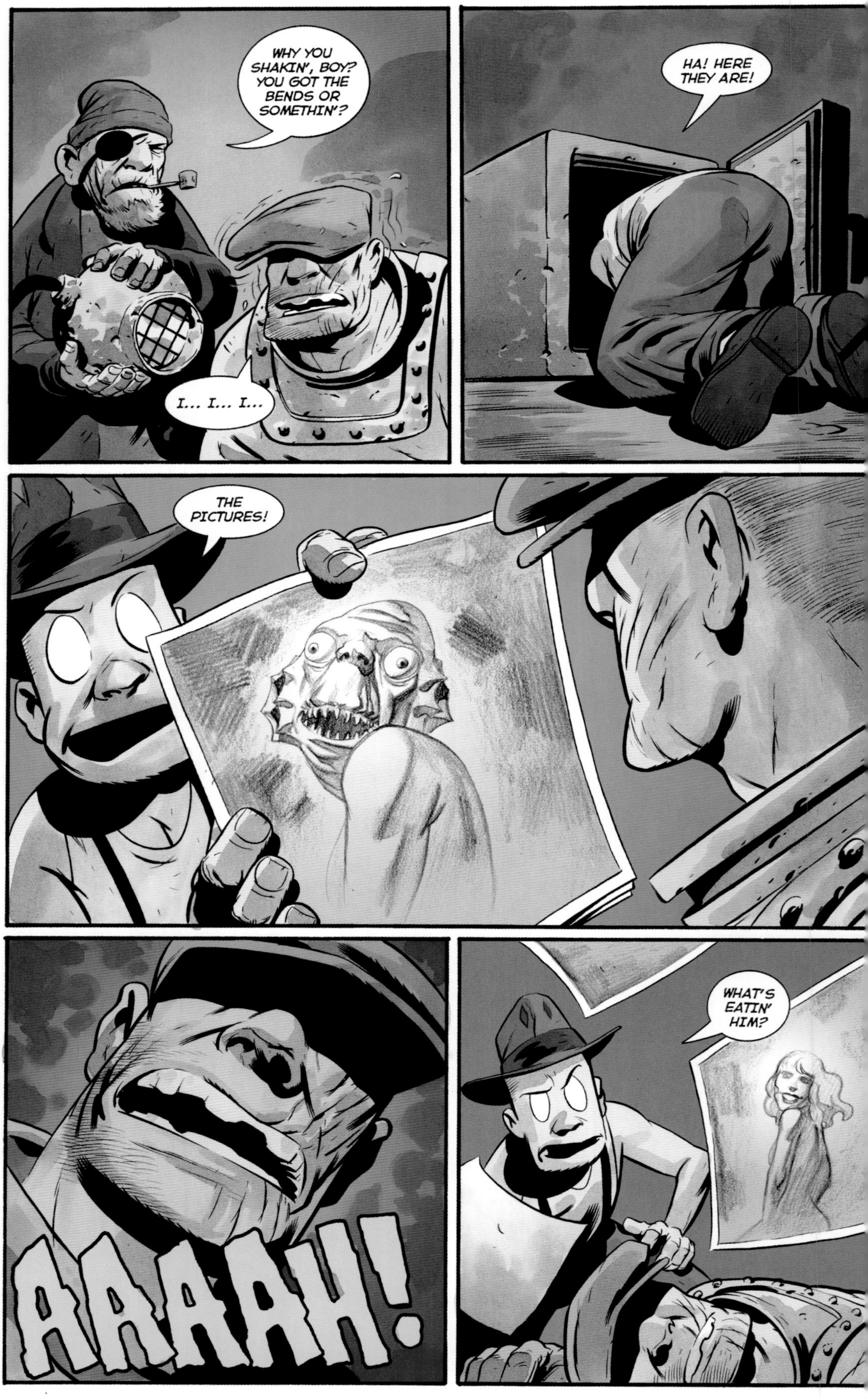
WHY YOU SHAKIN', BOY? YOU GOT THE BENDS OR SOMETHIN'?
I... I... I...
HA! HERE THEY ARE!
THE PICTURES!
AAAAH!
WHAT'S EATIN' HIM?

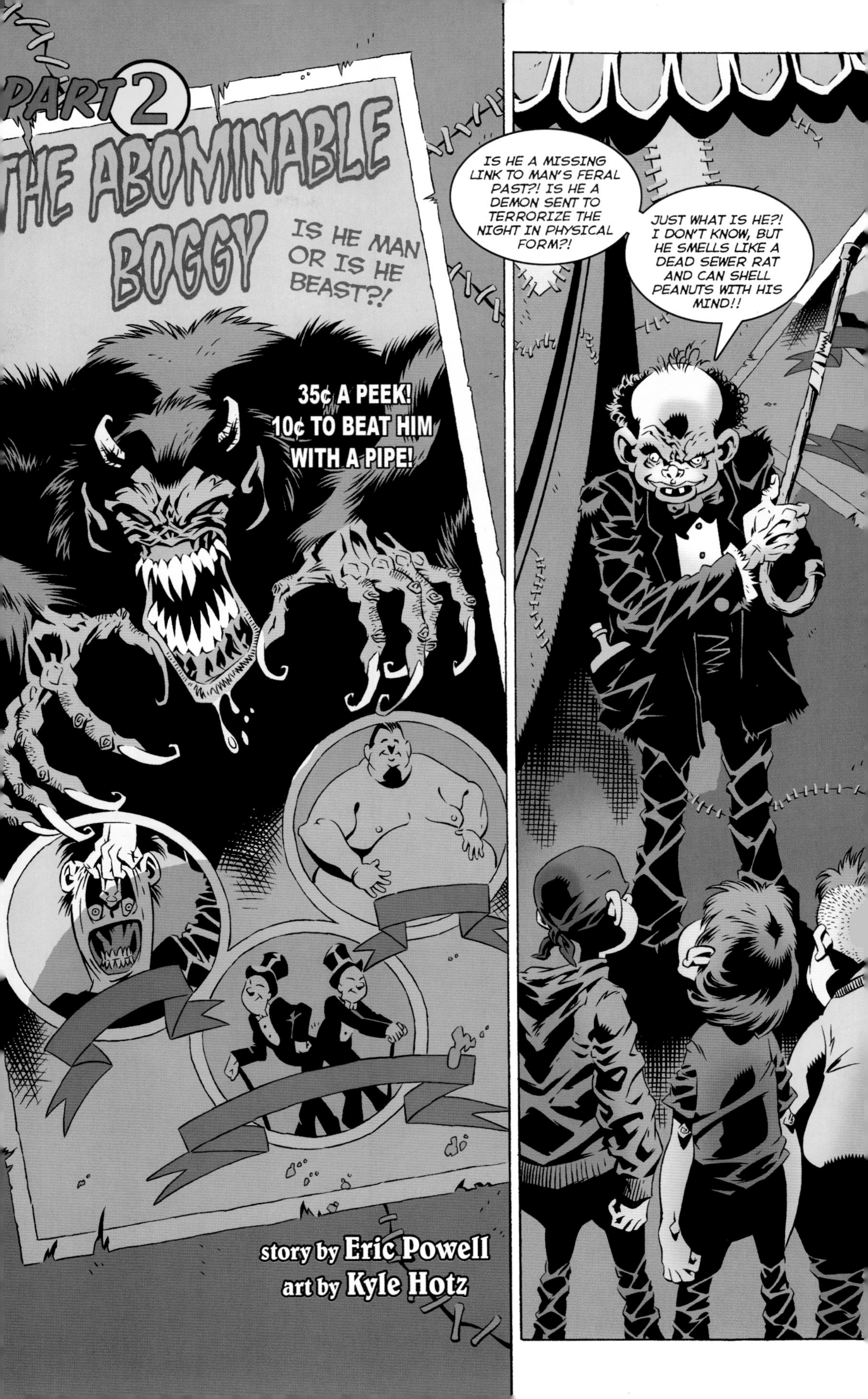
PART 2
THE ABOMINABLE BOGGY
IS HE MAN OR IS HE BEAST?!
35¢ A PEEK!
10¢ TO BEAT HIM WITH A PIPE!
story by Eric Powell
art by Kyle Hotz
IS HE A MISSING LINK TO MAN'S FERAL PAST?! IS HE A DEMON SENT TO TERRORIZE THE NIGHT IN PHYSICAL FORM?!
JUST WHAT IS HE?! I DON'T KNOW, BUT HE SMELLS LIKE A DEAD SEWER RAT AND CAN SHELL PEANUTS WITH HIS MIND!!

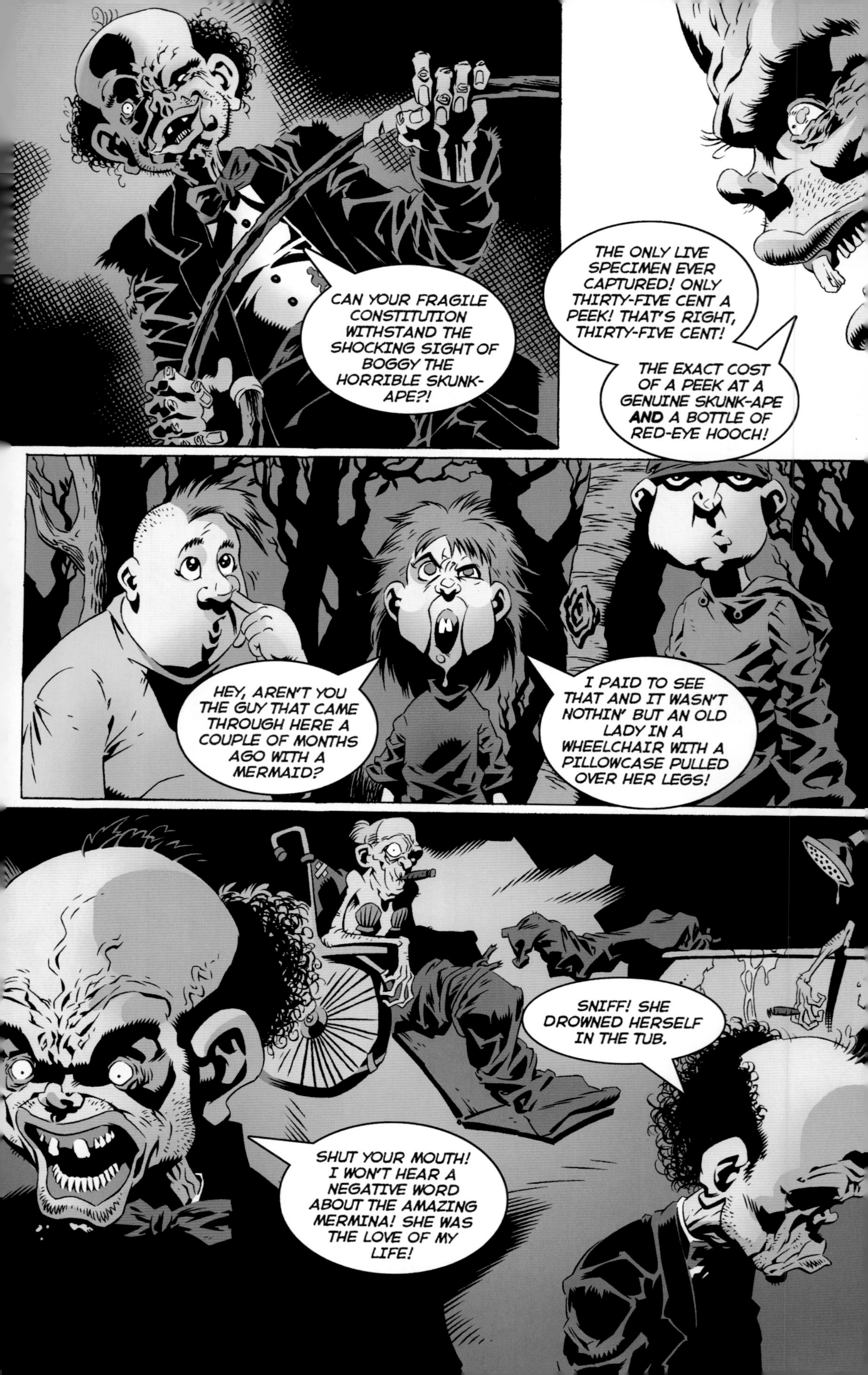
CAN YOUR FRAGILE CONSTITUTION WITHSTAND THE SHOCKING SIGHT OF BOGGY THE HORRIBLE SKUNK-APE?!
THE ONLY LIVE SPECIMEN EVER CAPTURED! ONLY THIRTY-FIVE CENT A PEEK! THAT'S RIGHT, THIRTY-FIVE CENT!
THE EXACT COST OF A PEEK AT A GENUINE SKUNK-APE **AND** A BOTTLE OF RED-EYE HOOCH!
HEY, AREN'T YOU THE GUY THAT CAME THROUGH HERE A COUPLE OF MONTHS AGO WITH A MERMAID?
I PAID TO SEE THAT AND IT WASN'T NOTHIN' BUT AN OLD LADY IN A WHEELCHAIR WITH A PILLOWCASE PULLED OVER HER LEGS!
SNIFF! SHE DROWNED HERSELF IN THE TUB.
SHUT YOUR MOUTH! I WON'T HEAR A NEGATIVE WORD ABOUT THE AMAZING MERMINA! SHE WAS THE LOVE OF MY LIFE!

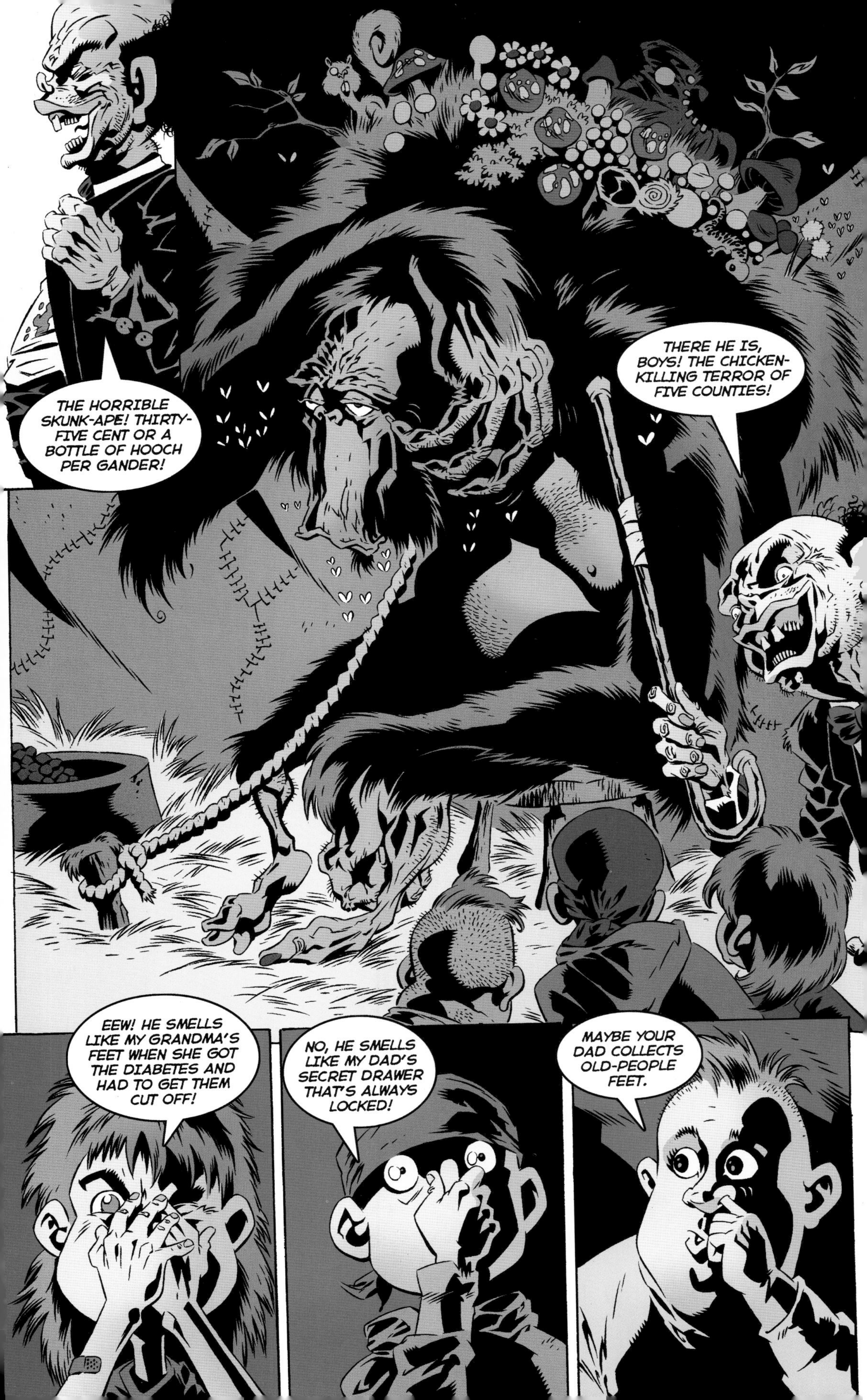
THE HORRIBLE SKUNK-APE! THIRTY-FIVE CENT OR A BOTTLE OF HOOCH PER GANDER!
THERE HE IS, BOYS! THE CHICKEN-KILLING TERROR OF FIVE COUNTIES!
EEW! HE SMELLS LIKE MY GRANDMA'S FEET WHEN SHE GOT THE DIABETES AND HAD TO GET THEM CUT OFF!
NO, HE SMELLS LIKE MY DAD'S SECRET DRAWER THAT'S ALWAYS LOCKED!
MAYBE YOUR DAD COLLECTS OLD-PEOPLE FEET.

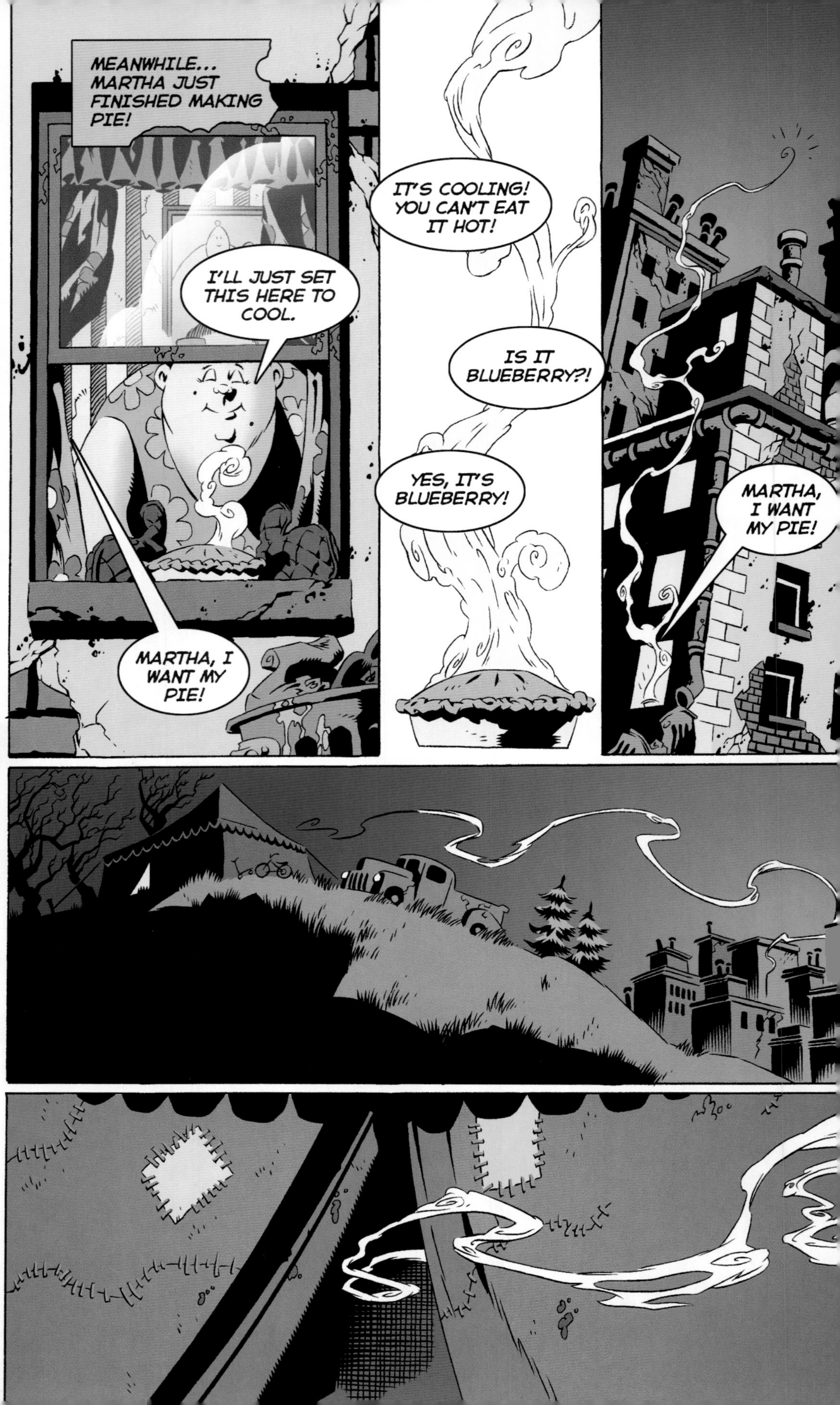
MEANWHILE... MARTHA JUST FINISHED MAKING PIE!
I'LL JUST SET THIS HERE TO COOL.
MARTHA, I WANT MY PIE!
IT'S COOLING! YOU CAN'T EAT IT HOT!
IS IT BLUEBERRY?!
YES, IT'S BLUEBERRY!
MARTHA, I WANT MY PIE!

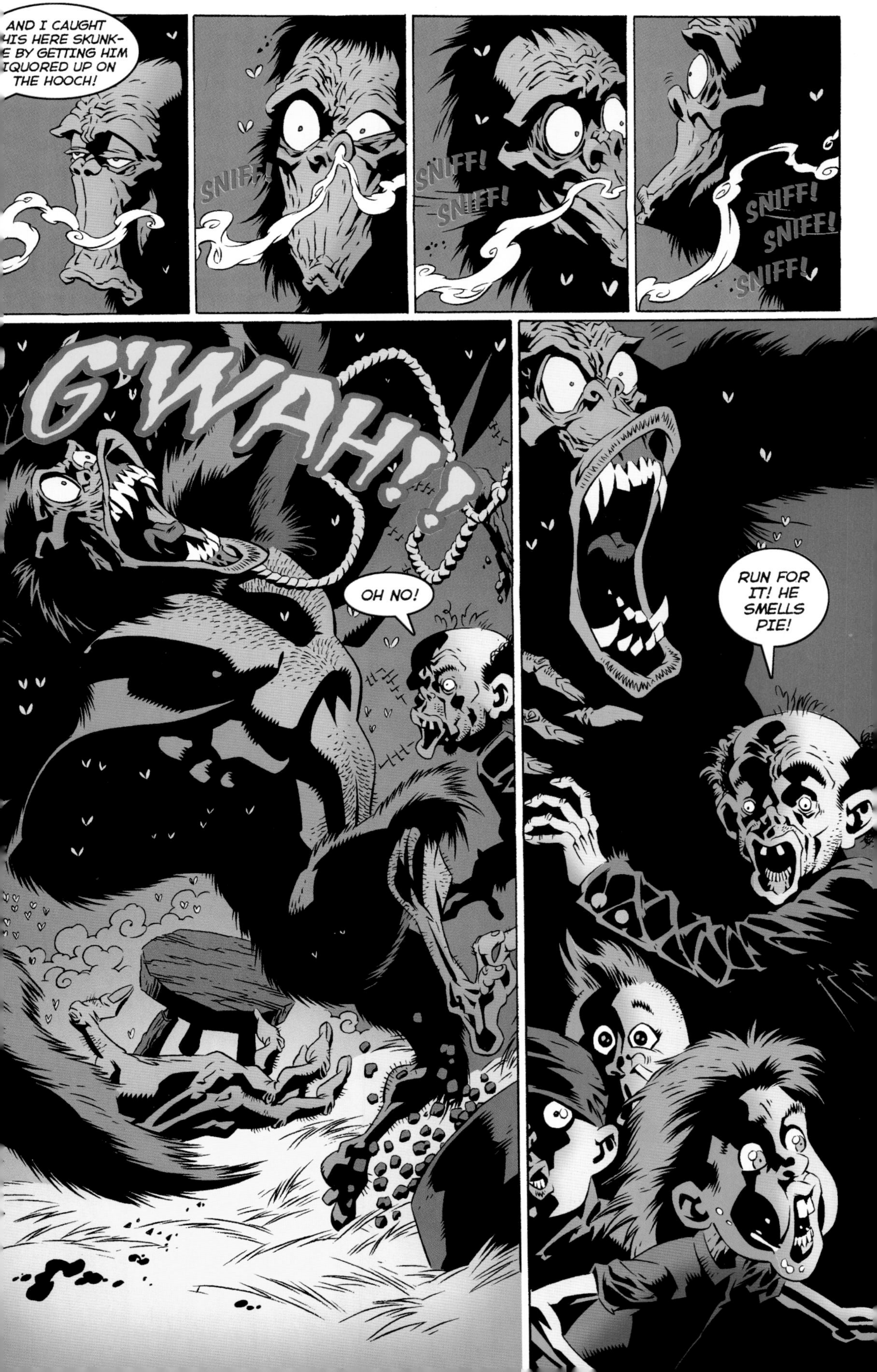
AND I CAUGHT
HIS HERE SKUNK-
E BY GETTING HIM
IQUORED UP ON
THE HOOCH!
SNIFF!
SNIFF!
SNIFF!
SNIFF!
SNIFF!
SNIFF!
G'WAH!!
OH NO!
RUN FOR
IT! HE
SMELLS
PIE!

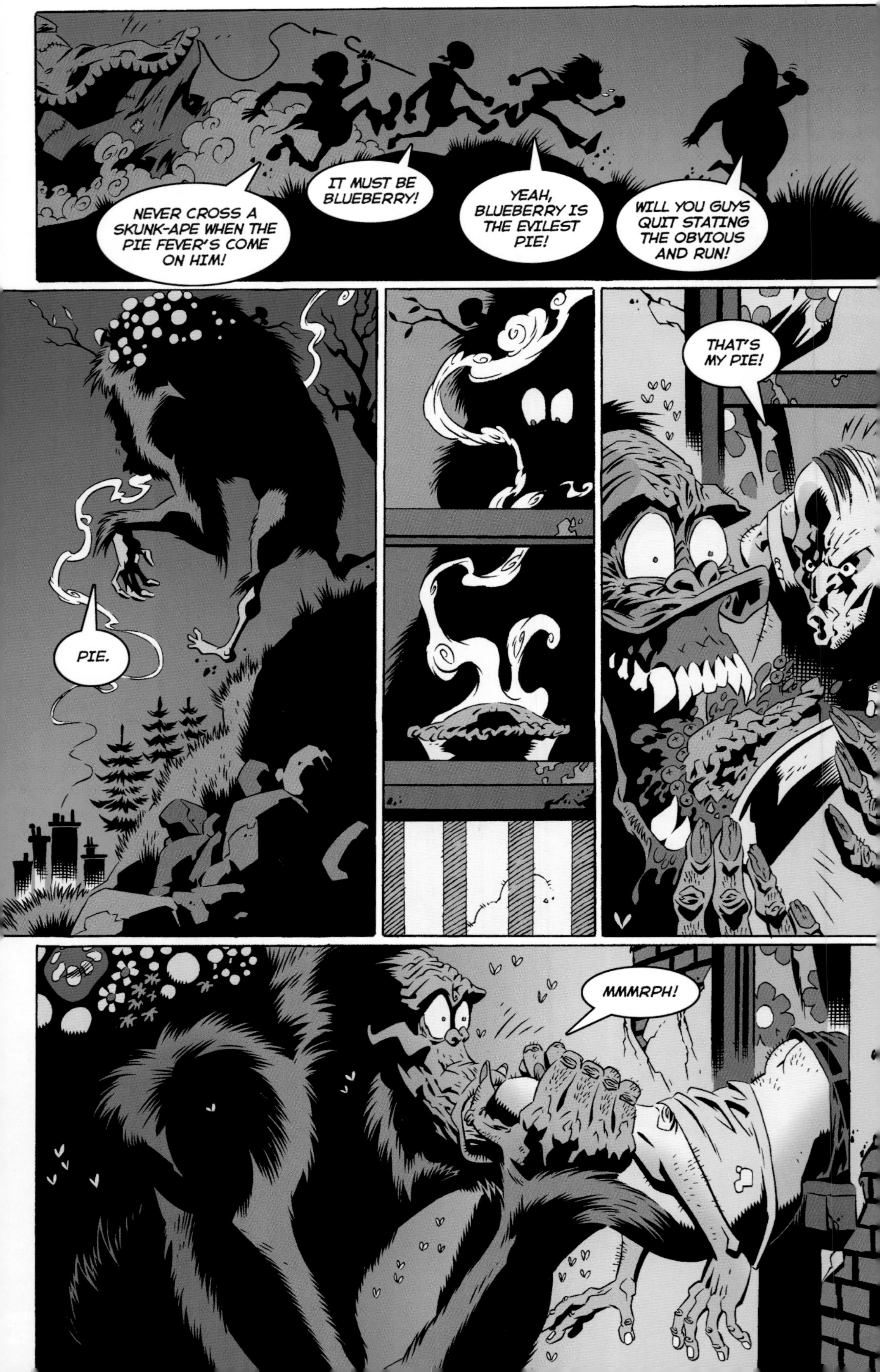
NEVER CROSS A SKUNK-APE WHEN THE PIE FEVER'S COME ON HIM!
IT MUST BE BLUEBERRY!
YEAH, BLUEBERRY IS THE EVILEST PIE!
WILL YOU GUYS QUIT STATING THE OBVIOUS AND RUN!
PIE.
THAT'S MY PIE!
MMMRPH!

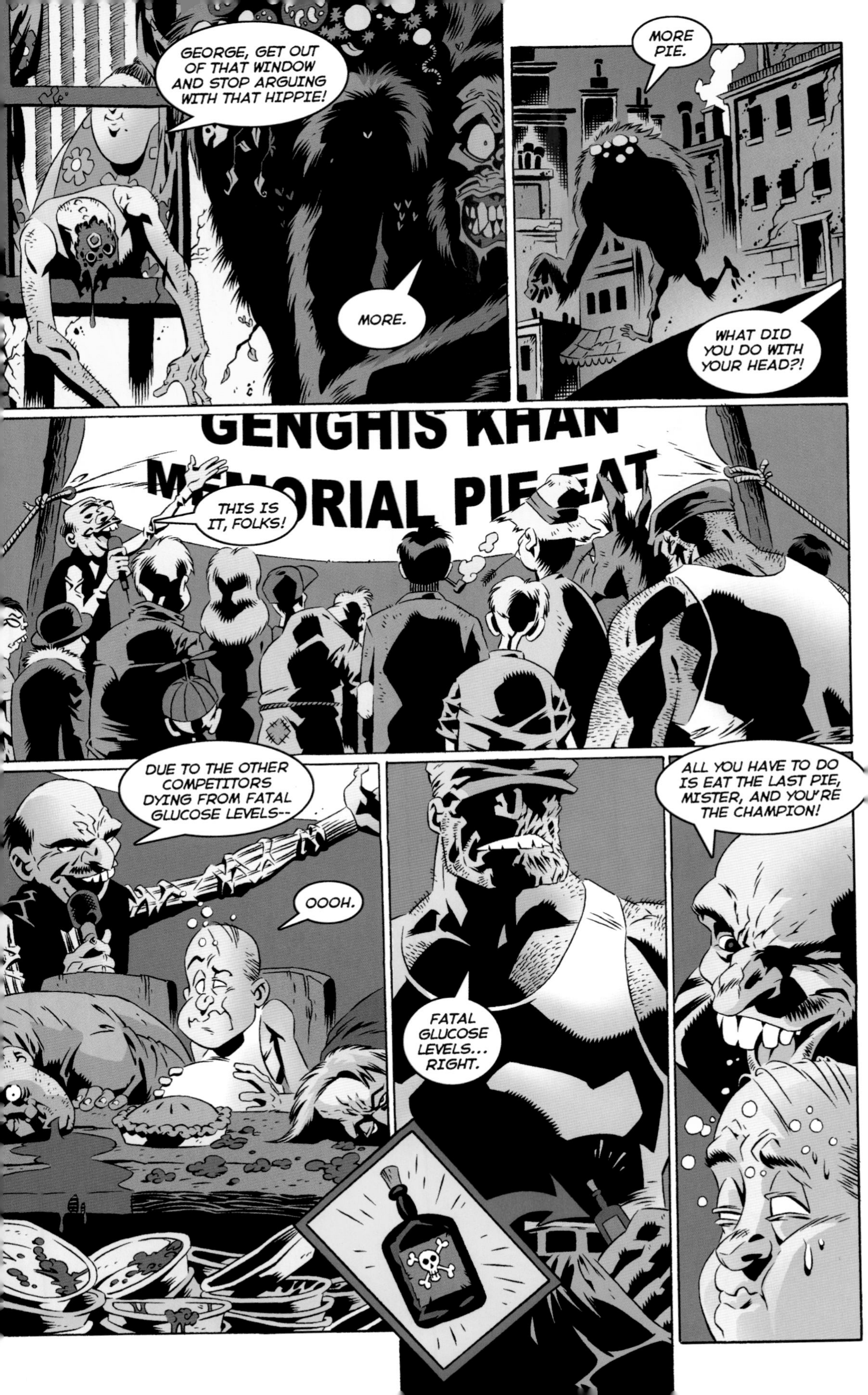
GEORGE, GET OUT OF THAT WINDOW AND STOP ARGUING WITH THAT HIPPIE!
MORE.
MORE PIE.
WHAT DID YOU DO WITH YOUR HEAD?!
GENGHIS KHAN MEMORIAL PIE EAT
THIS IS IT, FOLKS!
DUE TO THE OTHER COMPETITORS DYING FROM FATAL GLUCOSE LEVELS--
OOOH.
FATAL GLUCOSE LEVELS... RIGHT.
ALL YOU HAVE TO DO IS EAT THE LAST PIE, MISTER, AND YOU'RE THE CHAMPION!

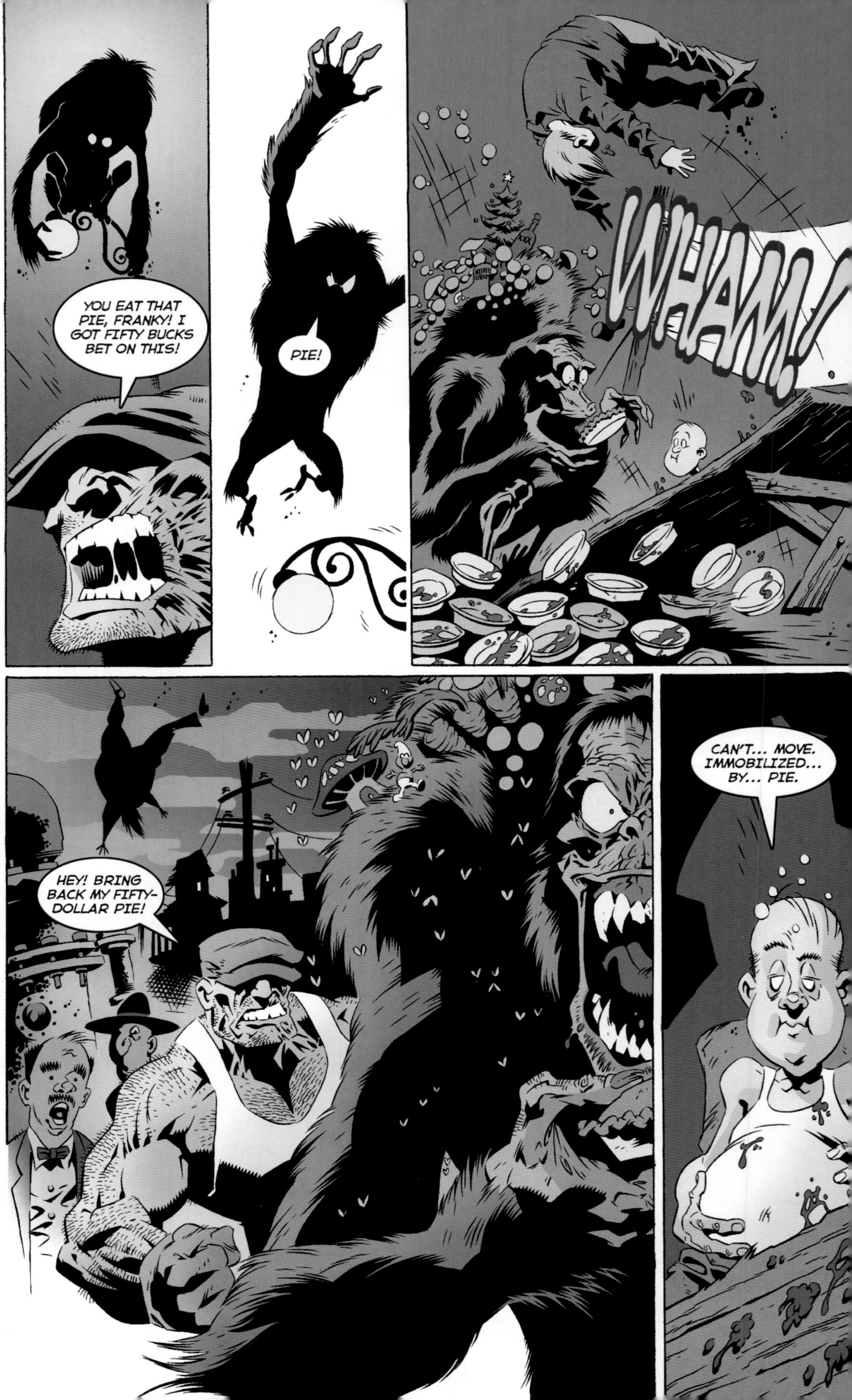
YOU EAT THAT PIE, FRANKY! I GOT FIFTY BUCKS BET ON THIS!
PIE!
WHAM!
HEY! BRING BACK MY FIFTY-DOLLAR PIE!
CAN'T... MOVE. IMMOBILIZED... BY... PIE.

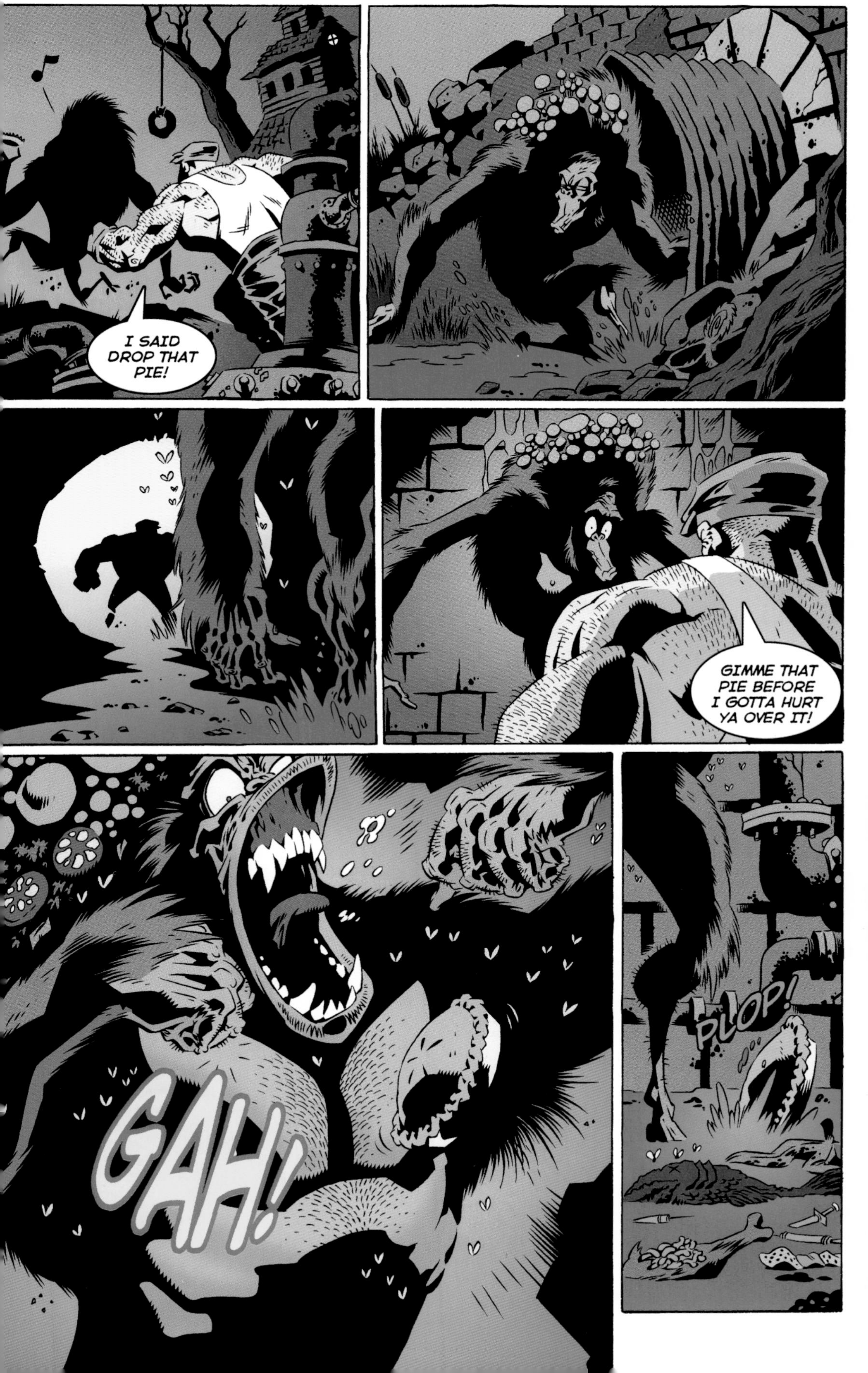
I SAID DROP THAT PIE!
GIMME THAT PIE BEFORE I GOTTA HURT YA OVER IT!
GAH!
PLOP!

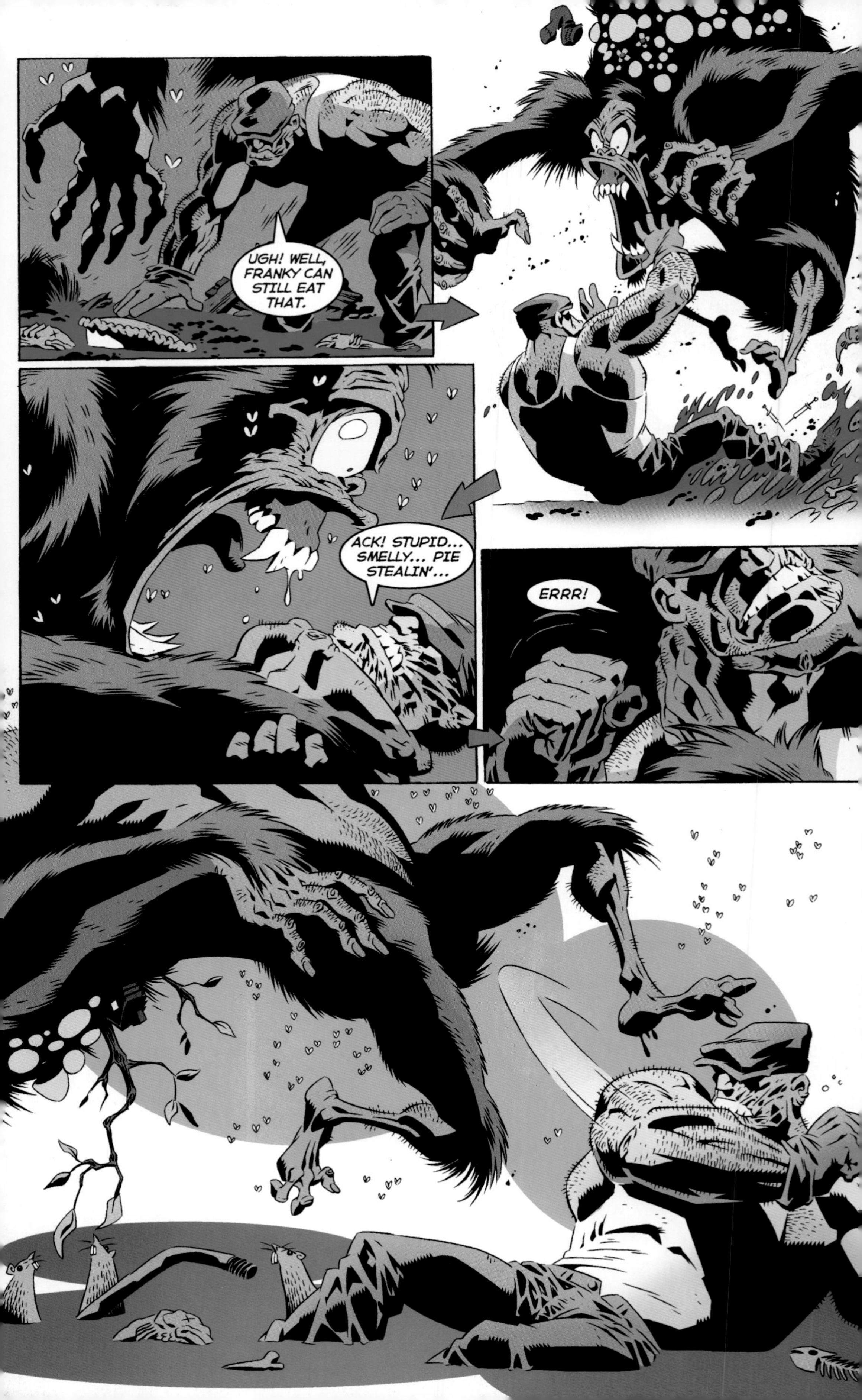
UGH! WELL, FRANKY CAN STILL EAT THAT.
ACK! STUPID... SMELLY... PIE STEALIN'...
ERRR!

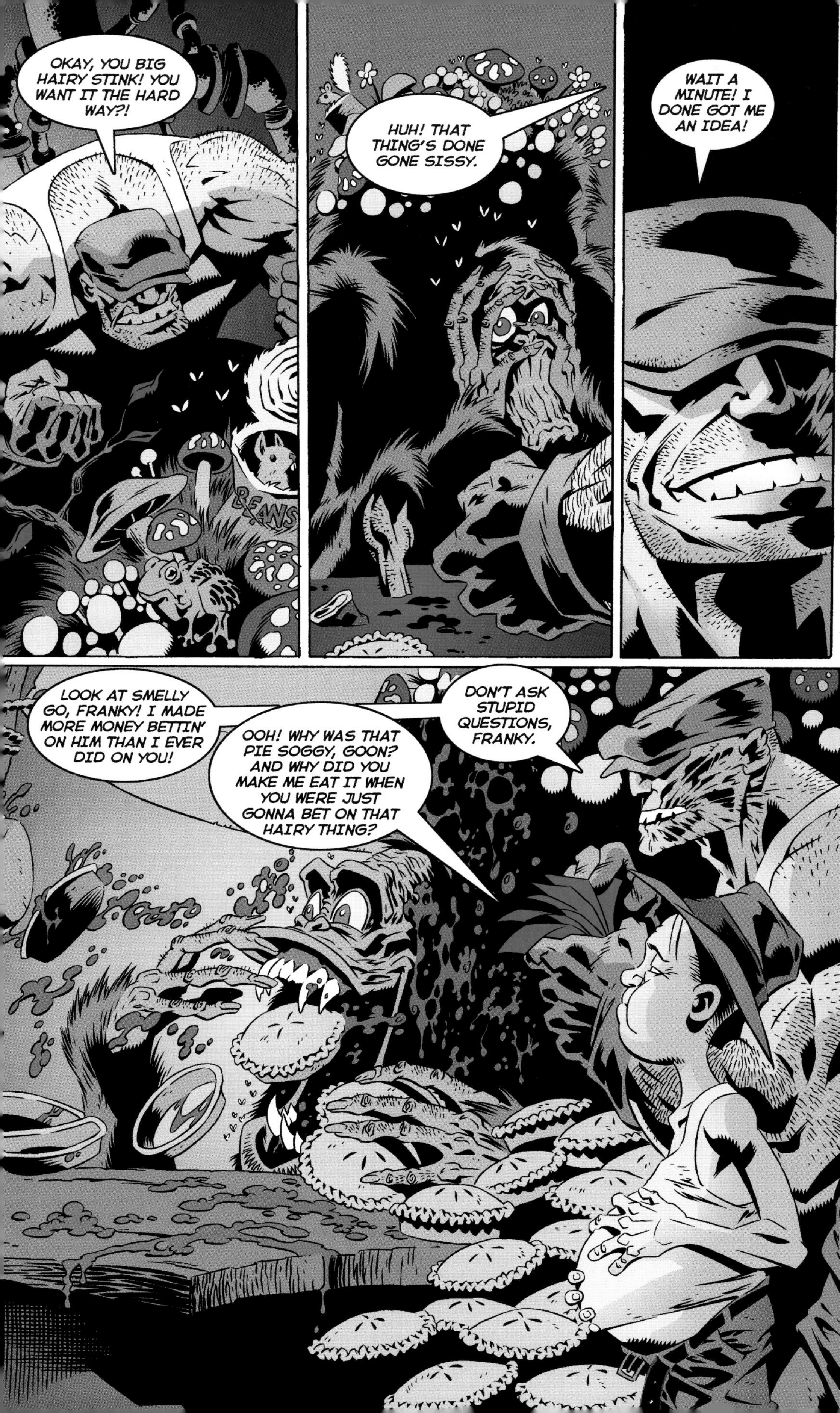
OKAY, YOU BIG HAIRY STINK! YOU WANT IT THE HARD WAY?!
BEANS
HUH! THAT THING'S DONE GONE SISSY.
WAIT A MINUTE! I DONE GOT ME AN IDEA!
LOOK AT SMELLY GO, FRANKY! I MADE MORE MONEY BETTIN' ON HIM THAN I EVER DID ON YOU!
OOH! WHY WAS THAT PIE SOGGY, GOON? AND WHY DID YOU MAKE ME EAT IT WHEN YOU WERE JUST GONNA BET ON THAT HAIRY THING?
DON'T ASK STUPID QUESTIONS, FRANKY.

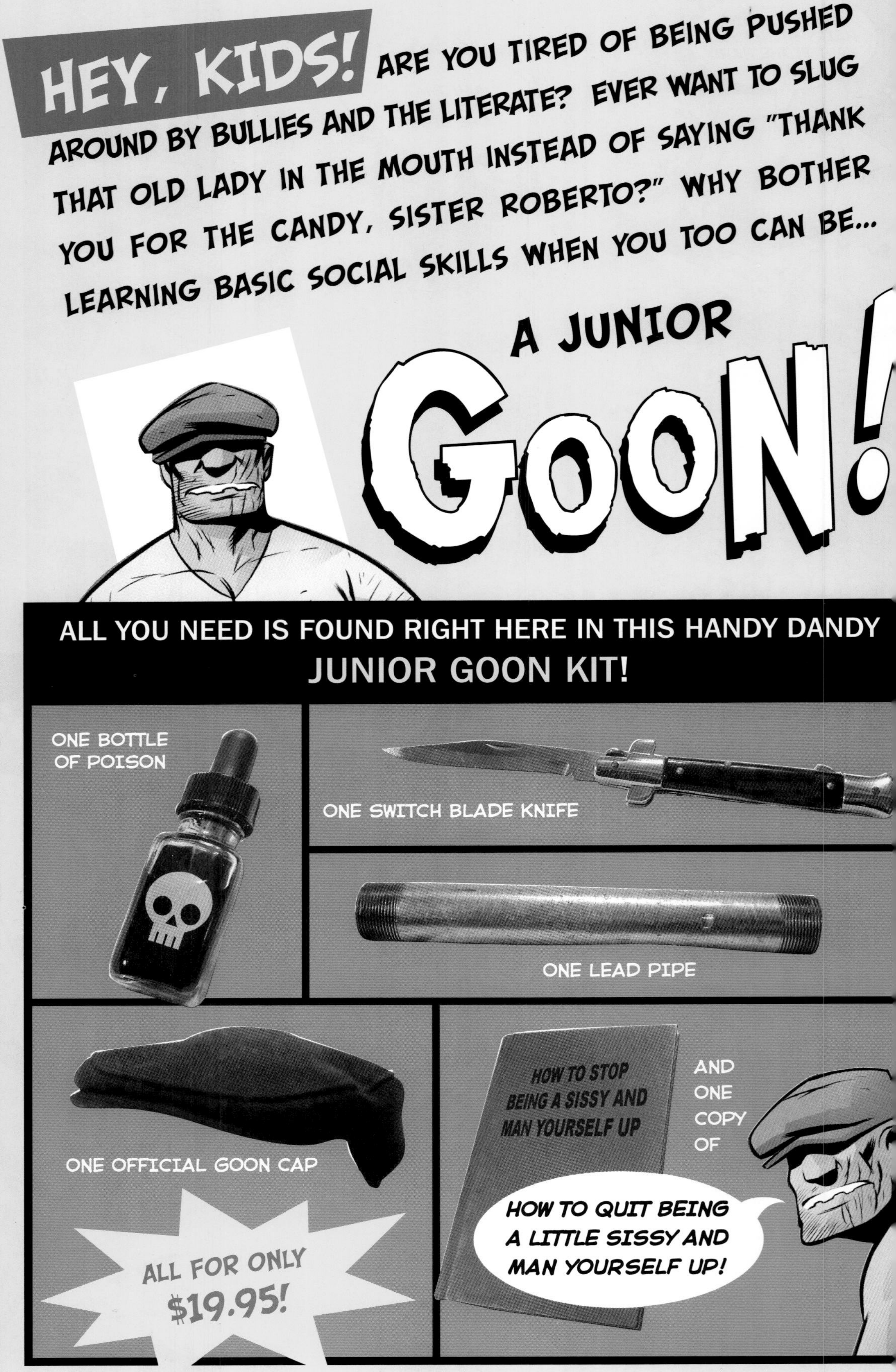
HEY, KIDS!
ARE YOU TIRED OF BEING PUSHED AROUND BY BULLIES AND THE LITERATE? EVER WANT TO SLUG THAT OLD LADY IN THE MOUTH INSTEAD OF SAYING "THANK YOU FOR THE CANDY, SISTER ROBERTO?" WHY BOTHER LEARNING BASIC SOCIAL SKILLS WHEN YOU TOO CAN BE...
A JUNIOR
GOON!
ALL YOU NEED IS FOUND RIGHT HERE IN THIS HANDY DANDY
JUNIOR GOON KIT!
ONE BOTTLE OF POISON
ONE SWITCH BLADE KNIFE
ONE LEAD PIPE
ONE OFFICIAL GOON CAP
ALL FOR ONLY $19.95!
HOW TO STOP BEING A SISSY AND MAN YOURSELF UP
AND ONE COPY OF
HOW TO QUIT BEING A LITTLE SISSY AND MAN YOURSELF UP!

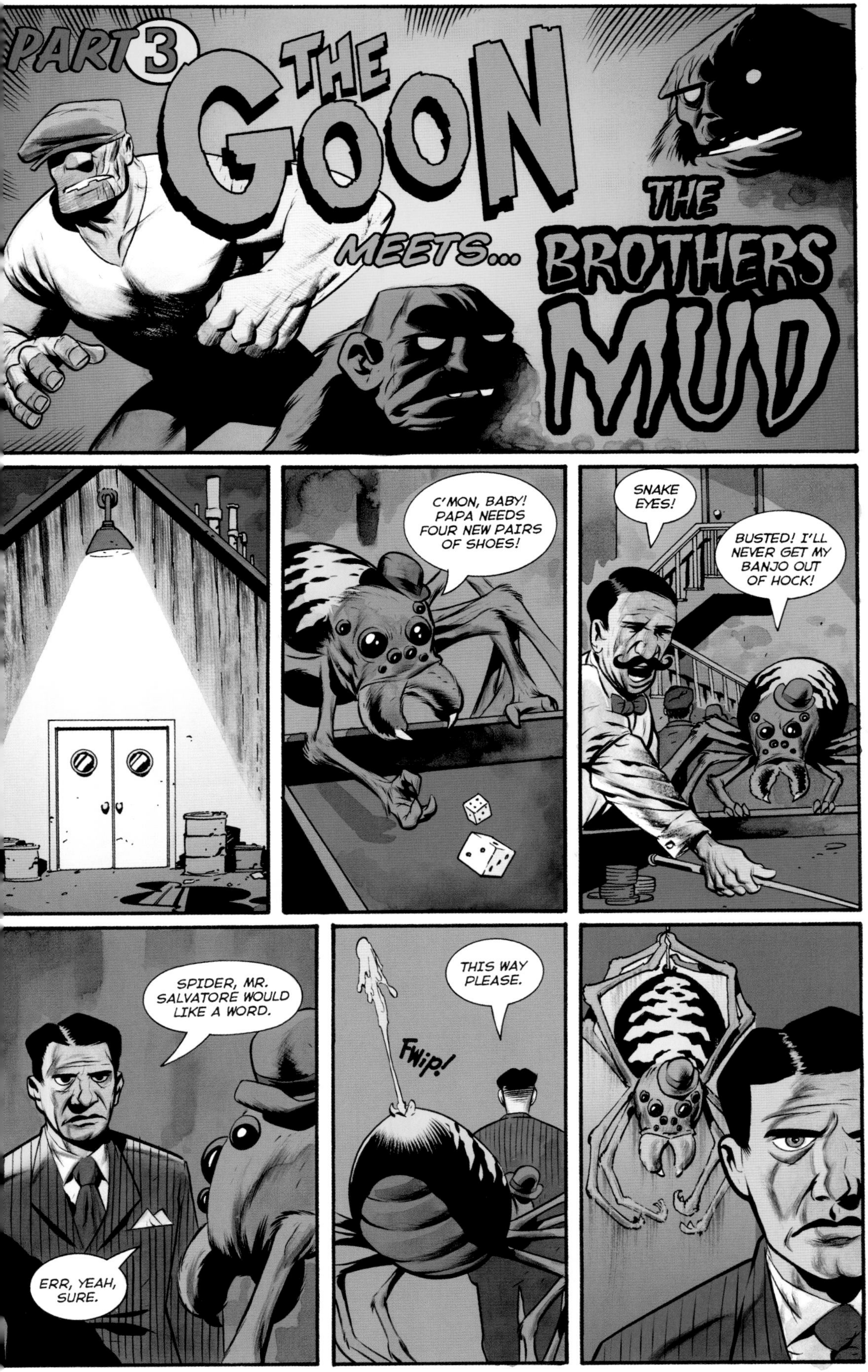

PART 3
THE GOON
MEETS...
THE BROTHERS MUD
C'MON, BABY! PAPA NEEDS FOUR NEW PAIRS OF SHOES!
SNAKE EYES!
BUSTED! I'LL NEVER GET MY BANJO OUT OF HOCK!
SPIDER, MR. SALVATORE WOULD LIKE A WORD.
ERR, YEAH, SURE.
THIS WAY PLEASE.
FWIP!

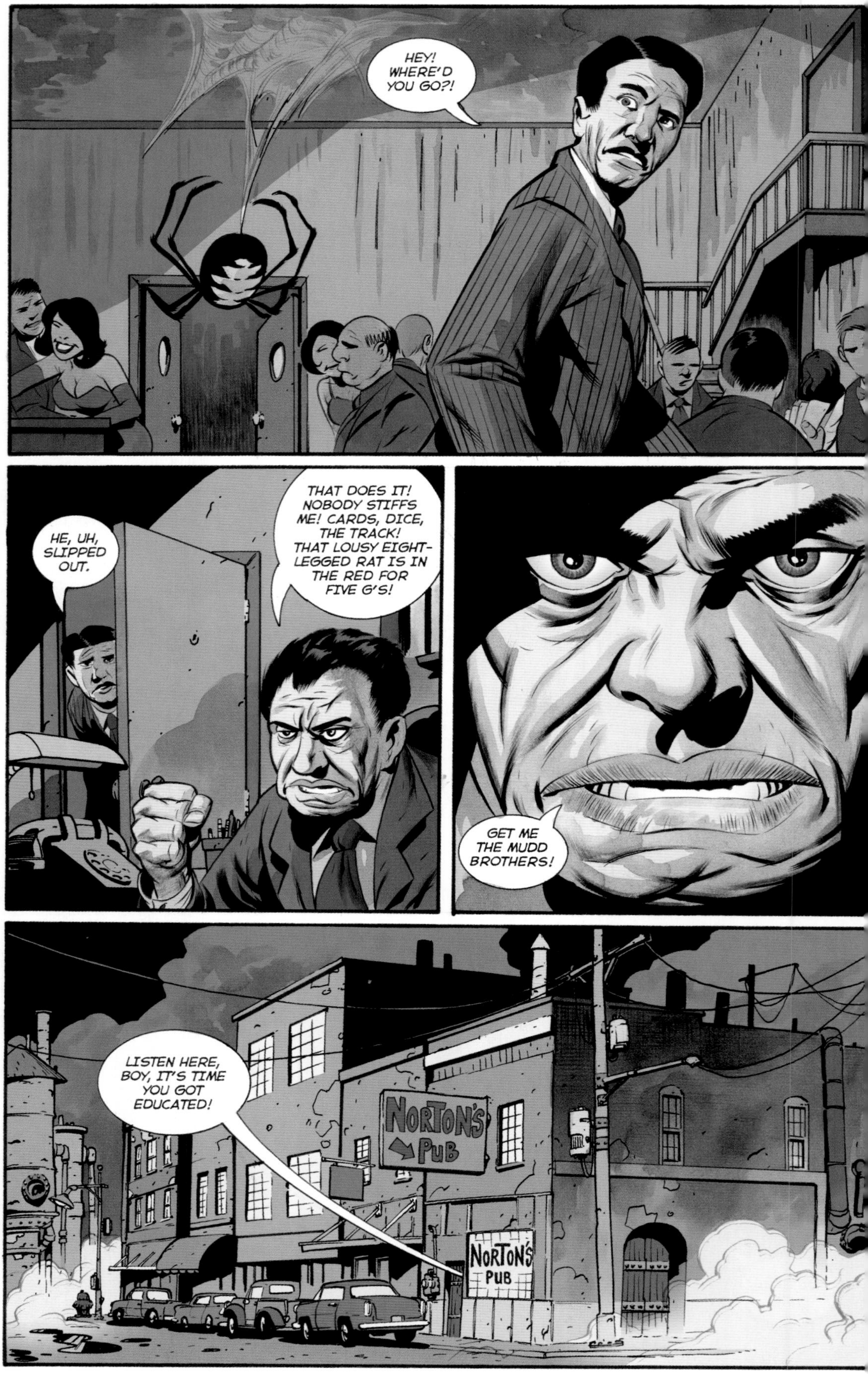
HEY! WHERE'D YOU GO?!
HE, UH, SLIPPED OUT.
THAT DOES IT! NOBODY STIFFS ME! CARDS, DICE, THE TRACK! THAT LOUSY EIGHT-LEGGED RAT IS IN THE RED FOR FIVE G'S!
GET ME THE MUDD BROTHERS!
LISTEN HERE, BOY, IT'S TIME YOU GOT EDUCATED!
NORTON'S PUB
NORTON'S PUB

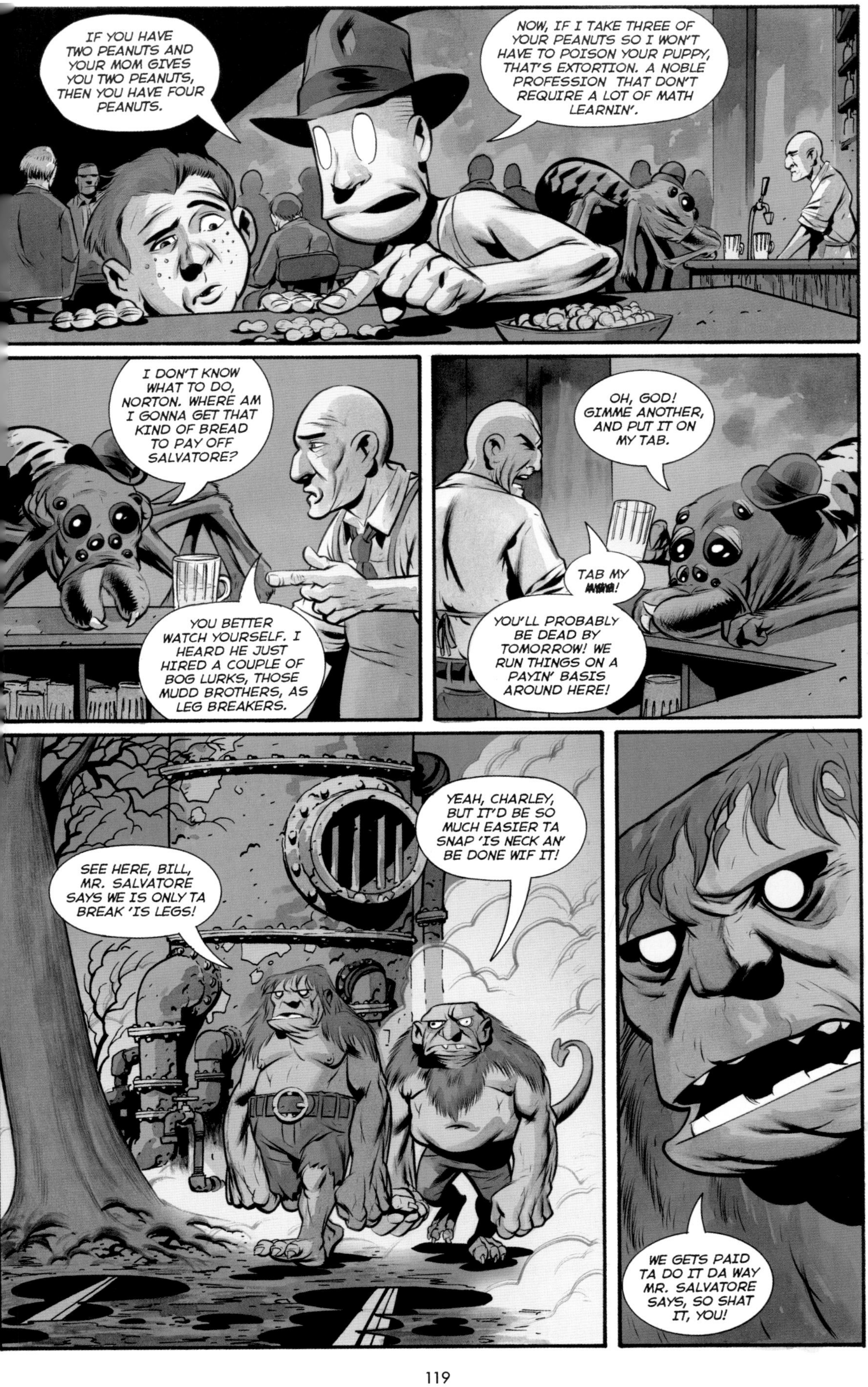
IF YOU HAVE TWO PEANUTS AND YOUR MOM GIVES YOU TWO PEANUTS, THEN YOU HAVE FOUR PEANUTS.
NOW, IF I TAKE THREE OF YOUR PEANUTS SO I WON'T HAVE TO POISON YOUR PUPPY, THAT'S EXTORTION. A NOBLE PROFESSION THAT DON'T REQUIRE A LOT OF MATH LEARNIN'.
I DON'T KNOW WHAT TO DO, NORTON. WHERE AM I GONNA GET THAT KIND OF BREAD TO PAY OFF SALVATORE?
YOU BETTER WATCH YOURSELF. I HEARD HE JUST HIRED A COUPLE OF BOG LURKS, THOSE MUDD BROTHERS, AS LEG BREAKERS.
OH, GOD! GIMME ANOTHER, AND PUT IT ON MY TAB.
TAB MY !
YOU'LL PROBABLY BE DEAD BY TOMORROW! WE RUN THINGS ON A PAYIN' BASIS AROUND HERE!
SEE HERE, BILL, MR. SALVATORE SAYS WE IS ONLY TA BREAK 'IS LEGS!
YEAH, CHARLEY, BUT IT'D BE SO MUCH EASIER TA SNAP 'IS NECK AN' BE DONE WIF IT!
WE GETS PAID TA DO IT DA WAY MR. SALVATORE SAYS, SO SHAT IT, YOU!

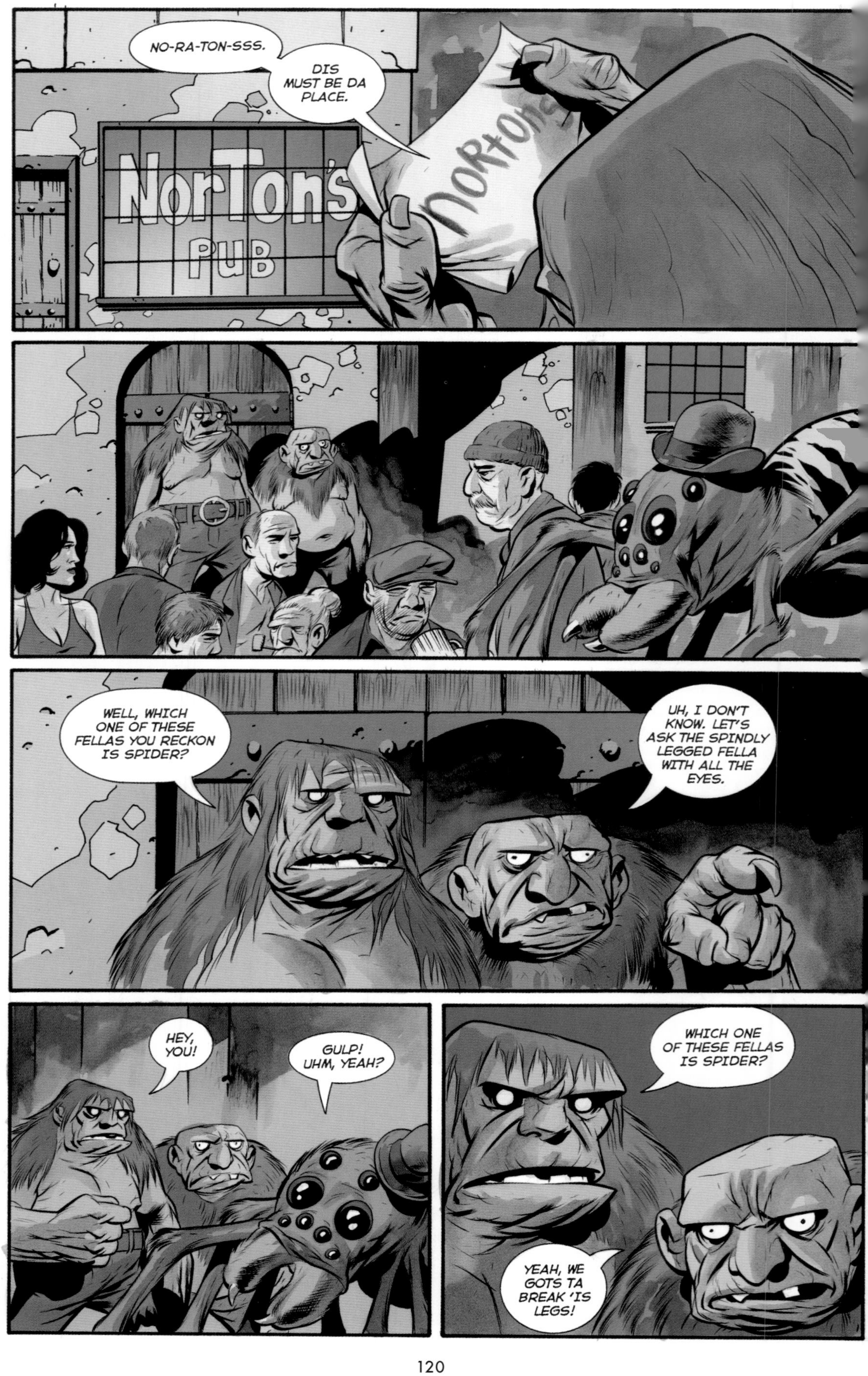
NO-RA-TON-SSS.
DIS MUST BE DA PLACE.
NORTON'S PUB
WELL, WHICH ONE OF THESE FELLAS YOU RECKON IS SPIDER?
UH, I DON'T KNOW. LET'S ASK THE SPINDLY LEGGED FELLA WITH ALL THE EYES.
HEY, YOU!
GULP! UHM, YEAH?
WHICH ONE OF THESE FELLAS IS SPIDER?
YEAH, WE GOTS TA BREAK 'IS LEGS!

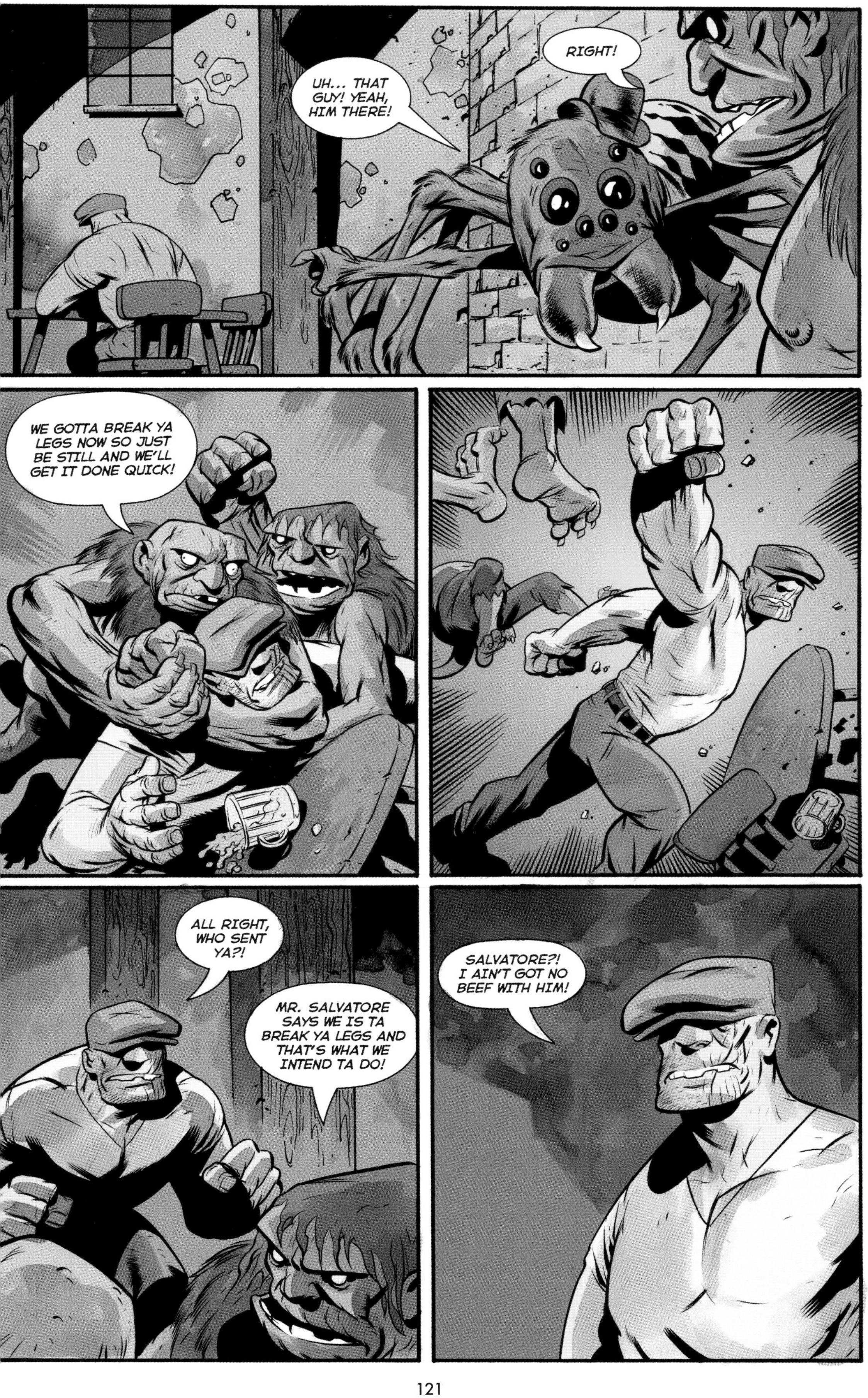
UH... THAT GUY! YEAH, HIM THERE!
RIGHT!
WE GOTTA BREAK YA LEGS NOW SO JUST BE STILL AND WE'LL GET IT DONE QUICK!
ALL RIGHT, WHO SENT YA?!
MR. SALVATORE SAYS WE IS TA BREAK YA LEGS AND THAT'S WHAT WE INTEND TA DO!
SALVATORE?! I AIN'T GOT NO BEEF WITH HIM!

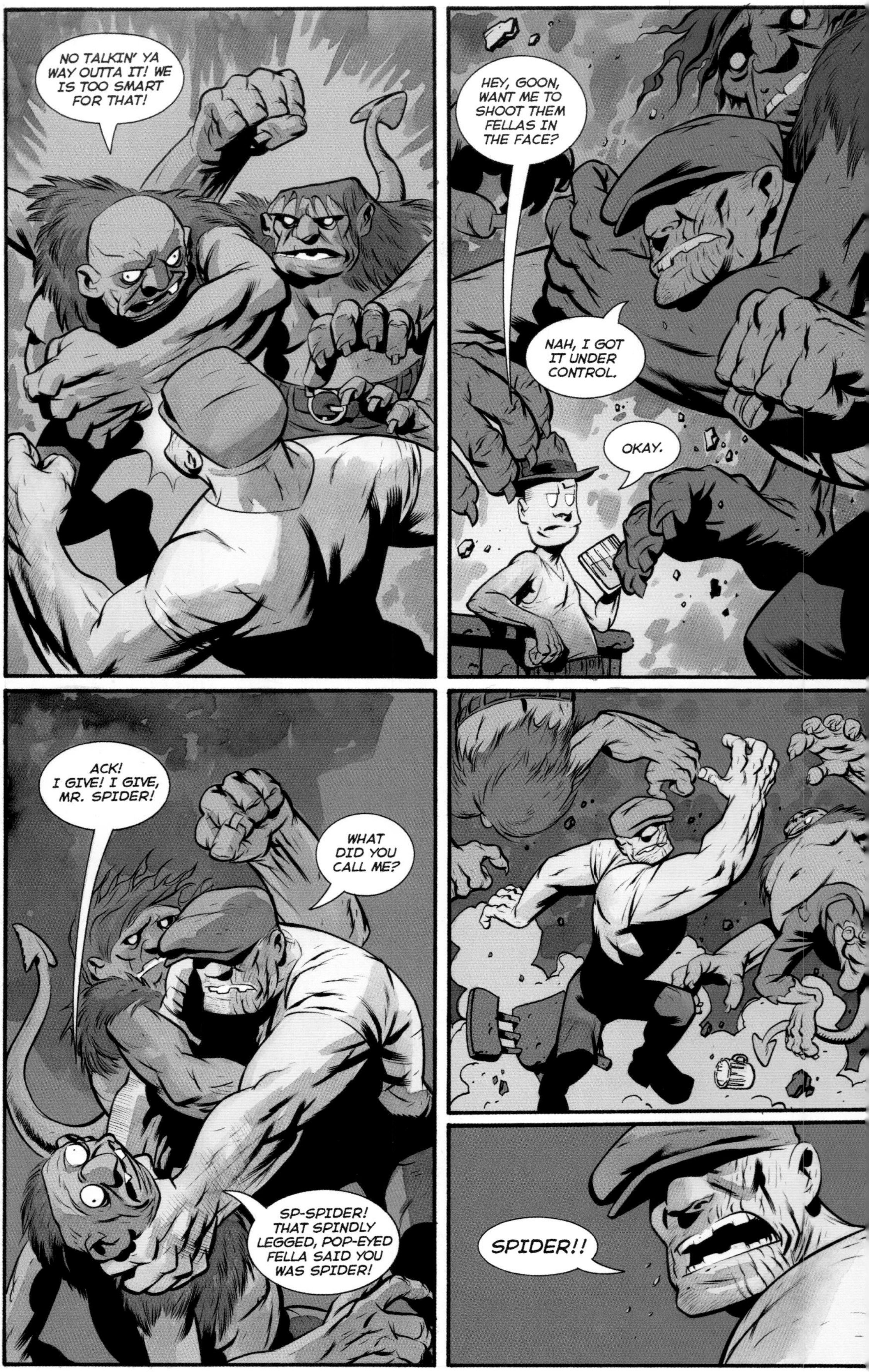
NO TALKIN' YA WAY OUTTA IT! WE IS TOO SMART FOR THAT!
HEY, GOON, WANT ME TO SHOOT THEM FELLAS IN THE FACE?
NAH, I GOT IT UNDER CONTROL.
OKAY.
ACK! I GIVE! I GIVE, MR. SPIDER!
WHAT DID YOU CALL ME?
SP-SPIDER! THAT SPINDLY LEGGED, POP-EYED FELLA SAID YOU WAS SPIDER!
SPIDER!!

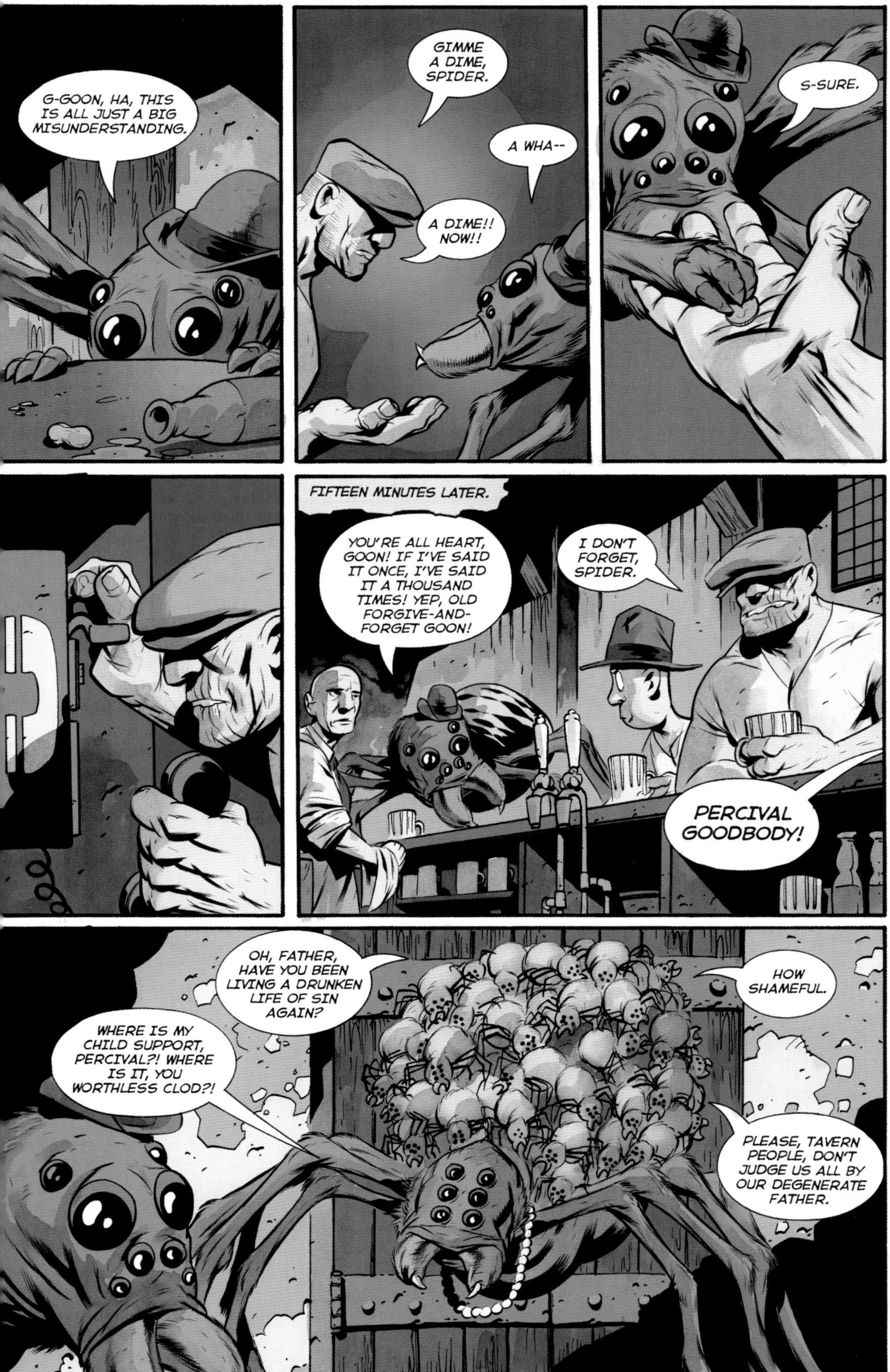
G-GOON, HA, THIS IS ALL JUST A BIG MISUNDERSTANDING.
GIMME A DIME, SPIDER.
A WHA--
A DIME!! NOW!!
S-SURE.
FIFTEEN MINUTES LATER.
YOU'RE ALL HEART, GOON! IF I'VE SAID IT ONCE, I'VE SAID IT A THOUSAND TIMES! YEP, OLD FORGIVE-AND-FORGET GOON!
I DON'T FORGET, SPIDER.
PERCIVAL GOODBODY!
OH, FATHER, HAVE YOU BEEN LIVING A DRUNKEN LIFE OF SIN AGAIN?
HOW SHAMEFUL.
WHERE IS MY CHILD SUPPORT, PERCIVAL?! WHERE IS IT, YOU WORTHLESS CLOD?!
PLEASE, TAVERN PEOPLE, DON'T JUDGE US ALL BY OUR DEGENERATE FATHER.

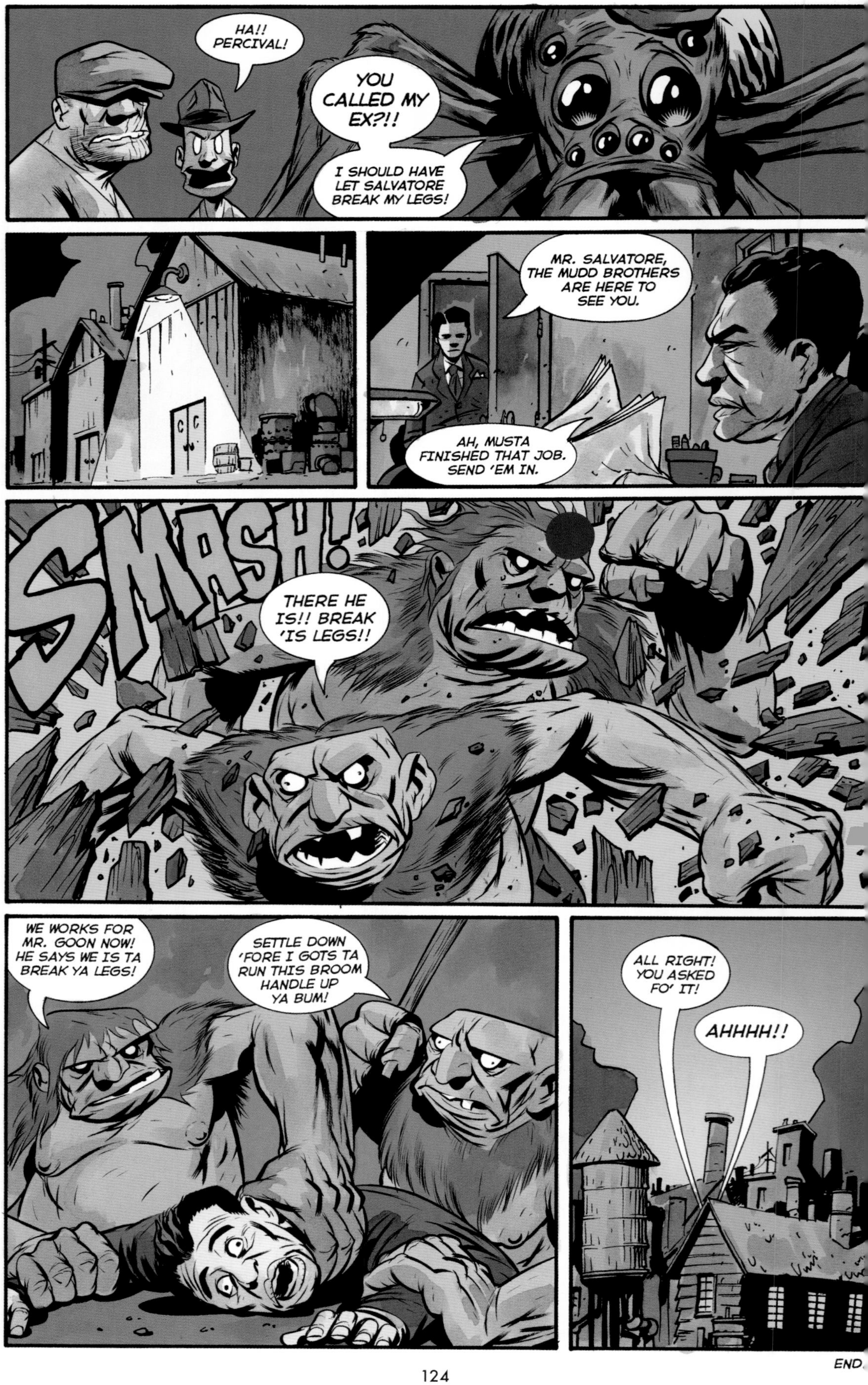
HA!! PERCIVAL!
YOU CALLED MY EX?!!
I SHOULD HAVE LET SALVATORE BREAK MY LEGS!
MR. SALVATORE, THE MUDD BROTHERS ARE HERE TO SEE YOU.
AH, MUSTA FINISHED THAT JOB. SEND 'EM IN.
SMASH!
THERE HE IS!! BREAK 'IS LEGS!!
WE WORKS FOR MR. GOON NOW! HE SAYS WE IS TA BREAK YA LEGS!
SETTLE DOWN 'FORE I GOTS TA RUN THIS BROOM HANDLE UP YA BUM!
ALL RIGHT! YOU ASKED FO' IT!
AHHHH!!

END.

THE GOON™

SKETCHBOOK

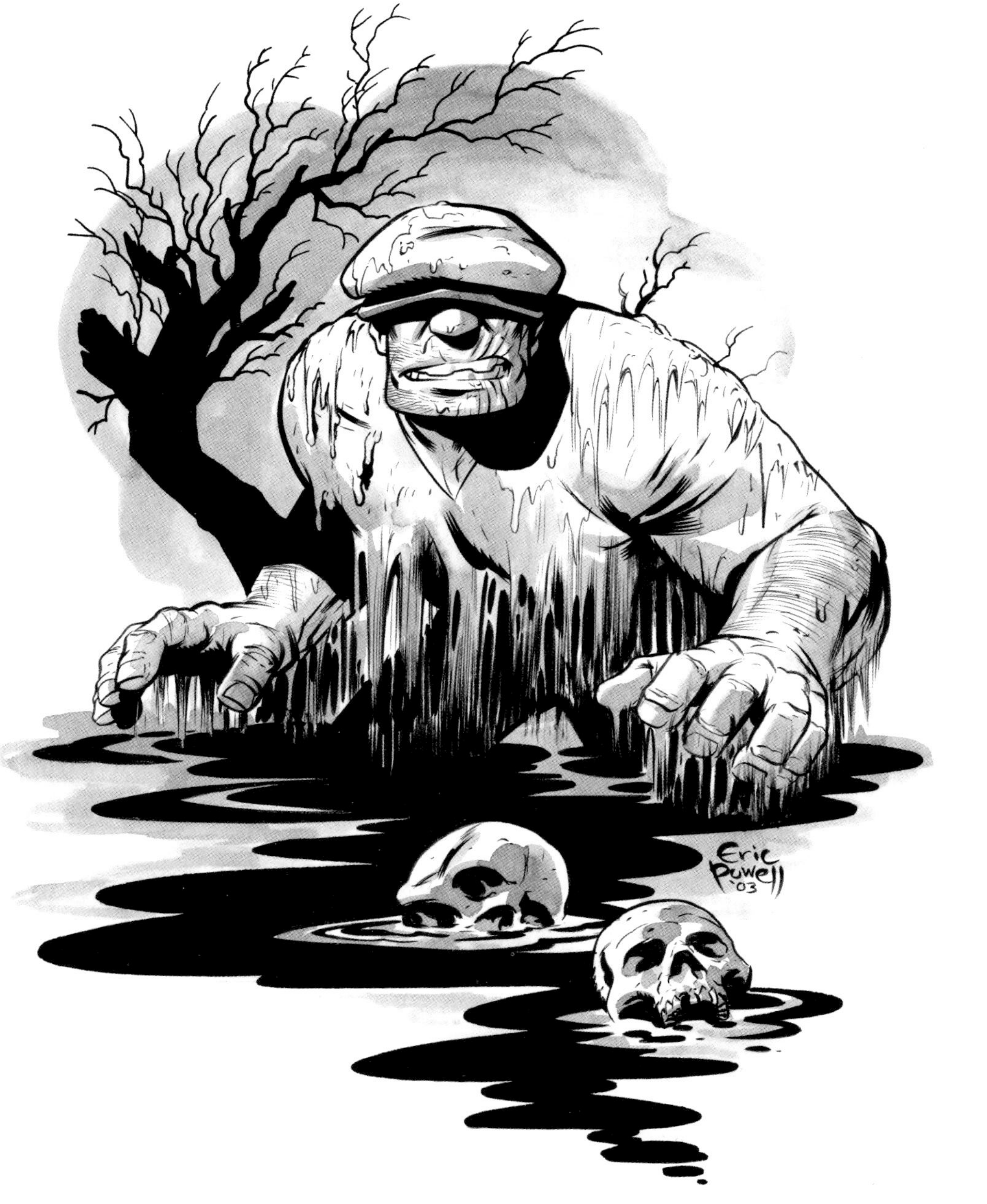
Eric Powell '03

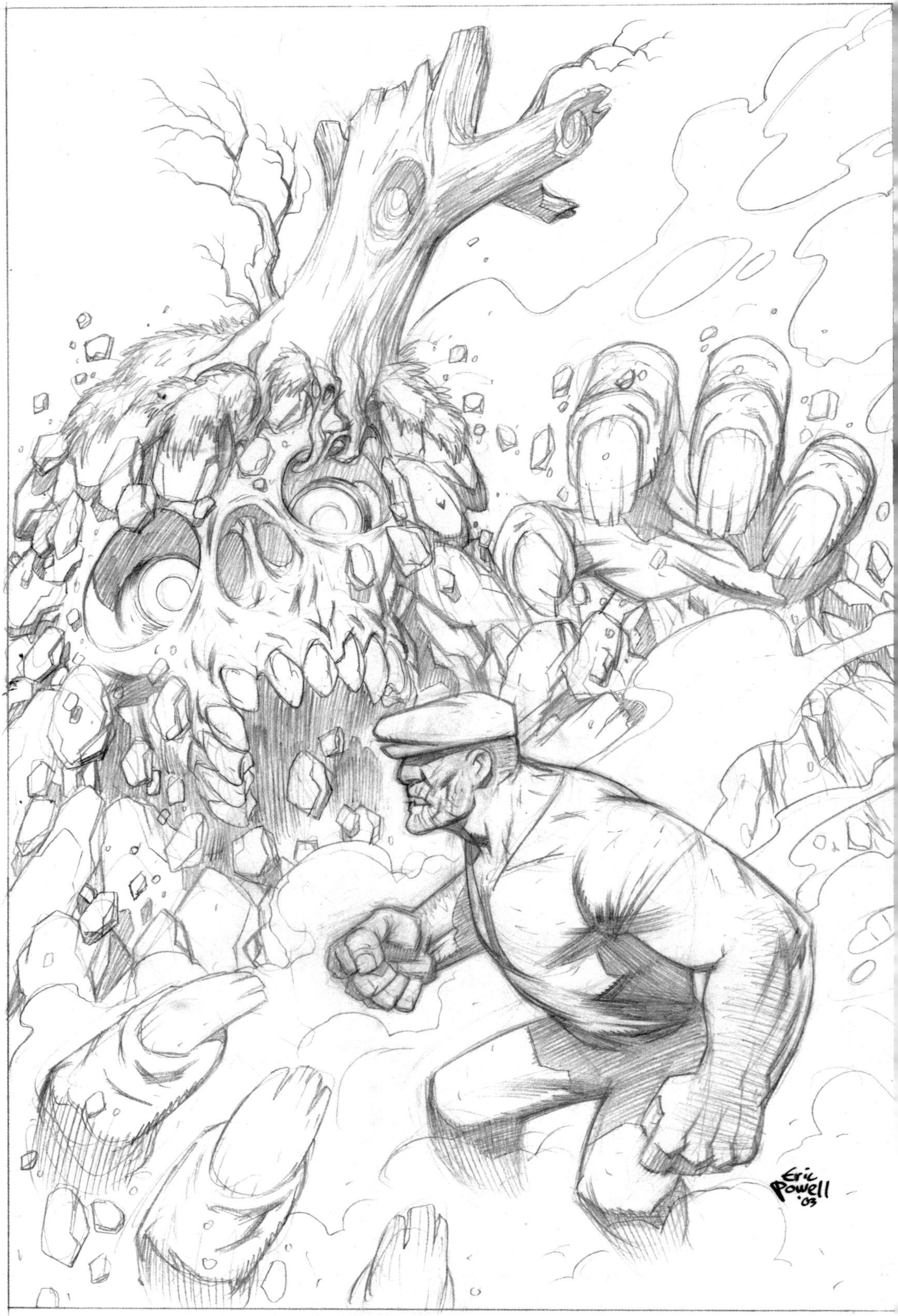
Eric Powell '03

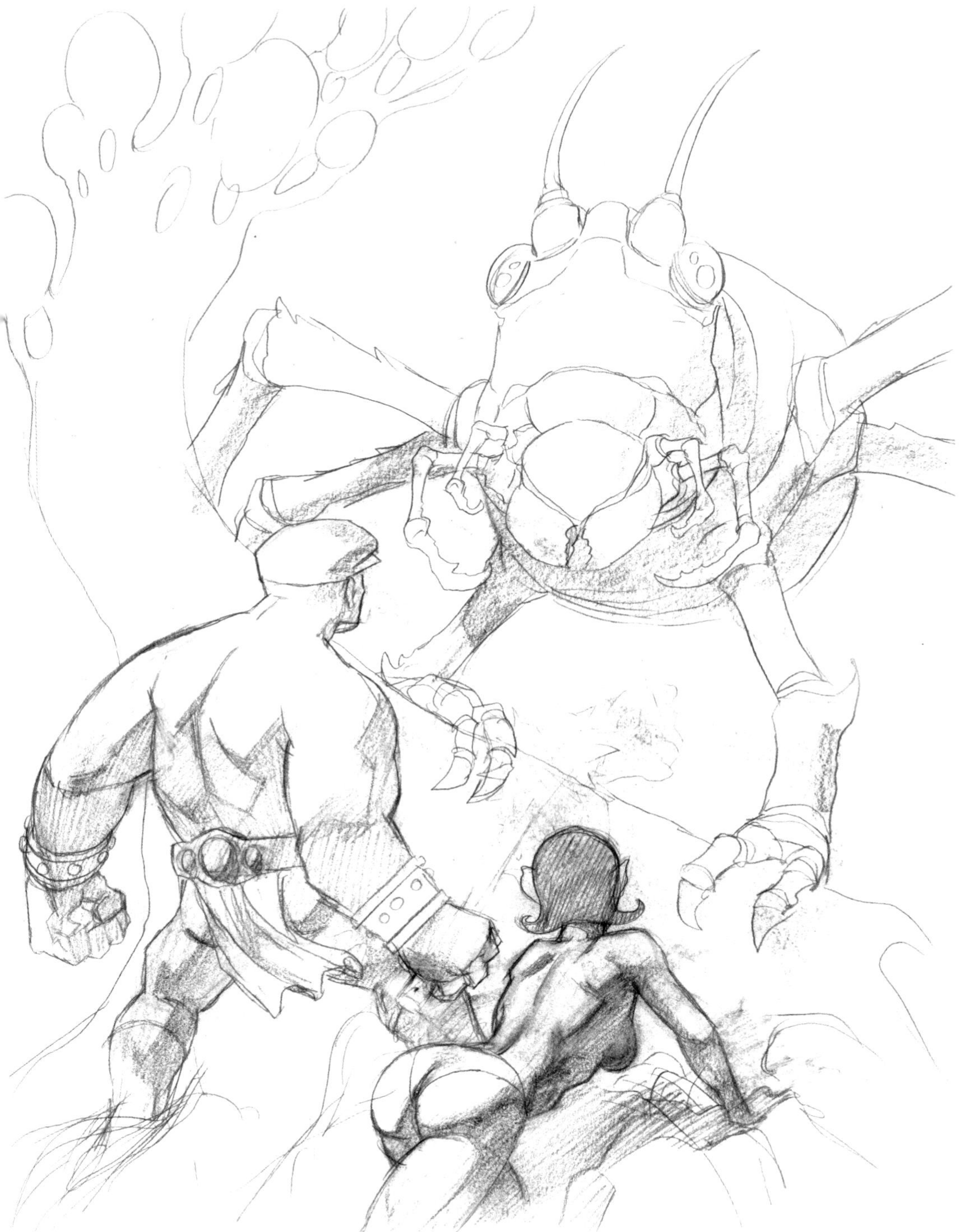

This is a sneak peak at a sketch for the *Goon in Space* book.

Buzzard was initially conceived as a separate series. The initial concept was of a ghoul who guarded a cemetery that happened to be a gateway to hell. Sort of like that movie *The Sentinel*, but with big monsters and a hero who eats dead people. I even wrote a short introductory script, but never did anything with it. I figured there was only so far I could take that concept with the main character tied to a cemetery. It then became a fantasy concept about a cursed assassin having to eat the flesh of dead men to survive. Buzzard was on a quest to kill the thing that cursed him with a young farm boy and a baron's concubine in tow. I drew a three-page intro story. It might have been a good book, but my main focus was on the Goon. "Hell, why not throw this guy in *The Goon*?" I says. "Anything works in *The Goon*! And why not make the Zombie Priest the guy who cursed him? Even better!"

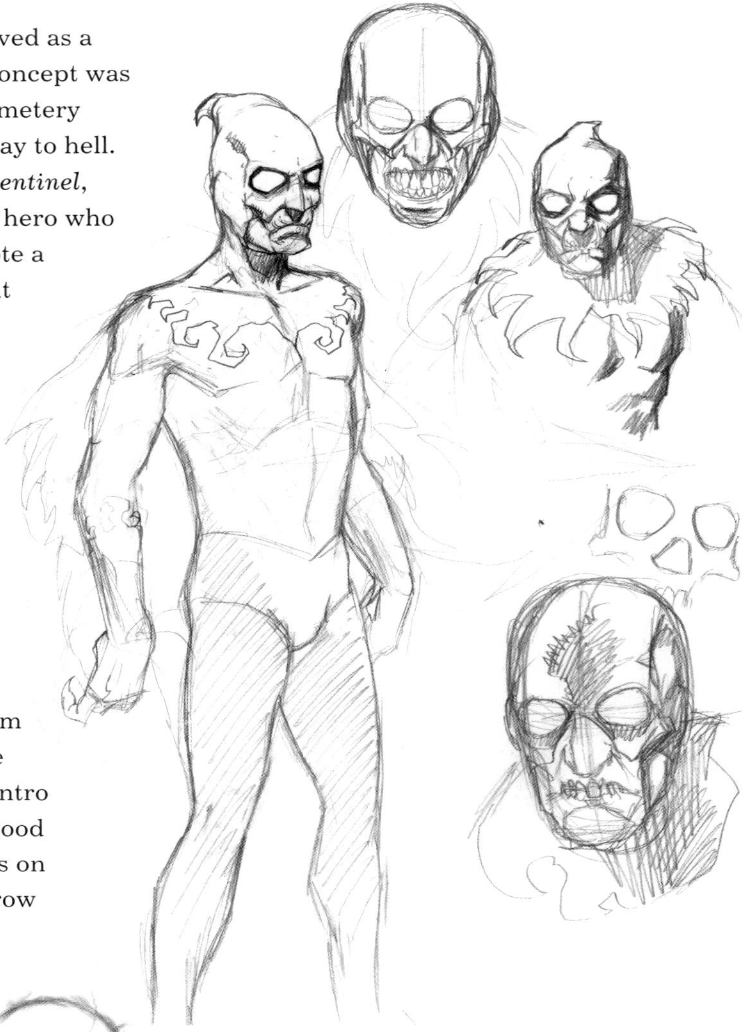

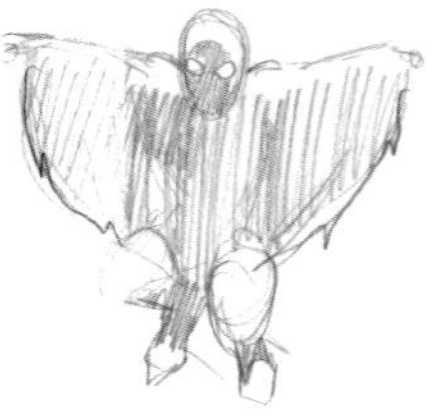

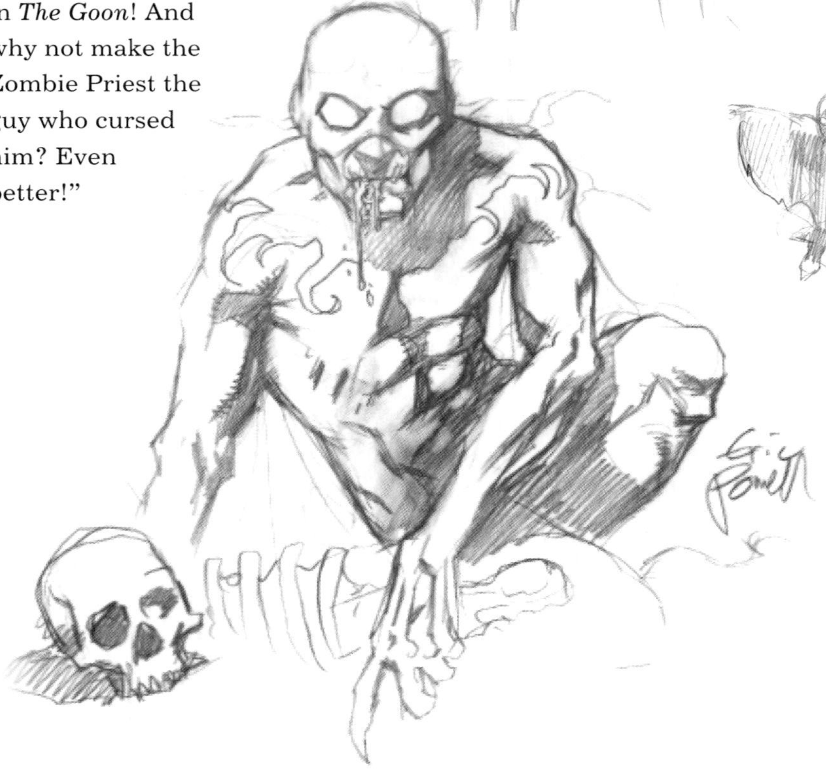

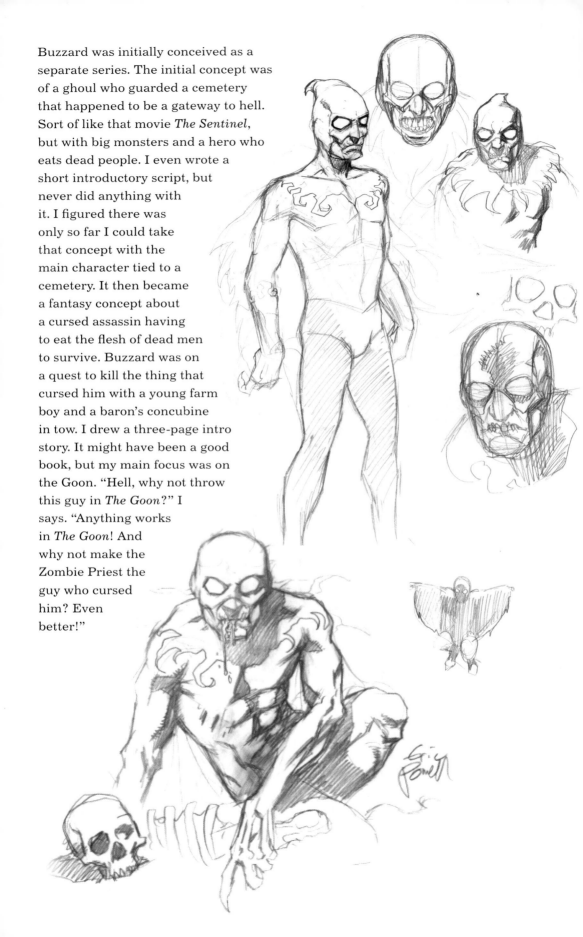

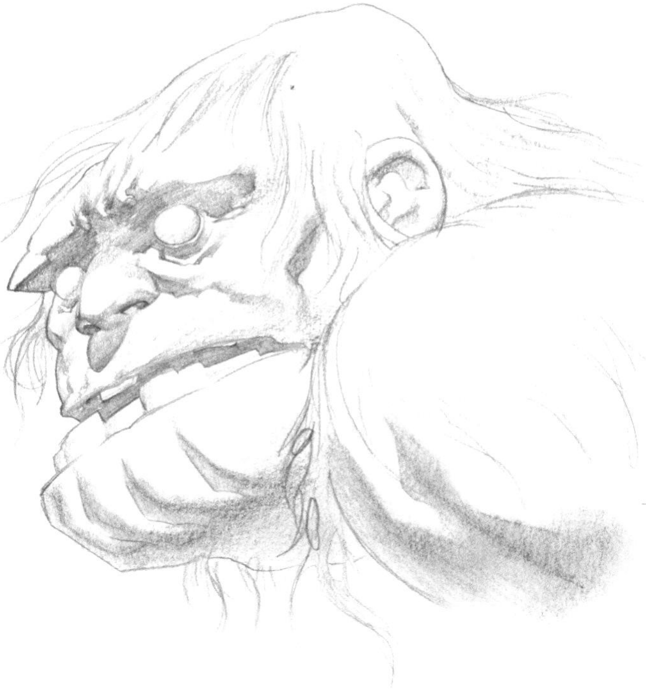

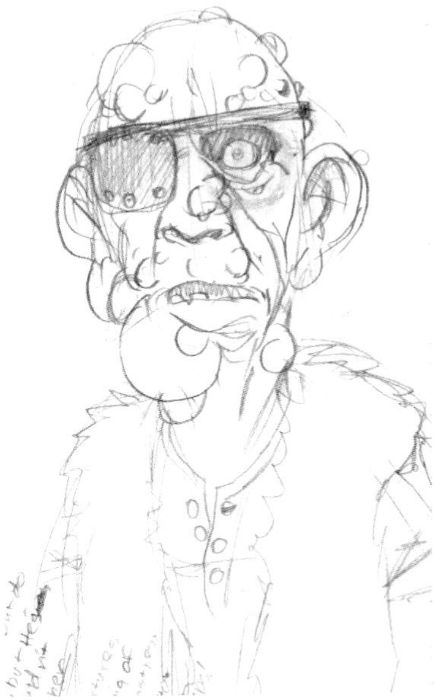

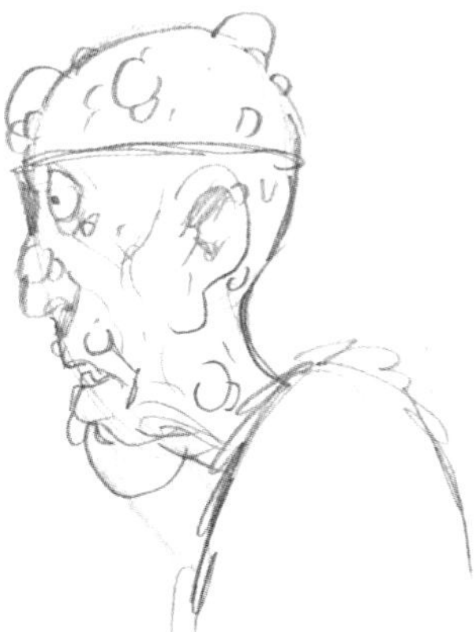

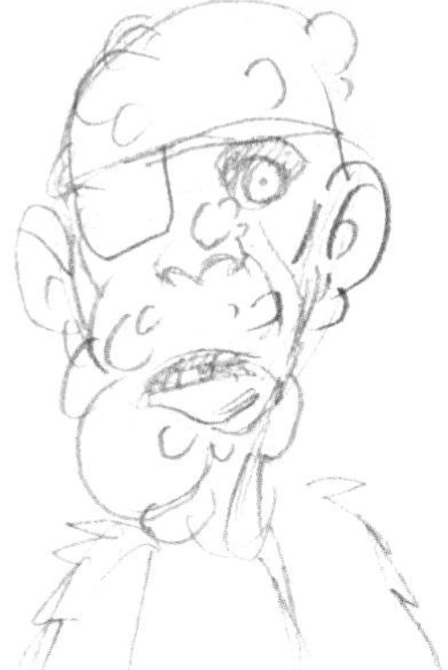

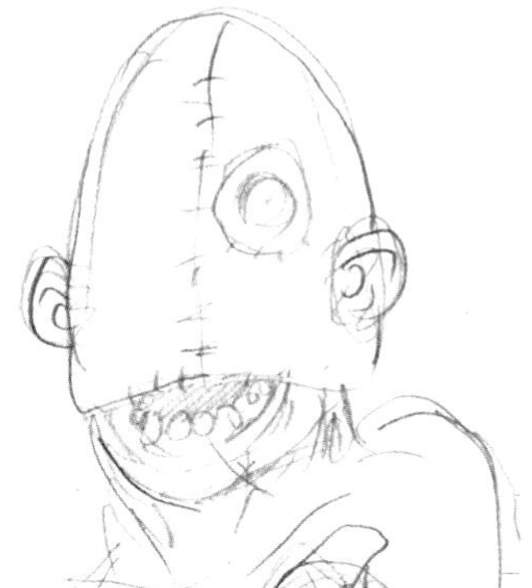

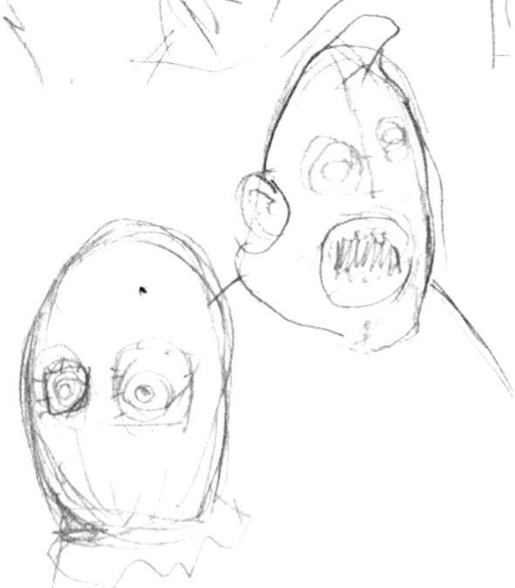

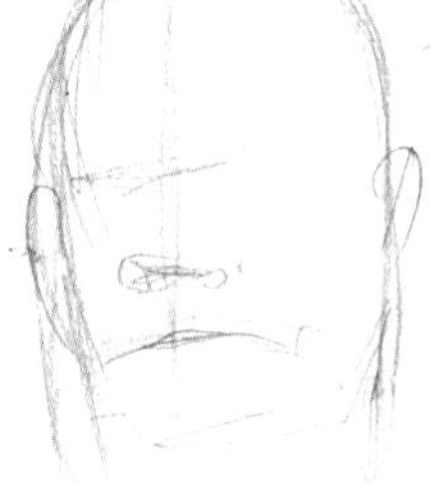

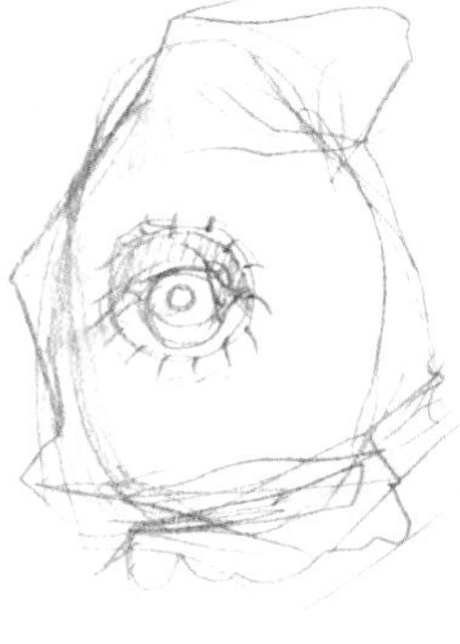

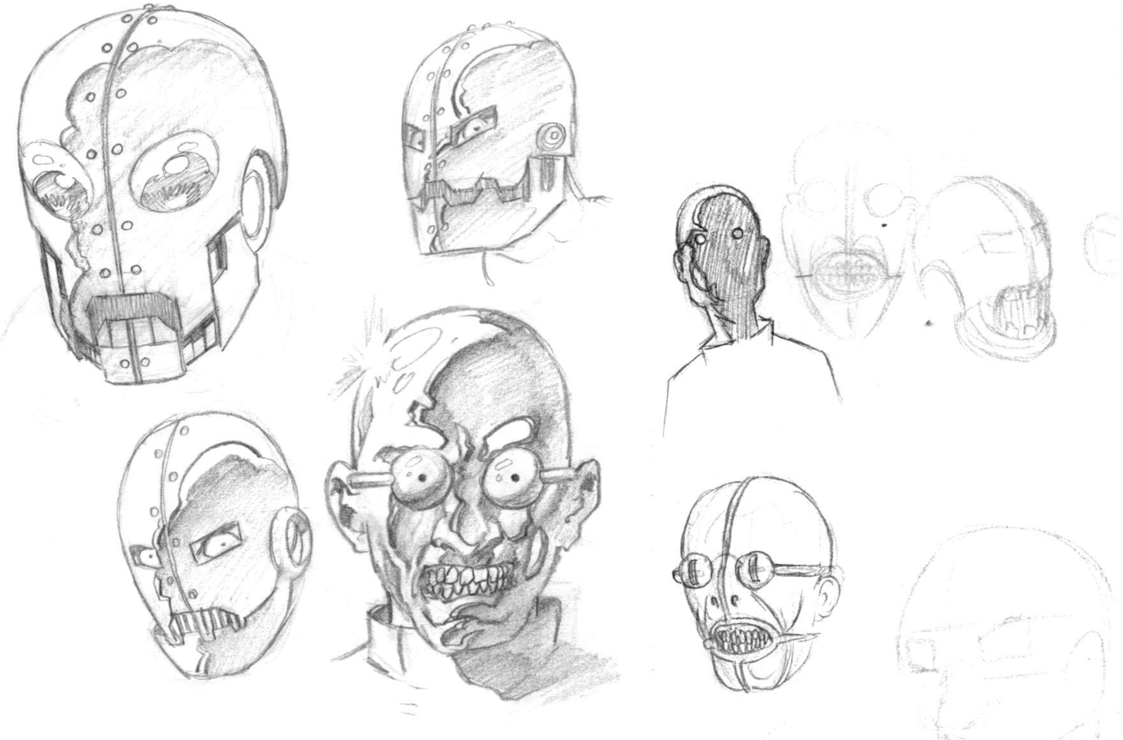

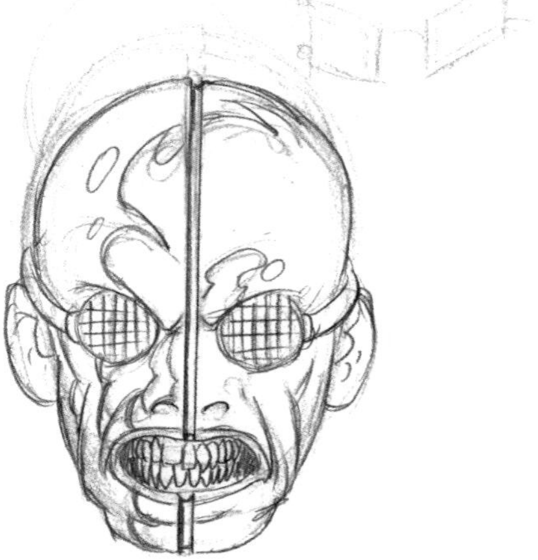

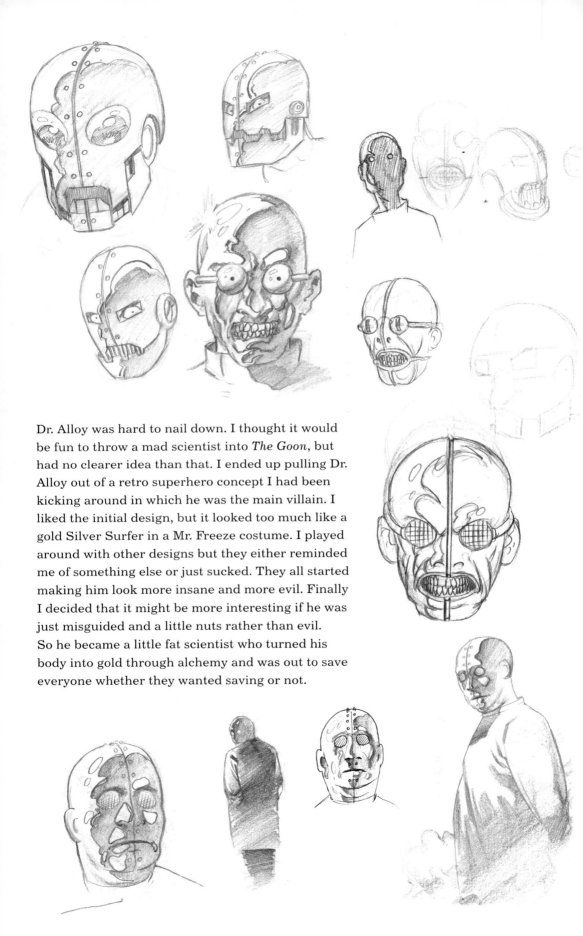

Dr. Alloy was hard to nail down. I thought it would be fun to throw a mad scientist into *The Goon*, but had no clearer idea than that. I ended up pulling Dr. Alloy out of a retro superhero concept I had been kicking around in which he was the main villain. I liked the initial design, but it looked too much like a gold Silver Surfer in a Mr. Freeze costume. I played around with other designs but they either reminded me of something else or just sucked. They all started making him look more insane and more evil. Finally I decided that it might be more interesting if he was just misguided and a little nuts rather than evil. So he became a little fat scientist who turned his body into gold through alchemy and was out to save everyone whether they wanted saving or not.

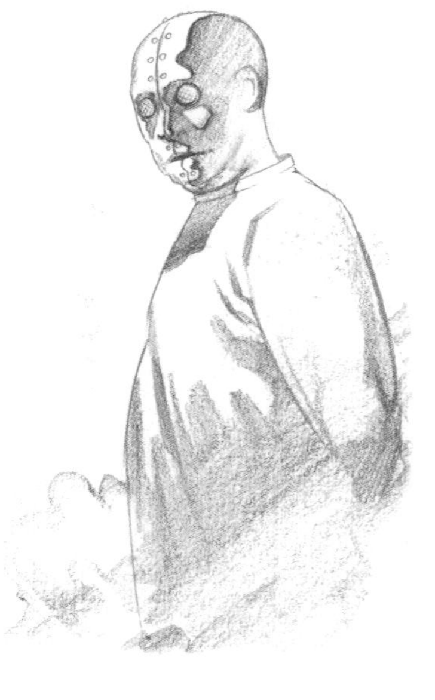

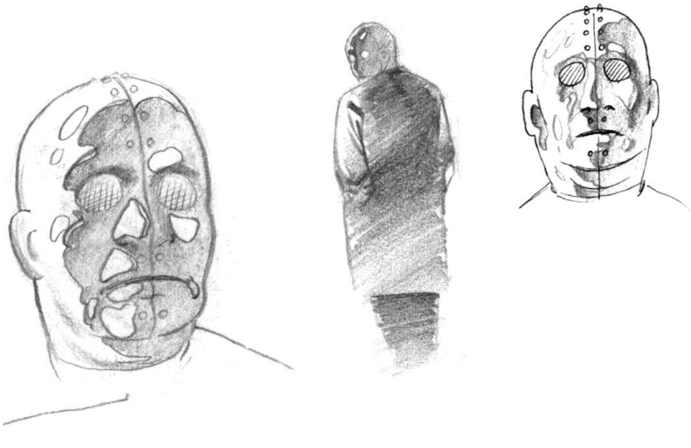

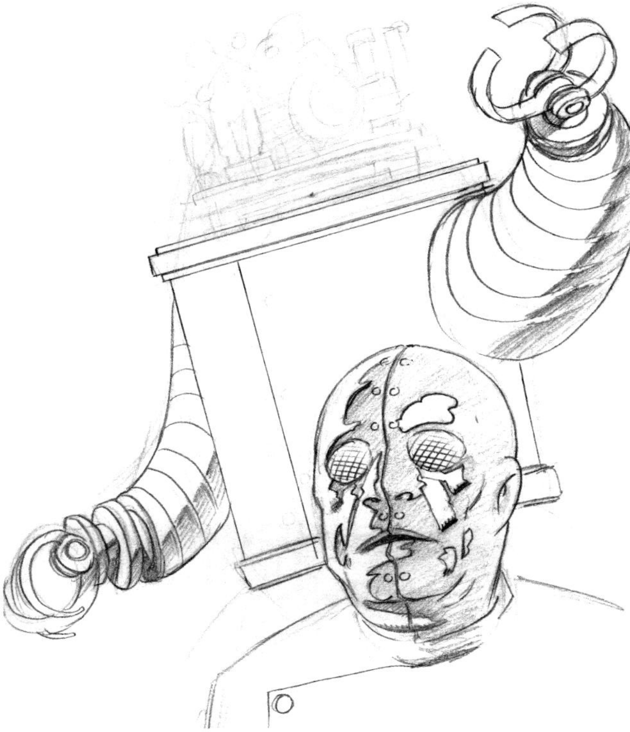

Bruno was no easier. I went through several designs trying to find the right retro feel.

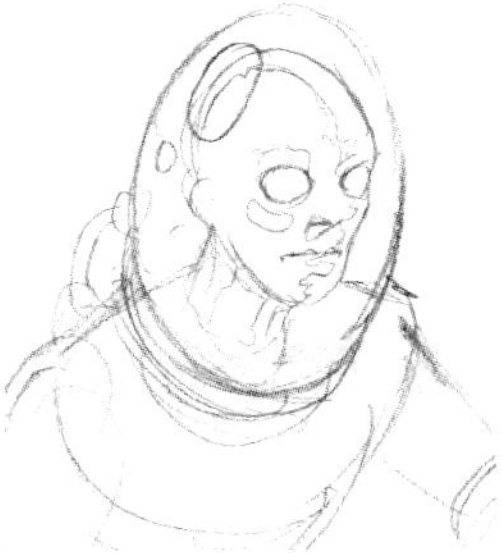

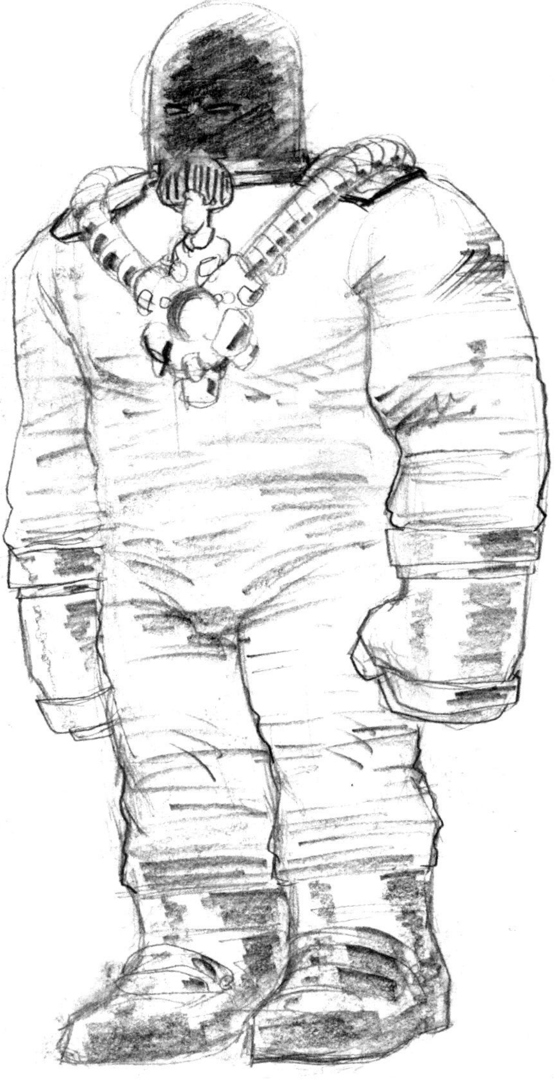

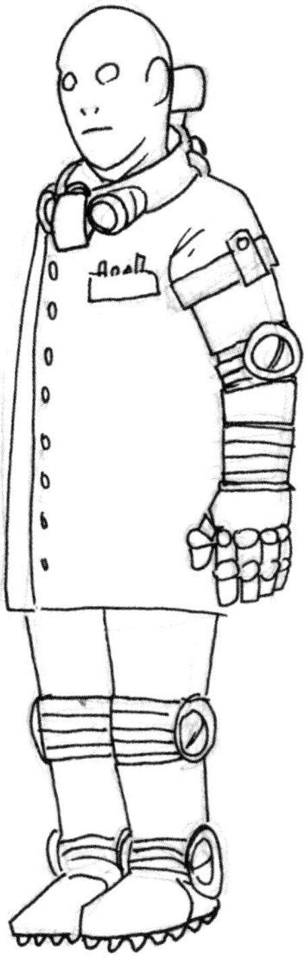

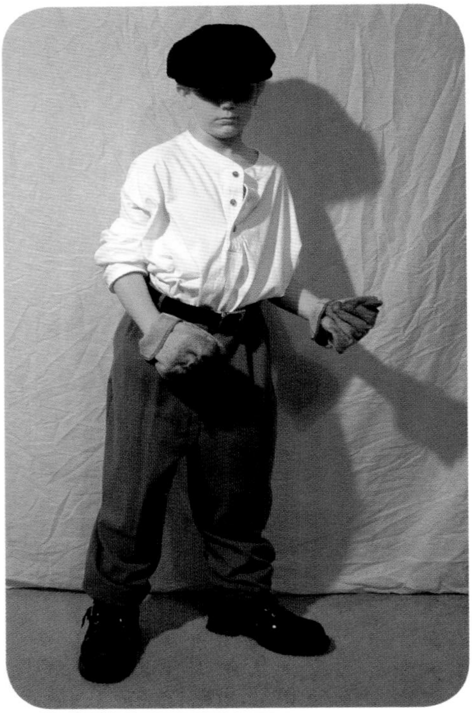

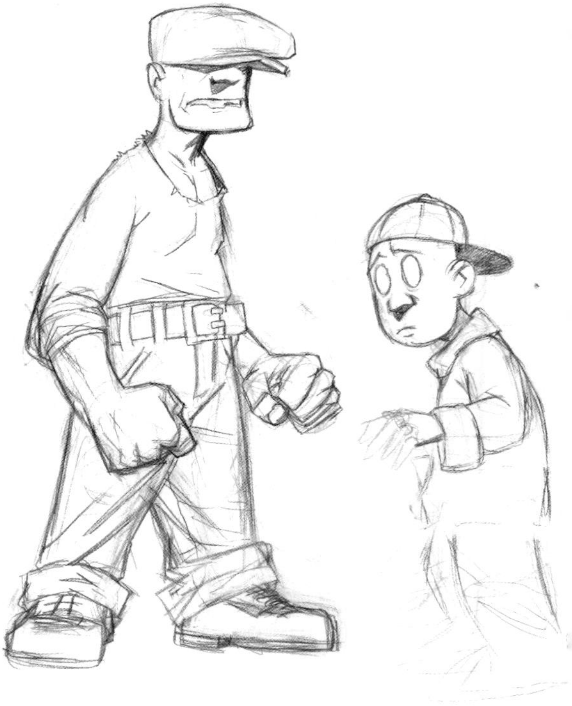

Best reason to have children . . . free kid reference. Just kidding. Being the big ham that he is, Gage was more than willing to help me out by posing as the adolescent Goon. This shot was used for the cover painting.

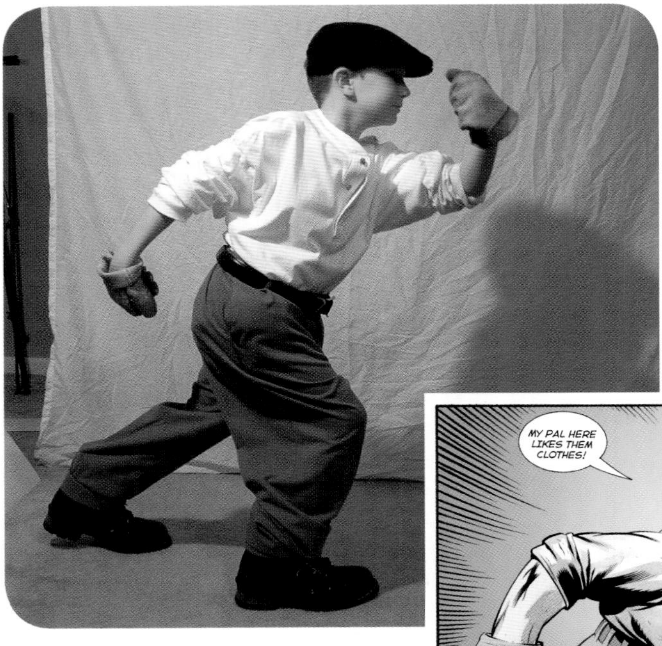

This was used for the shot where Goon is punching Nicky in the head.

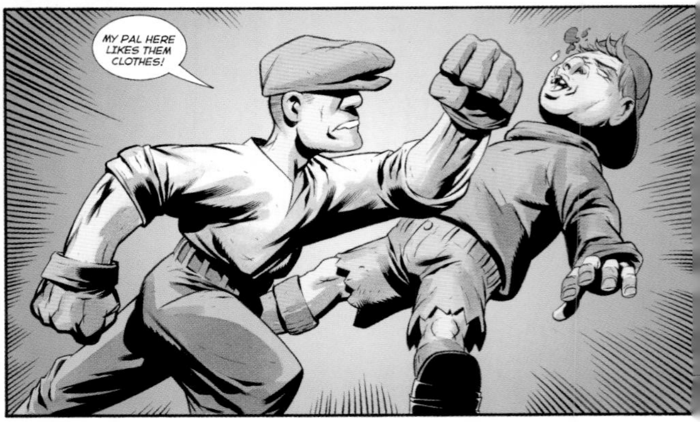
MY PAL HERE LIKES THEM CLOTHES!

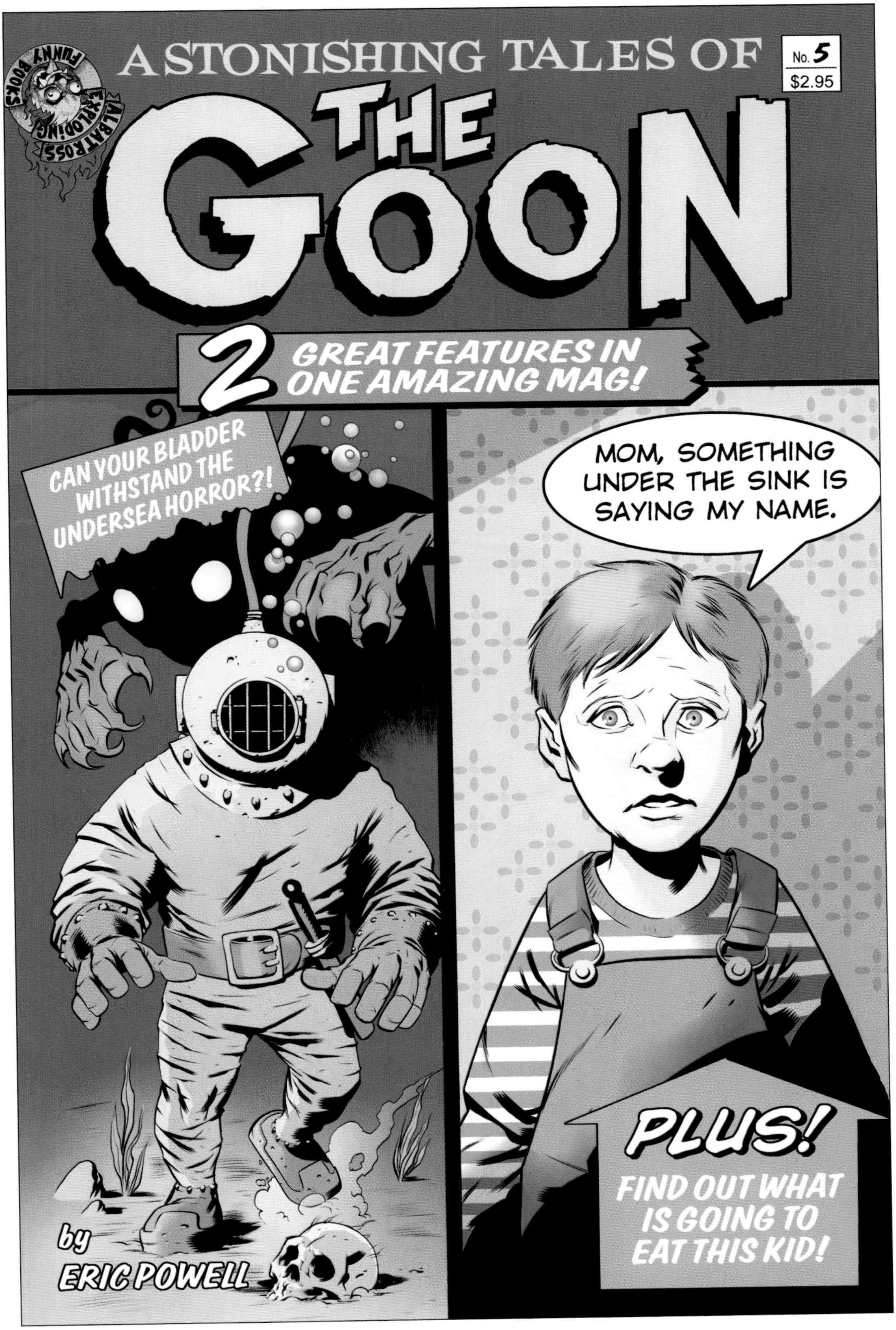
FUNNY BOOKS
EXPLODING ALBATROSS
ASTONISHING TALES OF
No. 5
$2.95
THE GOON
2 GREAT FEATURES IN ONE AMAZING MAG!
CAN YOUR BLADDER WITHSTAND THE UNDERSEA HORROR?!
MOM, SOMETHING UNDER THE SINK IS SAYING MY NAME.
by ERIC POWELL
PLUS!
FIND OUT WHAT IS GOING TO EAT THIS KID!

This was going to be the Albatross *Goon* #5 cover, but we moved to Dark Horse before the issue could be completed.

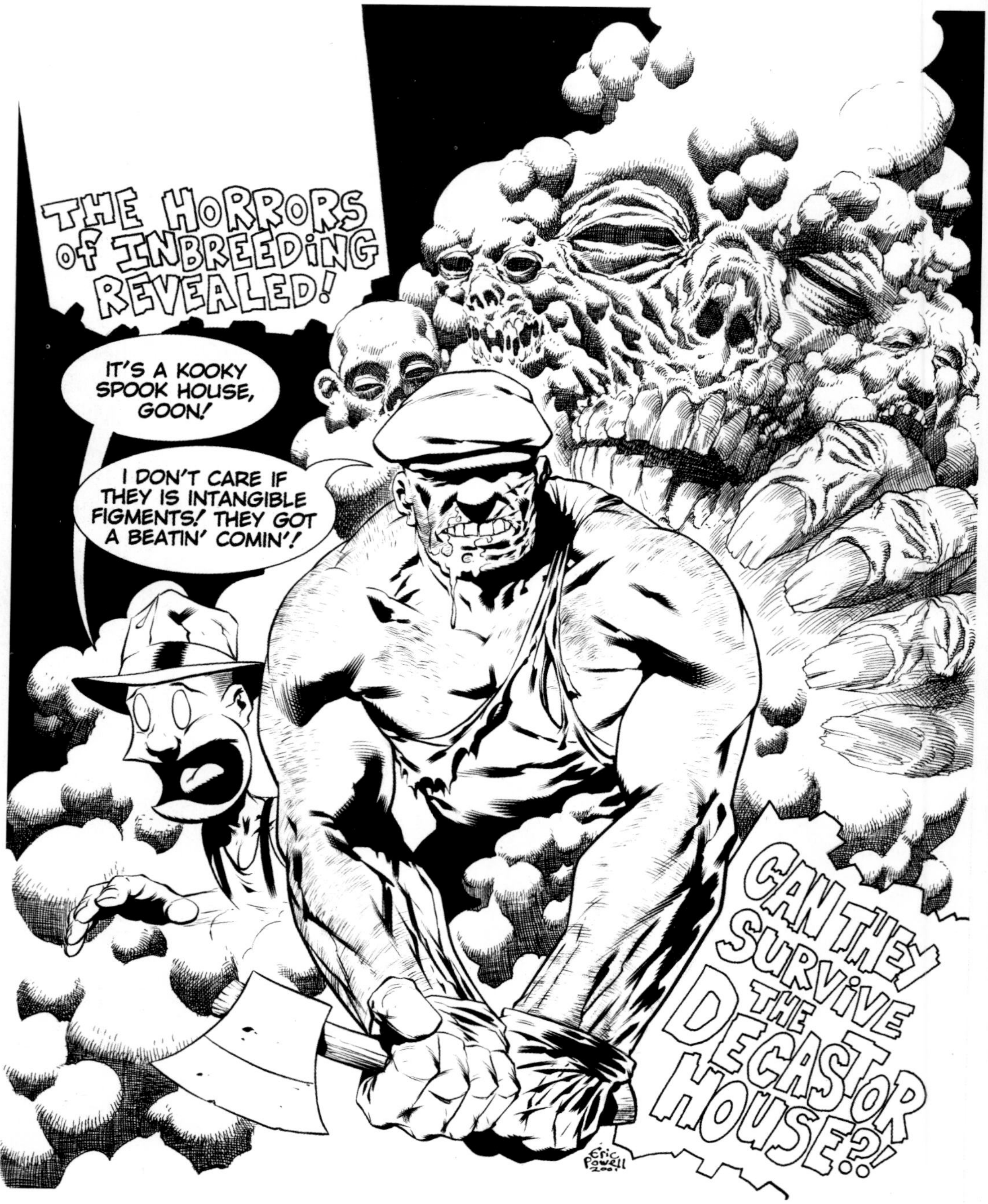
THE HORRORS of INBREEDING REVEALED!
IT'S A KOOKY SPOOK HOUSE, GOON!
I DON'T CARE IF THEY IS INTANGIBLE FIGMENTS! THEY GOT A BEATIN' COMIN'!
CAN THEY SURVIVE THE DECASTOR HOUSE?!
Eric Powell

An early version of the cover to the Albatross *Goon Color Special*.

RECOMMENDED DARK HORSE READING . . .

ABSENT
BODIES
THE CLEANERS
MARK WHEATON JOSHUA HALE FIALKOV RAHSAN EKEDAL

THE CLEANERS
Mark Wheaton, Joshua Hale Fialkov, and Rahsan Ekedal
Contracted with sanitizing some of the nastiest crime and accident scenes in the tricounty LA basin, ex-surgeon Robert Bellarmine and his team of specialists battle against what could only be described as the grim, unknowable face of the supernatural.
ISBN 978-1-59582-370-0 | $14.99

CREEPY
VOLUME ONE
COLLECTING CREEPY 1-5
WEIRD AND HAUNTING TALES OF FRIGHT!
DARK HORSE ARCHIVES

CREEPY ARCHIVES VOLUME 1
Various
Dark Horse Comics further corners the market on high-quality horror storytellir with this series of hardcover archive collections of legendary *Creepy* magazin delivering a horrifying adventure into the darkest corners of comics history.
ISBN 978-1-59307-973-4 | $49.99

BEASTS of BURDEN
ANIMAL RITES
EVAN DORKIN JILL THOMPSON

BEASTS OF BURDEN: ANIMAL RITES
Evan Dorkin and Jill Thompson
Beneath its shiny exterior, the picturesque town of Burden Hill harbors dark and sinister secrets, and it's up to a heroic gang of dogs—and one cat—to protect the town from the evil forces at work. These are the Beasts of Burden Hill.
ISBN 978-1-59582-513-1 | $19.99

GUY DAVIS
THE MARQUIS
INFERNO

THE MARQUIS VOLUME 1: INFERNO
Guy Davis
In eighteenth-century Venisalle, faith governs life and death, the guilty hide their shame behind masks, and the souls of Hell have escaped to possess the living. One man is blessed with the clarity to recognize the demons—and the means to return them to Hell.
ISBN 978-1-59582-368-7 | $24.99

AVAILABLE AT YOUR LOCAL COMICS SHOP OR BOOKSTORE! • To find a comics shop in your area, call 1-888-266-4226.
For more information or to order direct, visit darkhorse.com or call 1-800-862-0052 Mon.–Fri. 9 AM to 5 PM Pacific Time. Prices and availability subject to change without notice.

DARK HORSE BOOKS *drawing on your nightmares*
darkhorse.com

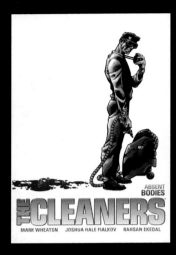

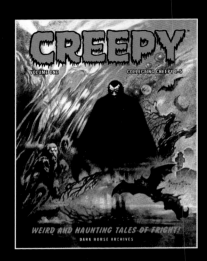

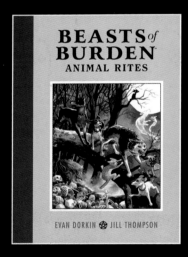

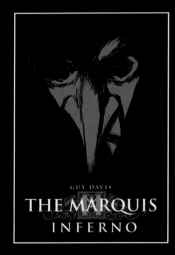